INFALLIBLE?

AN INQUIRY

"There is no doubt that from one point of view Hans Küng's book is important. This would seem to be the first time a theologian of note has, while remaining with the Roman Church, openly rejected the doctrine of papal infallibility in the sense in which it was defined. Theologians will not be able to ignore Hans Küng. His views, therefore, will demand discussion by other ecclesiologists . . . This book may, then, mark the opening of a new phase in the history of the papacy."
Commonweal

"Küng has presented a clear and closely reasoned argument which, despite its technical terminology and broad historical reference, can be read and understood by most educated laymen. He has focused on a key issue and has proposed a responsible solution . . . He offers a formula for a major breakthrough to a new self-understanding for the Roman Catholic Church."
The New Republic

"His work combines solid scholarship on the Church with unfeigned love of that church. I hope it receives the hearing it deserves not only from other theologians but also, and indeed especially, from those who can *effect* structural change."
The Christian Century

"Though Küng appears to be a man who enjoys a good fight, his book was not written solely as polemic. Rather, it is a cry *de profundis*. This man not only knows the good things the Church has done and ought to do; he is aware of the burden of wrong done in and through the Church, and has been deeply hurt by it. Love alone can inspire so urgent a plea."
Saturday Review

"As I read it I felt more and more as if I had an atom bomb in my hand. For if these ideas are taken up in Catholicism an entirely new situation will arise. Then Protestantism will no longer have any important reason for protesting."
Dr. Willem Visser 't Hooft, former General Secretary of the World Council of Churches

". . . above all, [Küng's] work is illuminated and supported by the intensity of his own belief. It is this which allows him to probe so radically without, as so many are tempted to do, fearing that this probing will cause the whole construction to come tumbling down about his ears. Thus in *Infallible?* he sees the Achilles heel of the Roman theory of infallibility as a lack of faith—in this case faith in God's promise of the Church's essential indefectibility despite all the errors into which its leaders or theologians may fall on the way."
The Critic

INFALLIBLE?

AN INQUIRY

HANS KÜNG

Translated by Edward Quinn

DOUBLEDAY & COMPANY, INC.
GARDEN CITY, NEW YORK
1983

Library of Congress Cataloging in Publication Data

Küng, Hans, 1928–
Infallible? an inquiry.

Translation of: Unfehlbar? eine Anfrage.
Includes bibliographical references.
1. Popes—Infallibility.   2. Catholic Church—
Infallibility.   I. Title.
BX1806.K8613   1983   262'.131
Library of Congress Catalog Card Number: 82–45641
ISBN 0-385-18483-2

I ask my readers to make common cause with me
when they share my convictions;
to keep an open mind
when they share my doubts.
I ask them to correct me
if I make a mistake,
to return to my way of thinking
if they do.

Augustine
De Trinitate I, iii, 5

CONTENTS

INFALLIBLE?
AN INQUIRY

INTRODUCTION TO THE
NEW AMERICAN EDITION

Nearly three years have gone by since church officials attempted by means of disciplinary measures to suppress a question which still troubles Catholic theology: the question of papal infallibility. But can a great public question be laid to rest before it has found an answer? The old infallibility of kings, emperors, and tsars reigning by the grace of God has long since ceased to be an issue. And the newer infallibility of autocrats, dictators, duces, führers, and general secretaries reigning on their own has now become—after two world wars, Auschwitz, the Gulag Archipelago, democratization in Spain, and the first signs of a turning away from Mao in China—distinctly brittle. Of course, debate over infallible *parties* (and their current representatives) is still being stifled as usual, from Moscow to Havana, with every oppressive and repressive means available. And then, many people are asking in turn, what about the infallibility of *churches,* which, like certain political parties, "are always right"? What about the Church's representatives, past or present, who invoke the Holy Spirit to justify their decisions? Whatever other differences may separate the Catholic Church from totalitarian societies, this one at least is clear: In the wake of the Second Vatican Council it is simply impossible for the Church to bury the issue of infallibility.

On the occasion of the hundredth anniversary of papal infallibility (defined by the First Vatican Council in 1870), I tried to give a precise formulation to this widely discussed but vague question in my book *Infallible? An Inquiry* (1970).

This was something like a parliamentary interpellation by His Majesty's loyal opposition in a free commonwealth. Religious authorities in Rome, with the help of bishops' conferences, were doing their best to mandate silence on this problem, which had suddenly sprung to life again, and to get rid of the whole thing once and for all. But, though condemned to death, the issue remained alive, and discussion among believers could not be throttled.

And surely, unprejudiced observers in Rome never imagined that in this day and age the Church could dispose of such an inquiry merely by repeating conciliar decrees whose infallibility had been dubious from the very beginning and which were once more being challenged. Well before the 1970s a similar line used to be taken by kings and generals, fathers, teachers and, often enough, professors trying to rescue their jeopardized infallibility: We are infallible because we have said that we are infallible!

But there was no avoiding the reply: With what right have you—and your forebears—said that you were infallible? And in the Church of all places. With what right do you lay claim to the infallibility of the Holy Spirit of God, which "blows where it wills," you who are men and not God? Doesn't "to err is human" hold true for you? Or has God anywhere ascribed to you his own infallibility? If so, that would have to be attested to in the most unambiguous language. People in the Bible (and in the Church of the New Testament, beginning with Peter, the "Rock") do not exactly convey an impression of infallibility. Peter was not the only one—Peter, whom the Lord once called "Satan," who denied the Lord three times, who, even after Easter, and above all in Antioch, proved to be quite fallible in his controversy with Paul—for whom the cock crowed. And thus, for many long decades nobody mentioned any infallibility of the bishop of Rome (nor, for the time being, of the ecumenical councils either). In fact, upon close inspection the historian must judge infallibility to be an innovation of the second millennium, and really only of the nineteenth century. So what is left of the argument that papal and conciliar infallibility are rooted in Scripture and old Catholic tradition?

Or may one not ask that question? Should even asking it be a sin and full-fledged inquiry a mortal sin? No, once the Vatican has gotten over its first (and understandable) shock, it can't seriously say things like that anymore. That would be a sign of fear, and would only provoke the child's question about the emperor's new clothes. No, a church that has nothing to fear from the truth, that has nothing more to fear than untruth, that claims to be the "pillar and foundation of the truth"—a church like that has an altogether vital interest in seeing that the truth is not stifled but continually "revealed" anew. Too much is at stake here to let silence become the long-term policy. For, after all, isn't the problem of infallibility now as ever the biggest obstacle to renewal within the Church? Isn't the doctrine of infallibility the most serious stumbling block on the road to ecumenical understanding? Isn't it the claim to infallibility which costs the Church its credibility and makes it seem so inept, despite all its unquestionably positive contributions and its still greater potential for good in today's society? Poverty and underdevelopment in the Third World, the population explosion, birth control, the encyclical *Humanae vitae,* the infallibility of traditional church doctrine—all these things are now so tightly connected that people who preach such loud sermons to outsiders actually ought to shout this message to those inside the Church instead of keeping silent on the whole business of infallibility.

The Catholic Church and its leaders, in fact, ought not to view questions and inquiry as an attack from outside but as help from within. For they themselves have the greatest interest of all in seeing

1) that the process of undoing the ideology of the absolutist-authoritarian magisterium, which began with John XXIII

and Vatican II, be completed so as to create a genuine spiritual authority and to free the Church from the arrogance, coercion, and dishonesty of a curialist theology and administration;

2) that a conscious effort be made to exploit the new beginnings of Vatican II, which, under the inspiration of John XXIII, deliberately chose to forego infallible definitions, and in opposition to traditional dogmatism called for a new way of proclaiming the Christian message—and to some degree made such a proclamation itself; and

3) that the historicity of truth and of its formulations be given fresh recognition in the Church, thus making possible a better foundation for the Christian faith, furthering the modernization and renewal of the Catholic Church, and in all this helping the cause of Jesus Christ to make a new breakthrough in a "church" system which in many ways contradicts the message of him in whose name it speaks.

Fortunately, the latest phase of the theological infallibility debate—as early as 1973 there was uncontested evidence of progress here—has already clarified a good number of points:

I. *Justification for the inquiry:* The uncomfortable texts from Vatican I and II—on this point both the critical inquirers themselves and the Roman authorities agree—are to be taken literally. Their original meaning may not be softened or watered down, as Catholic theologians in recent days (for reasons which are transparent) have continually tried to do. Opportunistic reinterpretation, ultimately leading to outright denial of the text, is a common feature of all authoritarian systems, but it only obscures the problems, violates intellectual integrity, and delays a comprehensive solution. Of course, read in their original sense, knowing what we know today, the texts on infallibility pose a still greater challenge to every

Catholic than they did one hundred years ago. But sticking one's head in the sand, theologically speaking, leads nowhere: An enlightened attitude here is as indispensable as it once was on the issue of Galileo. Catholic belief need not degenerate to the level of blind faith, where one believes only because the pastor says so. On this matter our examination must go beyond the (so-called "extraordinary") infallibility of the pope making dogmatic definitions ("how the pope became infallible"). A second question, much neglected by the anti-Infallibilist minority at Vatican I, is the (likewise "extraordinary") infallibility of definitions made by an ecumenical council. And a third is even more explosive: the (everyday, usual, "ordinary") infallibility of the entire episcopate all over the world. According to Vatican II, this body is also supposed to be infallible whenever pope and bishops concur in teaching that a specific theological or moral doctrine (e.g., the immorality of "artificial" contraception) is definitively binding. This question of doctrinal agreement between pope and bishops was a determining factor in the promulgation of *Humanae vitae*. Vatican II guaranteed the infallibility of such joint declarations ("Thus they proclaim in infallible fashion the teaching of Christ"), even in the absence of any explicit definition. This has proved to be the chemical agent that keeps the question of infallibility in constant ferment. Traditionally minded theologians often see this connection more clearly than the ones thought of as progressive. Such clarity, however, only throws into sharper relief the general perplexity vis-à-vis the infallibility of this "ordinary" magisterium.

II. *The contemporary Catholic consensus:* There is fundamental agreement on three important points:

A. The errors of the magisterium are a fact. Nowadays Catholic theologians concede with heretofore unwonted frankness that even the organs responsible for "infallible" doctrinal decisions can err, at least in principle (though perhaps not in specific situations), and often have erred. "No one who observes the history of the Church with any objectivity can deny that it has often enough promulgated errors. This is true both of the Church as a whole and of those church authorities which view themselves as the source of infallible doctrinal decisions, namely, the pope and the ecumenical councils, as well as the entire episcopate in the daily exercise of proclaiming the faith—insofar as it does this in a body." (O. Semmelroth)

B. Skepticism has been eating away at the concept and practice of infallibility: Even some conservative theologians consider the notion misleading, in fact, largely incomprehensible in today's world. One cannot help noticing that since the recent debate on the issue began, the word "infallible" has largely disappeared from theological and even official ecclesiastical terminology. Nobody wants infallible definitions anymore, neither to foster piety nor to clarify complex contemporary problems. If it hadn't already been defined, papal infallibility would certainly not be defined today. The plausibility structures—the political, social, cultural, and theological presuppositions—supporting the Vatican definitions in the nineteenth century no longer exist. All that remains for the Catholic people is the definition itself, and neither the laity nor the theologians nor even the popes have a very good idea of what to do with it. The "exaggerations" and "misuse" of the papal magisterium over the past hundred years are often bemoaned, but those who complain are less willing to admit that such negative developments are not accidental but built right into the structure of the Vatican dogmas. Still, there is no longer any ignoring the pattern leading from Pius IX and Vatican I through the campaign against modernism under Pius X to the *Humani generis* purge under Pius XII. The era of the Sodalitium Pianum (see Chapter 8) in nineteenth- and twentieth-century church history only ended with John XXIII.

C. Despite all its errors, the Church will remain preserved in the truth: Even for conservatives who defend infallible pronouncements, the Church's indestructible link with the truth (indefectibility) is more basic than the infallibility of particular statements. And now that no one can argue about the existence, in general, of errors by the magisterium, there is agreement, at least in principle, on the positive thesis that the Church will be preserved in the truth of the Gospel, for all its errors. But what this means concretely will have to be discussed later on.

III. *The decisive question:* Beyond this fundamental inde-fectibility, aren't there perhaps judgments, statements, defini-tions, and *credal propositions* which are not only de facto true (which no one denies) but *infallibly true?* That is, are there not certain officials or authoritative institutions which, owing to the special assistance of the Holy Spirit, in a certain speci-fied situation find themselves a priori incapable of making a mistake? This is a clear and precise phrasing of the question in the wake of Vatican I, which taught that the repositories of authority (pope and bishops) were not continually infallible, but only in delivering themselves of carefully specified judg-ments, sentences, definitions, and "propositions." In the recent debate on infallibility, critics have taken direct aim at these infallible propositions, which are not only not false de facto but can in no way be false because of the help of the Holy Spirit (e.g., the Marian dogmas). And what was the result? Briefly put, to date not a single theologian and not a single official authority have managed to make a case for the possi-bility of such infallible credal propositions which, together with the authorities behind them, would be guaranteed by the Holy Spirit. The altogether exhaustive discussion we have had thus far shows that there are no solid grounds in Scrip-ture or the body of Catholic tradition for accepting such infallibly true propositions or authorities. And to adduce as proof for them the very doctrinal texts from Vatican I and II that are in dispute is a transparent begging of the question. It only stands to reason that Vatican I and Vatican II never solved problems whose existence neither Council recognized.

IV. *Unexpected confirmation:* The newer (older, in point of fact) Catholic position on infallibility has been unexpectedly confirmed by Catholic scholars:

A. With regard to *Peter:* Recent exegetical studies by Catholics have elaborated on Peter's genuine but fallible authority, and the problems related to succession in the "Petrine service." The symbolic figure of Peter kept its importance for the Church in the generations that followed him, but there is little support in the New Testament and the first three centuries for any infallibility on his part (the biblical evidence characteristically combines Peter's positive *and* negative qualities at every turn), and still less for the infallibility of the bishops of Rome. The main proof text cited at Vatican I for papal infallibility, Luke 22:32 ("I have prayed for you that your faith may not fail") was never used even by medieval canonists to document this dogma—and rightly so. In this passage Jesus does not promise Peter freedom from error but the grace to persevere in the faith till the end. Still, the same medieval canonists applied this not to the Roman bishops but to the faith of the entire Church. To construe Luke 22:32 as referring to the infallibility of the bishop of Rome turns out to be an innovation with no textual basis.

B. With regard to the *ecumenical councils:* The first Ecumenical Council of Nicaea (325) got along without any claim to infallibility. Recent historical research has pointed out the way in which the leader of this Council, Athanasius, along with many Greek Fathers of the Church and Augustine as well, explained the true—but in no sense infallible—authority of a council: A council speaks the truth not because it was convoked in a juridically unobjectionable manner, not because a majority of the bishops in the world were in attendance, not because it was confirmed by any sort of human authority, not, in a word, because it was, from the start, incapable of being deceived; but because, in spite of new words it says nothing new, because it hands on the old tradition in new language, because it bears witness to the original message, because it breathes the air of Scripture, because it has the Gospel behind it. One must distinguish this classical Catholic notion of a council from, in the East, the later mystical or juridical *Byzantine* "conciliar revalorizations," and, in the West—especially with reference to the authority of the papacy—from the *Roman Catholic* versions. The latter began to take on a distinctly Roman character with the popes of the fifth century, became dominant after the reform of Gregory VII, and was finally made a dogma at the First Vatican Council.

C. With regard to the *origin of the Roman doctrine of infallibility:* The latest historical studies—this was perhaps the biggest surprise of the whole debate—have discovered the unorthodox origins of the Roman doctrine of infallibility at the end of the thirteenth century. Scholars have the American historian Brian Tierney to thank for the discovery that the doctrine did not slowly "develop" or "unfold," but rather was created in one stroke in the late 1200s. And the "inventors" of papal infallibility and irreformability (both go together from the very beginning) were not at all, as previously suspected, the orthodox papalist theologians and canonist-popes of the High Middle Ages but an eccentric Franciscan, Peter Olivi (d. 1298), repeatedly accused of heresy. At first no one took Olivi's notion seriously, and in 1324 it was condemned by John XXII as a work of the devil, the Father of Lies. Even the Reformation popes could not invoke any generally accepted concept of infallibility, and the Council of Trent, it is worth noting, likewise never defined the pope's infallibility.

Intellectually speaking, it was the ideologues of the counter-revolution and the Restoration, de Lamennais and above all de Maistre, who were primarily responsible for Vatican I's definition of infallibility: The dogma was essentially a "new idea of the nineteenth century" (C. Langlois). The medieval canonists—and in those days the Church's teaching was their business—had never claimed that the Church needed an infallible head to preserve its faith. Instead they maintained that, however its head might err, the Church as a whole would never be led astray.

With the historical reconstruction of Vatican I finally out of the way, the first half of the theological business at hand has been taken care of. But no less momentous than the question of "how the pope became infallible" is another one: "How can the pope (once more) be pope without infallibility?" Here are some thoughts on that subject as I framed them in connection with the infallibility debate back in 1973.

How could the pope "function" without infallible doctrinal definitions? As a matter of fact, we have in our time come to know two possibilities here. There was a pope—Pius XII—who, not quite a century after Vatican I, felt he had to lay claim to the full power which the Council had ascribed to the popes but which they had never used. He did this in order to proclaim an infallible doctrinal definition, a new dogma on Mary, *urbi et orbi*. Yet none of his other pronouncements were ever so controverted, throughout the Christian world and even in the Catholic Church, as this "infallible" definition. Pius XII had high hopes then that the dogma would foster devotion to Mary among Catholics and help to convert the world—hopes which, thirty years later, we can only judge to have been intemperate. The fact that Vatican II dissociated itself from Mariolatry has made the questionableness of that definition still more apparent.

The other example: The next pope, John XXIII, had, from

the start, no ambition whatever of proclaiming an infallible definition. On the contrary, he continually stressed in the most varied ways his own humanity, his limitations, and now and again even his fallibility. He lacked the aura of infallibility. And yet none of the popes in this century had as great an influence on the course of Catholic history and of Christianity itself as this pope who put no stock in infallibility. Pope John and Vatican II ushered in a new era of church history. Without any infallible proclamations he succeeded in getting the Church to listen to the gospel of Jesus Christ once more. This is what gave him the authority he had both inside and outside the Catholic Church, in a way that would have been unthinkable back in the days of his predecessor. In any event, with all his weaknesses and mistakes—his approach was more spontaneous than planned, more sketchy than programmatic—he demonstrated in rough outline how the pope could be pope without claiming infallibility: no jealous insistence on full power and prerogatives, no exercise of authority after the fashion of the ancien régime, but an authority of service, in the spirit of the New Testament, with a view to the needs of today—fraternal partnership and cooperation, dialogue, consultation and collaboration, above all, with the bishops and theologians of the entire Church, participation in the decision-making process of everyone affected by it, and an invitation to share responsibility. In other words, even when teaching and proclaiming the faith, the pope is most emphatically to see his function as *in* the Church, *with* the Church, *for* the Church, but not *over* or *outside* the Church.

On the other hand, this does not exclude the possibility of a pope's taking a decisive stand *against* something or, under certain circumstances, having a duty to take a stand. There was no need of any sort of infallible definition in the face of the blitzkrieg in Poland or the mass murder of the Jews: A clear, understandable statement from the "Deputy" truly reflecting the Christian message would have been enough. It is remarkable how seldom the popes have spoken "infallibly" in modern times just when countless millions of people would have expected them to. Conversely, in spite of all his fallibility, the pope can (together with the rest of the bishops) serve the community of the Church, promote its unity, inspire the missionary work of the Church in the world, and intensify his efforts for peace and justice, disarmament, human rights, the social liberation of nations and races, and the disadvantaged everywhere. Without making any claim to infallibility, he can let the voice of the Good Shepherd ring out time and again in the Christian ecumene and far beyond it through his life and work. He would then become a source of inspiration in the spirit of Jesus Christ and a leader in Christian renewal, and Rome would become a rendezvous for conversation and candid, friendly cooperation.

It follows from all this that the pope can indeed function without infallible doctrinal definitions. He can, in fact, *better* fulfill his obligations in the Church and the world such as they are today without such definitions. To raise doubts, then, about the infallibility of papal pronouncements is not to call the papacy itself into question. This point must be stressed as firmly as possible to correct the continual errors, distortions, and insinuations one hears on this topic. Many aspects of the Petrine office *have* become dubious, most notably the medieval and modern forms of absolutism, which have been retained right up to the present. The papacy has a future only if it is understood in the light of the Petrine symbolism found in the New Testament. The exegetical and scholarly grounds for a *historical* succession of the bishops of Rome have also become questionable. But the papacy will have kept its real meaning if it functions as a *practical succession* of servants to the entire Church: a primacy of service in the full biblical sense.

Such a primacy of service, as we saw it, at least sketched out if not completed, in the figure of John XXIII, offers the Catholic Church and the whole Christian world a great *opportunity*. A primacy based on service would be more than a "primacy of honor." The latter would be unforgivable in a church that aimed to serve mankind; it would, in its very passivity, be of no help to anyone. A primacy of service would also be more than a "primacy of jurisdiction": Seen purely in terms of power and authority, that would be a fundamental misunderstanding of the ideal, and if taken literally would leave out the most important thing of all, namely, service. The papacy, as the Bible would have it, can only be a "pastoral primacy": a service of ministry to the entire Church. This sort of papacy is fully supported by the New Testament, despite all the problems of historical succession which have not yet been cleared up and probably never will be. This sort of papacy could greatly benefit all of the modern Christian world.

There is one last question left: Can a person who criticizes infallibility *remain a Catholic theologian?* Is not a position, which has no New Testament or several hundred years of Catholic theology on its side, acceptable within the Catholic Church? Once again: disciplinary Church measures cannot silence the request. The number of doubters is too high. Opinion polls, were they taken, might well show that in many countries only a minority of Catholics believe in papal infallibility. And so the previous attempt to brand the critics of infallibility before all the world as un-Catholic proved to be a failure. The same thing happened with the critics of the Papal States, who were threatened with excommunication but who have finally been vindicated—many of them, of course, only after their death.

We have to make a distinction here. "Un-Catholic" does not mean someone who turns against the *Roman system,* that is, Roman Catholicism, which achieved a position of dominance in doctrine, ethics, and church government in the eleventh century, and which has been continually accused of over-centralization, absolutism, triumphalism, and imperialism, both at Vatican II and in the postconciliar period, by bishops, theologians, and laymen. From the standpoint of the Gospel, there is no reason to reject the notion of a unique role—in connection with Peter and the great Roman tradition—for the pope as servant ministering to souls. But that absolutist curial system which views the free community of the Catholic faith as a religious version of the Roman Empire violates the spirit of the Gospel and is chiefly responsible for the schism with the Eastern Church, for the Protestant Reformation, and for the petrifaction of the Catholic Church.

"Un-Catholic" refers to anyone who voluntarily turns his back on the Catholic (or whole, universal, all-encompassing) Church. Or, more precisely, anyone who abandons the dogged continuity of belief and of communion in that belief (catholicity in time), which has persisted through all the Church's failures; anyone who gives up on the universality of belief and of communion in that belief (catholicity in space), which embraces all different groups; anyone, then, who falls prey to a "Protestant" radicalism and particularism, which has nothing to do with genuine evangelical radicalness and orientation to local communities. Today, more clearly than ever before, the question poses itself: Does not the infallibility of doctrinal propositions (like the Papal States in the last century) belong more to the curialist system than to the Catholic Church, as it has understood itself from the very first? What will the future bring?

The French theologian Yves Congar has called for a "re-reception" of Vatican I's papal doctrines. And it is my strong conviction that the Catholic Church has to go through this process. More than anyone else it was Congar who laid the groundwork for the modern understanding of the Church characteristic of Vatican II. Historical studies (Aubert, Torrell, Schatz), historical-theological analyses (Thils, Dejaifve, Pottmeyer), radical questions (Küng), then the fact of Vatican II itself, the revival of local and particular churches and, lastly, the revived appreciation of the principles of Eastern ecclesiology—all this, Congar maintains, has made more people realize how trapped in its own time Vatican I was. It also impels us "with our Catholic loyalty" to "re-receive" the Vatican dogmas, and especially the dogma of papal infallibility. Taking into consideration an authentic conception of the magisterium, the best exegetical, historical, and theological studies of the past few decades, the ecumenical contacts (made in such a changed environment) with the theology and concrete existence of the local churches, Congar thinks Catholics should get together with the other Christian churches to re-examine and reformulate the dogmas first defined by Vatican I in 1870 and subsequently accepted by the rest of the Church under the conditions prevalent during that epoch. If one were to take up Congar's suggestions, one would have to take the following points into consideration: why not have a fresh investigation into the problem of infallibility from the exegetical, historical, and theological point of view judging the matter with objectivity, scientific integrity, fairness, and justice?

Why not set up an *ecumenical commission* to deal with this issue (as was done before with birth control) made up of internationally recognized experts from the various disciplines (exegesis, history of dogma, systematic theology, and relevant nontheological fields)?

In carrying out this investigation, why not put more emphasis than before on the positive, constructive side of the question and less on the negative, critical side? Why not ask whether the notion that *the Church will remain in the truth despite all errors* doesn't have a more solid foundation in the Christian message and the great Catholic tradition than does infallibility, and whether this wouldn't make for a better life in the Church today?

One application of this idea: Pope Paul's rejection of every form of contraception was based on the Roman concept of the authority, continuity, universality, and therefore de facto infallibility and irreversibility of traditional doctrine. Since that time Rome seems to have come to an impasse on this question, as it has on some others. *Non possumus* (we cannot) is still the response today, as it once was to the demand that the Church relinquish the Papal States. The only way to solve the problem of contraception is to solve the problem of infallibility. The Church's leadership is all too often satisfied with admonishing everybody. In this case it could, in an act of humility and self-criticism, lend the world some active help by courageously revising the doctrine of the supposed immorality of all (!) contraception. This teaching, which forms the basis of *Humanae vitae,* has laid a heavy burden on the conscience of innumerable people, even in industrially developed countries with declining birthrates. But for the people in many underdeveloped countries, especially in Latin America, it constitutes a source of incalculable harm, a crime in which the Church has implicated itself. High birthrates are linked in a cause-effect relationship with poverty, illiteracy, unemployment, malnutrition, and disease. In the last two decades most of the gains (by no means insignificant) in food production among Third World nations were wiped out by population growth.

Pope John Paul II has traveled to many countries and has come back with a store of new experiences. While abroad, he spoke out clearly against poverty, underdevelopment, and the misery endured by children, and for human rights and ecumenism. Is it hoping for too much, then, to expect him to take a decisive step towards clearing up this vexing question of infallibility—in an atmosphere of mutual trust, free research, and fair-minded discussion?

Tübingen, July 1982

Hans Küng
Director of the Institute
for Ecumenical Research,
University of Tübingen

A CANDID PREFACE

The renewal of the Catholic Church sought by the second Vatican Council, with its prospect of ecumenical understanding with other Christian Churches and a new opening out toward the modern world, has come to a standstill. Five years after the close of Vatican II, this state of affairs can no longer be overlooked. And it would be imprudent and dangerous to remain silent about the fact in Church and in theology. After long, postconciliar years of patient but vain waiting, a more outspoken and blunt manner of speaking may be permitted today, in order to reveal the seriousness of the situation and perhaps gain the attention of those responsible.

For the sake of the Church and of the human beings for whom the theologian does his work, the reasons for this stagnation must be exposed, so that hope and action again in the postconciliar period, as before and during the Council, can break through in force. Let no one assume (we are anticipating here the objections and reproaches that will inevitably be raised) a lack of faith or charity on our part, when now, in view of our concern and understanding for so much human suffering in the Church, appeasement and concealment are no longer appropriate, but courageous and hopeful speech (*parrhesia*) is required.

It should scarcely be necessary to insist that what follows is not an attempt to bring unrest and uncertainty into the Church, but only to give expression to the unrest and uncertainty already to be found on all sides; that the author is not driven on by his own arrogance, but only wants to help to gain a hearing for the undeniable grievances of the believing community; that if perhaps occasionally the tone is sharp and the style harsh, this is a reflection, not of the author's aggressiveness, but of the way in which the matter affects him.

There could be two main reasons why we have not made more progress at the present time into the solution of a number of questions, which to most people inside and outside the Catholic Church seems overdue:

In spite of the impetus of the Council, it has hitherto not been possible decisively to change the institutional-personal *power-structure of the Church leadership* in the spirit of the Christian message: pope, Curia, and many bishops, in spite of the unavoidable changes which have taken place, continue to carry on in a largely preconciliar way; they seem to have learned little from the Council. Now as before, both in Rome and in a number of areas of the Church, at the controls of spiritual power are personalities who are interested more in maintaining the comfortable status quo than in serious renewal. Now as before, decisive institutional reforms are prevented which would lead to fewer conservatives' being in key positions of leadership, people who keep to the party line, men imbued with the Roman mentality. Now, as before, the existing Roman canon law (to be confirmed and strengthened by a "basic law" already planned) prevents the renewal of the Church, as it is wanted and sought by the most active groups of laity and clergy, from having any effect on the most urgent problems.

What is to be done in this field has been explained elsewhere. In our book *The Church* (1968), we developed in principle an understanding of the Church for modern times in the light of the biblical message and there said what was necessary about service in the Church and a renewed Petrine ministry. In another book, *Truthfulness: On the Future of the Church* (1968), we tried to apply these principles and to work out the practical requirements which emerge logically in the light of the gospel from the Second Vatican Council (as one of the most urgent requirements, we need mention only a new arrangement for papal elections: in the present system the pope is chosen by a completely superannuated body, consisting largely of pensioners and still dominated largely by a single nation and a single mentality). What has been said in these two books will not be repeated here, but only confirmed in a more or less general way.

It would be for the bishops—who all according to Vatican II bear a common responsibility for the whole Church—to see that justified demands are carried out in Rome and at the same time to go ahead courageously and resolutely with the renewal in their own countries and dioceses. In any case, nothing will be achieved without untiring struggle and patient effort, nor without constant, legitimate pressure on Church leaders by individuals, priests and laity, men and women, and by the various newly created bodies in parishes and dioceses and in the Church as a whole. Nor without the creation of counterstructures: priest-groups and lay groups, with definite, concrete objectives (reform of the regulations for mixed marriages, the putting into practice of the concept of co-responsibility, a change in the law of clerical celibacy). Nor finally without prudently considered, abundant self-help, perhaps even against particular regulations in cases where—because of human need—further waiting cannot be justified. Hitherto, in spite of the impetus of the Council, it has not been possible to consider critically and determine afresh, in the spirit of the Christian message, the *nature and function of the Church's teaching authority*. Even in the field of doctrine astonishingly little seems to have been learned from the Council; the ecclesiastical "teaching office" is conceived by the Pope and also by a number of bishops largely in a preconciliar authoritarian way, without the co-operation with theology tested at the Council and much more necessary after it. Now as before, a preconciliar theology feebly touched up in individual cases is dominant in Rome. Now as before, the Church is presented with encyclicals, decrees and pastoral letters which in decisive matters are not supported by the Gospel, are not really understood by most people today, and cannot be substantiated by theology. Now as before, the Holy Spirit is invoked in all possible questions great and small; apostolic plenary powers are asserted, in fact with such a display of infallibility that five years after the Council the authority and credibility of the Catholic Church have been exposed to a test the severity of which has scarcely been paralleled.

The critical-constructive theological reflection of this book will therefore be devoted to the complex of questions relating to the ecclesiastical teaching authority. The author did not seek out this dangerously tricky subject: it is simply imposed on him as on other theologians by the needs of the Church and the requirements of the time. The centenary of the First Vatican Council might perhaps have been passed over in 1970 as unceremoniously as the fourth centenary of the Council of Trent at the time of Vatican II. But in the postconciliar period no one has contributed more to critical reflection on Vatican I and its definitions than the Vatican itself. No one has done more in recent years to provoke the demythologizing of the ecclesiastical teaching office than this teaching office itself. And no one has raised the question of ecclesiastical infallibility more than those who themselves act as if infallible in all possible questions relating to the Church's doctrine, morals, and discipline.

If we look back—not "look back in anger," but certainly "look back in anxiety"—the context which has led to the composition of this book, which some may consider provocative but which is meant to be constructive, becomes clear. There can be no question of romanticizing the time of the Council and John's pontificate or—consequently—of creating resentment against the present holder of the Petrine ministry. Nevertheless, to get the right perspective, the ecclesial reality —even in its negative aspect—must be described with no holds barred. John XXIII, by his whole attitude, by his words and deeds, had exercised the ecclesiastical "teaching office" in a new, Christian way—or perhaps in reality in a more original way, a way therefore more potent for the future. People listened to him, both inside and outside the Catholic Church. Together with the Council, he produced for the Catholic Church an astonishing increase in internal and external credibility. But many a person who actively co-operated in this renewal is now saddened at having to see how the store of confidence gained in those few years has been dissipated in a still shorter time and how much hope and joy has thereby been destroyed.

Paul VI is a serious man, a man of integrity, who suffers under his responsibility and perhaps also under the weight of excessive demands. He personally unselfishly wants only the best for the Church and mankind and sincerely thinks he must act in this way. He has shown this concern for mankind clearly in matters where he does not feel tied by dogma or ecclesiastical policy: in his initiatives for world peace and disarmament, for social justice, the third world and development aid, for the extension of liturgical reform, for a restricted personnel and structural reform in the Roman Curia, etc. By comparison with some high curial advisers, he can be described as a moderate. Although for some in the Church and in the world he seems to be on the extreme right, for others within the Vatican ghetto he is too much to the left. And just as John XXIII was not without faults, so Paul VI does not lack strength. All this is not to be disputed or belittled. And yet (would it help the Church to pass over this in silence?) it can no longer be ignored that, contrary to the best intentions of the Pope and his advisers, the longer the teaching office is exercised by pope and Curia, the more it is exercised in a way which—as previously in Church history, and from Rome—inflicts the worst damage on the unity and credibility of the Catholic Church.

The most important facts are known and no one should be criticized for enumerating them. For they indicate better

than any abstract-critical reflection the tendency adopted by
the official Church in the postconciliar period. The signals
of a negative development could already be seen at an early
stage of the Council, when the newly elected Pope Paul,
after his great and hopeful address at the opening of the
second session in 1963, from about the middle of the session
—out of increasing apprehension, theological uncertainty, curial tradition, consideration for those around him and because
of the fluctuating political situation of his native Italy, or
for one reason or another—began to make speeches very
different in tone. As opposed to the Council, full of the joy
of renewal, the Pope more and more frequently supported
the Curia—backward-looking, unecumenical, traditionalistic,
nationalistic, thinking in terms of power politics—to which he
himself had belonged for thirty years.

Paul VI rejected the demand of a number of members for
a free election by the Council of the presidents of the commissions, and thus for a renovation of the commissions, which
had been dominated by the curial machinery. In a personal
address to the Council he committed himself to the schema
on the Missions, wholly conceived from the standpoint of
the Roman Congregation on the Missions, which was afterward rejected by the great majority of the assembly as
completely inadequate. There were acts of real sabotage on
the part of the Curia against the Declaration on the Jews and
the Declaration on Religious Freedom and only the solid
protest of the bishops and the theologians prevented the final
torpedoing of these important projects. In the schema on
Ecumenism, already frequently approved by the Council, the
Pope at the last minute introduced changes which were
scarcely friendly toward other Christians and which had
ostensibly been approved by the Secretariat for Unity.

The commissions of the Council and particularly the theological commission were generally harassed on certain questions (not least on those which are discussed in this book) by
postulates "from higher authority," which were inspired by

curial theologians and repeatedly led to changes for the worse in the text. Discussion on birth control was forbidden by the Pope and—like the question of mixed marriages by the Council itself—referred to a papal commission: actions for which the postconciliar Church was to pay dearly. Names of bishops who wanted to raise the question of celibacy were deleted from the list of speakers and at the papal behest no discussion on the celibacy question as such took place at the Council, so that the burden of grappling with it was again loaded on to the postconciliar Church. On the question of the relationship between pope and bishops, decisive for the future of the Church, the Pope imposed on the Council a *nota explicativa*, watering down episcopal collegiality, which was never submitted to a vote: ideological security for all isolated, uncollegial papal actions in the subsequent period. Against the express will of the majority of the Council, Paul VI proclaimed for Mary the misleading title Mater Ecclesiae, which roused great hostility and doubt about the Pope's genuine desire for ecumenical understanding, and not only outside the Catholic Church. The author publicly referred to these notorious facts and the dangerous consequences for the credibility of the Church and Pope at the end of the third session of the Council in 1964:[1] a move which led to his being called to account in Rome and to a "colloquium" first with Cardinal Ottaviani and then with two commissioners of the Inquisition, which however took place in an atmosphere of mutual respect.

With the fourth session the Second Vatican Council came to an end. In spite of all the difficulties, reverses, and defects, seen as a whole, it was a magnificent success. Even now, and particularly now, this cannot be sufficiently emphasized. No doors were closed, but innumerable doors were opened: in regard to the other Christian Churches; in regard to the Jews; the great world religions; and the problems of the secular world generally; and finally in regard also to the internal structure of the Catholic Church herself. A new spirit, a new freedom of thinking, discussing and acting, a new approach to truth, had become reality. Constitutions, decrees and declarations, in spite of all their negative features, contained so much that was positive that it could rightly be said at the time in an account of the Council's achievements:[2]

> In spite of all, what is now important is not to complain of the indisputable obscurities, compromises, omissions, imbalance, retrograde steps and mistakes as defects of the past, in a critical manoeuvre directed backward, but to see them in forward-looking hope as *tasks of the future*, in the spirit of the Council which did not want to close any doors. For in a sense the Council, the true realization of the Council event, *began* on December 8, 1965. And precisely in order to prepare the better future, we must at the present time not make the better the enemy of the good, but the good the herald of the better.

The Council offered a splendid program for a renewed Church of the future.[3] And in innumerable parishes and dioceses throughout the world people set to work energetically to implement it. The Pope too exhorted his reluctant curial officials to take the Council's conclusions seriously. Subsequently he appointed new, more moderate men, including foreigners, especially Frenchmen, to important posts and in various respects the Roman central administration was reformed, but it was also internally strongly centralized.

In a short time there began to prevail, at least theoretically, in the Catholic Church a new concept of the Church as the people of God and of ecclesiastical office as a service to this people. Reform of the Mass and the introduction of the mother tongue, with a new arrangement of Scripture readings meant substantial progress. Ecumenical co-operation, both at the parish level (common action and Bible services) and at the level of the Church as a whole (by mutual visits and mixed study commissions), was strengthened. The reform of priests' seminaries and religious orders was very energetically pressed forward, up to a point. Diocesan and parish councils with strong lay participation were founded and began to be active. New life began to appear in theology and a new opening-out of the Church toward the problems of modern man and society was clearly developing. Nothing was perfect, but everything was basically good and hopeful.

Important internal problems of the Church, meanwhile, were left unsettled as a result of the attitude of the Pope and of the bishops, who at that time did not protest. These were problems which in the course of time were to occupy the general public more than any others: birth control, the question of mixed marriages, priestly celibacy in the Latin Church, structural and personnel reform of the Roman Curia, the effective involvement of the areas concerned in the appointment of new, suitable bishops. These were certainly not the central theological questions of Christian proclamation, but nevertheless were of the utmost urgency particularly for the credible proclamation of the Christian message today and for the innumerable people affected by them.

But just at these neuralgic points, where solutions really were and are quite possible in every case, guidance was lacking: the great, strong, hopeful spiritual leadership which had emanated from John XXIII did not appear. Instead, increasingly, we had exhortations and warnings, often very gloomy, and complaints and accusations to bishops and bishops' conferences, to theologians, priests, young people in the Church and the world . . . The reasons, of a personal and structural character, for this reaction are manifold. As always, instead of taking the bold message of Jesus Christ himself and the new challenges of a new age as an orientation pole, there was an increasingly strong, fearful, and nervous concentration on the maintenance of the status quo and of one's own spiritual power, no part of which would be given up.

The traditional curial policy and theology again prevailed and in Rome there was largely a relapse into the preconciliar absolutism, juridicism, and centralism: all in accordance with the saying quoted at the time of the Council, "Councils may go, popes may go, but the Roman Curia remains." The Curia was expanded, instead of being cut down, and its centralization in the Secretariat of State means setting back all other curial authorities, so that now again, as in the time of Pius XII, responsibility for the most important decisions lies in fact less with the appropriate congregations than with some secret, but well-known "super-periti."

In view of this consolidation in Rome, many bishops and bishops' conferences remained undecided, wavering, passive, in the postconciliar period. Instead of at once boldly tackling the application of the Council's decisions to individual countries, they continued to wait. The Dutch bishops in a unique and admirable way seized the chance to identify themselves with the cares and needs of their own clergy and people; but the same opportunity was not grasped elsewhere. While some bishops attempted a new style, others again adopted a downright preconciliar-authoritarian attitude. Rome remained the model. The co-operation between bishops and theologians, which had functioned so well at the Council and contributed substantially to its success, came largely to a standstill in the postconciliar period. People wanted to be with their own kind again and the results were what might have been expected. Only when a fire broke out or when Latin documents were needed (as at the Council), was the help of theologians welcome. But otherwise theologians were regarded by a number of bishops as people to be avoided, an awkward species of men, who could easily be blamed for lack of humility, faith, love for the Church. It was not very readily admitted that the theologians had only given warnings about the crisis; they had not produced it. It took seven postconciliar years in Germany before a synod was finally announced for 1972, although it could have been envisaged even before 1965. In numerous other countries, in this respect, nothing at all has yet been done. But the hope that everything would remain as it was turned out to be deceptive.

The Roman Curia had meanwhile been making efforts to retain bishops with a preconciliar mentality in office even beyond the age limit envisaged by the Council (in principle, seventy-five): the old Roman system of royal dispensations and privileges was functioning again. And new bishops were selected—as far as Rome had a free hand—preferably according to the two "tried and tested" principles: sound moral standards and the utmost possible uncritical loyalty to the Roman party line (which was called "obedience"). Fortunately, mistakes were made in some cases and men were allowed to slip through the net who afterward distinguished themselves as bishops by their independence of judgment, courageous action, and unexpected initiatives. In Rome this was not appreciated at all—we may recall the irrelevant reactions to the initiatives of the Dutch episcopate and to the famous, very moderate, and objective interview with Cardinal Suenens, on which we shall comment later—and that type of bishop who always remains compliant toward Rome was preferred, even though—as is obvious in many cases—this resulted in the real leadership of the diocese more and more slipping out of such bishops' hands.

Under these circumstances, increasing solidarity particularly among the younger clergy in priests' groups and also among some laymen appeared to be a necessity and for many a veritable sign of hope in an ecclesiastical system again consolidating itself. It will have to be admitted, even on the part of those ruling the Church, that most of these groups of priests have behaved with extraordinary moderation, rationally and constructively.

Of course we should not put all the blame on Rome for the present critical situation. The numeous theologians too, who have been silent when they should have spoken, bear a considerable measure of responsibility. Nevertheless, the fact cannot be overlooked that Roman reaction carries the main

responsibility for the present intensifying of the crisis. Obviously the Pope is convinced that he has done much, very
much, for the renewal of the Church. Once again the sincerity
of his conviction and his good intentions are not in question
for a moment. But what appears to be revolutionary from
the narrow Roman perspective—the long overdue shaking
of some Vatican court traditions, the simplification of clothes
and titles that still seem odd, the acceptance of foreign but
blatantly very Roman-minded prelates into the Curia—is
scarcely worth mentioning so far as the world and the greater
part of the Church are concerned. For these there are more
important things that count.

It is true that the Index has been abolished and another
name given to the Roman Inquisition. But there are still
inquisitional processes against troublesome theologians and
the order of procedure of this "Congregation for the Doctrine
of the Faith," although settled by the Pope in 1965, has not
yet been published. It is true that an international commission
of theologians has been finally set up. But the more recent
conciliar and postconciliar theology has scarcely been admitted in the Curia, as—among other things—the painful in-
cidents connected with the Dutch Catechism prove. Theologians like Daniélou, formerly persecuted by the Inquisition,
but now themselves bringing an aura of scholarship to the
role of Grand Inquisitor, are nominated as Cardinals of the
Holy Roman Church.

Certainly a synod of bishops has twice been convoked
and the importance of the episcopal office is spoken of generally with great reverence. But even the modest recom-
mendations of this high-ranking representative body of the
whole Church have little visible effect and disappear into
those Vatican offices where—understandably—they prefer the
intimation of a personal wish to the expression of an official
standpoint. It is true that bishops have been given back
some of their original rights to grant dispensations. But, at
the same time, against the Council's wishes, the position of

nuncios was strengthened by a motu proprio (1969); and a papal commission for the reform of Canon Law—in which there was no representation of public opinion in the Church, not even of progressive specialists like those of the Canon Law Society of America—was allowed to work out a "Basic Law of the Catholic Church" which would use the words of Vatican II to strengthen the hold of Roman absolutism.

It is true that the Church's calendar has been "reformed" —in the clumsiest way—at the expense of some unhistorical saints, but at the same time the claim is made that the relics found under the main altar of St. Peter's can be officially identified as those of the Apostle Peter although this is rejected by the most competent historians. The reform of women's orders had been demanded, but in America, where it had been most seriously attempted, it was stopped by the Congregation for Religious. Cardinals' trains have been shortened but not cut off; indulgences "reformed" but not abolished; the expenses of canonization reduced but not abolished altogether.

It is true that during the Council, after more than 900 years, the excommunication of the Patriarch of Constantinople and his Churches was rescinded and mutual visits arranged. But after lifting the excommunication, the communio, the eucharistic community, was still not restored; instead, all the Roman privileges and prerogatives which have become customary since the middle ages have been rigidly maintained. It is true that relations have been established with the World Council of Churches and a call was made at the General Secretariat of the World Council on the occasion of a visit to the International Labour Office in Geneva. But only a few ecumenical deeds have followed all the ecumenical words. In the mixed marriage question a new motu proprio (1970) attempts by a discriminating use of dispensations to continue to avoid and prevent a general recognition of the validity of all mixed marriages, and opposes an ecumenical wedding ceremony based on equal rights of the

Churches and a responsible decision of the parents with regard to the baptism and education of the children.

It is true that a papal journey to Jerusalem was undertaken and greetings paid to the Israeli government. But now as before, because of political considerations, the state of Israel has not been recognized; and, in response to the threat to annihilate the Israeli nation, the same exhortation to peace was prudently sent to both sides, in the style of Pius XII. In contrast to journeys to the United Nations and addresses on human rights, there is diplomatic silence in regard to the persecution and torture of Catholic priests and lay people in South American military dictatorships; and a journey to Portugal, where at that time the suppression of freedom in Church and state with the crudest totalitarian methods was likewise passed over in silence, paid tribute instead to a Marian pilgrimage center historically and theologically dubious in every respect.

In Italy a violent protest and an intervention utilizing every possible means of opposition were raised against a reasonable civil divorce law, such as has long existed in several countries, although on the other hand the non-recognition of the validity of so many mixed marriages positively encourages divorce for frivolous reasons. It is true that papal journeys made to Africa, Asia, and South America were highly publicized as efforts on behalf of the third world. But the solution offered for the central problem there, the population explosion, is continence, and contraceptives are prohibited.

It is particularly depressing to have to view such actions and developments, but it brings us directly to our main theme: the more the Pope attempts to take his teaching office seriously, so much the more does this seem to happen at the expense of the credibility of this teaching office and of the inner cohesion of the Church.

Papal doctrinal statements seem to many to be party documents inspired by narrow Roman theology and ideology, and they have not made the desired impact on the Church. Only in the dogmatically innocuous field of the encyclical *Populorum Progressio* (1967), and of development aid, did the Pope venture to press forward, without however drawing any very clear conclusions about the role of the Church and the Vatican in regard to immediate assistance. The remaining important doctrinal documents, however, in essentials display a reactionary character. The first encyclical, *Ecclesiam Suam* (1963), was disappointing because of its not very ecumenical Romanism and its defective biblical substantiation. The encyclical, *Mysterium Fidei,* on the Eucharist (1965)—which Paul VI, to the scandal of many bishops, published just before the assembly of the Council for its fourth session, with an eye on Holland—also shows the Pope tied to a textbook theology on which neither the exegesis nor the historical studies of the last decades have made any sort of impression; John XXIII's statement that the clothing of formulas of faith may change, while the substance of faith remains the same, is disowned. The encyclical *Sacerdotalis Coelibatus* (1967), distorts the supreme truths of the Gospel in a really painful way, in order not to prove what it was supposed to prove: that the Church's rulers can impose a binding law abolishing freedom in regard to what should be a freely accepted vocation to celibacy in the spirit of the gospel. The encyclical *Humanae Vitae* (1968), makes the weakness and backwardness of Roman theology clearly evident to the astonished general public throughout the world and within the Catholic Church has aroused opposition such as had not hitherto existed, from simple Church members, theologians, bishops, and bishops' conferences. The papal *Credo* (1968), which the Pope in a typical Roman gesture of identification, without consulting the Church, declares to be the "Credo of the People of God," completely neglects the "hierarchy of truths" noted by Vatican II and in fact places problematic theologoumena of the Roman tradition on the same plane as central statements of the Christian faith. The latest mixed-marriage decree (1970) shows again, behind all the ecumenical assurances, the fundamentally unecumenical attitude of the Roman central administration.

It fits in with all this that Paul VI, answered the just and substantiated demand of the Dutch bishops and their Church for a re-examination of the law of celibacy with an abrupt "No" from the window of his palace, as if it were a question of a dogma of the Church or at least a matter to be decided by himself alone; instead of a dialogue with his Dutch brethren in the episcopal office, he sought a dialogue with the Cardinal Secretary of State living on the floor below and wrote a letter to him. Also betraying an abysmal lack of confidence, he attempted to impose on all the clergy that repressive measure—the annual renewal of priestly promises in connection with the Maundy Thursday liturgy. As if it were possible to compensate by promises and oaths for lack of intelligence and biblical substantiation.

Quousque tandem . . . we might cry out with the Roman Cicero, if we did not know that here is not simply an individual who fails in good faith, but rather that all this taken together is symbolic of the Roman system, which is still characterized by a spiritual absolutism, formalistic and frequently inhuman juridicism, and a traditionalism spelling death to genuine renewal that are really shocking to modern man.

At this point in order to avoid all misunderstandings and to quell the doubts expressed in letters from pious souls, let it be known that the writer of this book is and remains for all his criticism a convinced Catholic theologian. But just because he is a Catholic theologian deeply bound to his Church, he thinks he has the right and unfortunately also the duty, in all modesty and fully aware of his own human inadequacy *and* fallibility, to raise a protest, which cannot be misunderstood or unheard, against the way in which—with good intentions, but blindly—the people of God are being deprived of the fruits of the Council.

A Petrine ministry in the Church makes sense and every Catholic will affirm it. But the pope exists for the Church and not the Church for the pope. His primacy is not a primacy of ruling, but a primacy of service. And the holder of the Petrine ministry may not set himself up either as Lord of the Church or—still less—as Lord of the Gospel: this is what he does when today, after all the negative experiences of earlier times and the positive experience of the Council, he still interprets that ministry in the light of an uncritically adopted tradition, theology, and ecclesiastical policy.

It was this Roman theology and ecclesiastical policy which caused the separation of the Eastern Churches from Rome and then the breakaway of the Reformed Churches and finally encapsulated the Church in the Counter-Reformation ghetto. Would it not be better, in this fresh crisis provoked by Roman intransigence, opportunely, clearly, and publicly to sound a warning before still more priests give up their ministry, still more candidates for the priesthood leave, still more people noisily or noiselessly turn their backs on the Church and the Church is further degraded to the level of a subculture? The disappointment, the enervation, even defeatism and hopelessness that have spread lately particularly among the best of our clergy and people cannot be described.

The crisis must be endured and will be overcome. Without any bitterness or resentment, but also unimpressed by any sanctimonious exhortation to keep quiet and to practice obedient "humility" and "love" for the Church, by the power of the message of Jesus Christ himself and his Spirit, in the spirit of the Second Vatican Council, we shall continue to stand up in word and deed for the reform and renewal of our Church. For reform and renewal! Let this too be clearly stated: as we have no time for reaction in the Church, neither do we have any time for revolution—at any rate, in the sense of violently overthrowing her government and values.

Certainly the question may rightly be asked: can an absolutist system—and the Roman system is the sole absolutist system that has survived the French Revolution intact—be overcome without violent revolution? But, precisely in the light of the Christian message, which aims at radical conversion and not at violent subversion, a counterquestion may be raised. By the power of Christ's message, should not that which seems to occur rarely in the world and in world politics be possible in the Church: the overcoming of an absolutist system without violent revolution as a result of internal renewal of persons and structures? We cannot abandon the struggle for renewal and reform, but neither can we abandon discussion and the hope of mutual understanding.

In this book, then, the complex of questions relating to the ecclesiastical teaching authority and, at the same time, the question of infallibility in particular will be taken up. In our previous book on the Church infallibility was dealt with—for good reasons—merely marginally; but—likewise with good reasons—some reviewers demanded an *ex professo* treatment of the subject, and the present developments within the Church make such a treatment imperative. Roman abolutism and traditionalism in theory and practice will here be examined theologically at the point where they appear with particular sharpness and are also particularly influential. The claim to *infallibility* in the Church is always present subliminally, even when not given formal expression. This claim to infallibility will be examined with the encyclical of Paul VI which has so shaken the credibility of the Catholic Church and her teaching office by its apodictic rejection of all "artificial" birth control, as the starting point.

It has now become quite clear that the conception of continuity, authority, infallibility of the Church and the Church's teaching, on which there has not been sufficient reflection, has led the Catholic Church into a dangerous tight corner. If we have the strength (and humility) to make an effort to get out of that impasse, in the end the profit may be greater than the loss. For there would then be opened up to us a free area where we could walk without constantly going wide of the mark and without the constant need to reassure ourselves. Also we might find again our Christian brethren, who for so long have not understood us, particularly on this point.

There will be no Imprimatur for this book: not because the book is not meant to be Catholic, but because—as we hope—it is Catholic even without an Imprimatur. The Imprimatur, particularly in recent years, has become increasingly meaningless. On the one hand, the Imprimatur did not prevent my book *The Church* from becoming involved in a Roman Inquisition process which is not yet closed. On the other hand, more than one bishop has asked authors seeking an Imprimatur for their books voluntarily to do without it, since in Rome and elsewhere it might be understood as an episcopal recommendation of the book. The Imprimatur, as we know from experience, means in many cases the precensorship of one theological school by another and its abolition has long been urgent; but thinking in centuries often means that there is no time to solve the problems of the present moment. At the time of royal absolutism permission to print was the usual thing for publications of all kinds; the Church was no exception in this respect. But for modern times free expression of opinion is a basic human right, which cannot be denied even to a Catholic theologian in the ecclesial community, as long as he is striving for the truth of the Church's proclamation.[4]

Perhaps at the end of this frank preface we may quote what Cardinal Bernhard Alfrink said in another connection, in his important closing speech at the Dutch Pastoral Council (one of the few great, hopeful signs for so many people in the postconciliar period):

We have carried on the debate with the utmost frankness and given others the opportunity, as far as they wanted, to be witnesses of what we were doing and to be drawn into it. Once again, not as propaganda, but only to render a service. For what we discussed were really not our questions alone. No one can dispose of the message of the Lord as of an exclusive possession. We shall have to experience it always as a challenge and thus for ourselves too occasionally as a painful message. In this way too we hope to contribute something to the reconciliation of the Churches.[5]

It is in such a spirit and tone that the author would like to come before the public with this book and to provide some assistance to those who must patiently persevere on the "long road through the institutions." The unforgettable John F. Kennedy described this effort of ours in relation to his own task in these words:

All this will not be finished in the first 100 days. Nor will it be finished in the first 1,000 days, nor in the life of this Administration, nor even perhaps in our own life time on this planet. But let us begin.

In your hands, my fellow citizens, more than mine, will rest the final success or failure of our course.

Tübingen, Pentecost 1970

I. INFALLIBLE TEACHING OFFICE?

1. The errors of the ecclesiastical teaching office

The assertion of an "infallibility" of the teaching office in the Catholic Church has always been unacceptable to non-Christians and to Christians outside that Church. In recent times, however, it has become to a surprising extent at least questionable even within the Catholic Church. For this reason the question, sometimes more assumed than expressed, but discussed more and more openly among both theologians and laymen today, will be considered here theologically in the form of an *inquiry*, aiming at a definite answer.

It is easy to understand why the question is urgent. The errors of the ecclesiastical teaching office are numerous and serious: today, when frank discussion can no longer be forbidden, they may not be denied even by the more conservative theologians and Church leaders. What might be called classical errors of the ecclesiastical teaching office, now largely admitted, may be listed as follows: the excommunication of Photius, the Ecumenical Patriarch of Constantinople and of the Greek Church, which made formal the schism with the Eastern Church, a schism which is now almost a thousand years old; the prohibition of interest at the beginning of modern times, on which the ecclesiastical teaching office after a variety of compromises changed its mind, much too late; the condemnation of Galileo and the measures adopted as a consequence of this action, which are essentially responsible for the estrangement between the Church and the

natural sciences (not yet overcome today); the condemnation
of new forms of worship in the Rites controversy, which is
one of the main reasons for the large-scale breakdown of
the Catholic missions of modern times in India, China, and
Japan; the maintenance up to the First Vatican Council of
the medieval secular power of the Pope, with the aid of
all secular and spiritual means of excommunication, which
in large measure rendered the papacy incredible as a spiritual
ministry; finally, at the beginning of our century, the numerous condemnations of the approach of modern critical-his-
torical exegesis to the authorship of the books of the Bible,
to source-criticism in the Old and New Testaments, to historicity and literary forms, to the Comma Johanneum, to the
Vulgate; and also the condemnations in the dogmatic field,
particularly in connection with "modernism" (theory of evolution, conception of development of dogma) and most recently of all in connection with Pius XII's encyclical *Humani
Generis*, and the consequent ecclesiastical disciplinary measures, etc.

The errors of the ecclesiastical teaching office in every
century have been numerous and indisputable: a close scrutiny of the Index of Forbidden Books would be particularly
revealing in this respect. And yet the teaching office constantly found it difficult to admit these errors frankly and
honestly. Mostly the correction was made only "implicitly,"
in a veiled way, without any frankness and particularly
without honestly admitting the mistake. It was feared that
awareness of the admitted fallibility of certain important
decisions would restrict or even finally shut out the prospect
of claiming infallibility for certain other important decisions.

For a long time, too, Catholic theologians in their works on
apologetics, in the service of the teaching office, were able
very successfully to ward off any questioning of infallibility
by the use of a basically simple recipe: either it was not
an error or—when at last and finally an error could no longer
be denied, reinterpreted, rendered innocuous or belittled—

it was not an infallible decision. In this way theology helped the hierarchy and in this sense the hierarchy fostered theology. As an example from the distant past of such theological maneuvers, often creating a painful impression, we need only cite the case of Pope Honorius—also discussed at Vatican I—who had been condemned as a heretic by an ecumenical council and several subsequent popes. As a not-too-distant example of a mistaken reaction of the ecclesiastical teaching office, which does not allow for such theological maneuvers, the latest decision of that office—on the immorality of birth control—may be cited. We shall begin our analysis with this very latest test case, which is extraordinarily revealing in regard to the problem of infallibility.

It is not only in scientific experiments, but in theology too and in the Church, that unintended side effects are often more important than the intended main effect. Many a discovery has come about by "chance." Pope Paul VI's encyclical on birth control, *Humanae Vitae*, could have great historical consequences, but not as a result of its main aim: to prevent or at least check the use of "artificial" methods of contraception.

From opinion polls in the most diverse countries it seems that the encyclical has not succeeded, at least in this main aim. The reasons advanced in the encyclical were plainly not sufficient to convince the majority, even within the Catholic Church, and the use of such methods in the future may well increase rather than decrease. Karl Rahner wrote at the time: "From all that has been said up to now we must certainly draw the sober conclusion that, in this respect, the mentality and practice of the majority of Catholics will not be changed after the encyclical."[1] But the unintended side effect of this encyclical, the consequences of which cannot yet be foreseen, is an examination of conscience on a large scale about the meaning of authority—in particular, teaching authority—in the Church.

2. An encyclical as occasion for
an examination of conscience

This question of an examination of conscience has been raised on such a universal scale and in so radical a manner that it has surprised even those who had earlier been worried about the consequences of a possible negative papal decision. But isn't this understandable?

For one thing, it is a question which cannot be a matter of indifference either to the unskilled laborer or to the university professor, to the peasant or to the official; a question that interests New Yorkers just as much as Romans, Asians as much as Europeans. In brief: everyone feels that it is aimed at him and that he is challenged, positively or negatively. Secondly, it is a question that compels a radical answer, an either-or: may I take the pill or no? Here even theologians engaged in playing the Catholic game of "Both this and also that," in a virtuoso dialectic, must answer finally with a definitive "Yes" *or* "No."

Whatever we think of the encyclical, Pope Paul deserves respect for having had the courage to make an unpopular and at the same time *unambiguous* decision. In spite of all the conflicting motives behind its intentions and demands, the text is formulated with Gallic clarity (we know who was the main author).

It might have been worse. An answer could have been presented in the Roman style: in the main clause the traditional "No" and, stuck away in the subordinate clause, an expansible "Yes." But, fortunately, there is nothing like this. All theological-political hermeneutic breaks down, misunderstandings are excluded and subterfuges—such as a broad interpretation of "therapeutic treatment" with hormones, morally permissible according to the encyclical—are offenses against scientific honesty.

The encyclical is clear and unequivocal: "artificial" methods of contraception—by contrast with "natural" periodical abstention—are not permitted, and this on account of the natural law, emanating from the Creator himself. Although the Pope strives—visibly—to speak, not harshly, but pastorally, and although he also recommends sympathy and compassion for the individual sinner, this really only makes it all the more clear: for him it is a question of guilt and sin. So this time we are grateful for knowing quite clearly just where we are. And, in view of the determined tone of the encyclical on the decisive point, it would also be an illusion to think that this document might be withdrawn or revised in the foreseeable future. The Church will have to learn to live with this encyclical.

One thing is novel about the whole discussion: it is centered not so much on the objective arguments of the encyclical as on its authority. In view of the aims of the present exposition, we do not need to discuss what are the problematic aspects of these objective arguments. The reasons put forward against the encyclical largely repeat the arguments already raised in the report of the progressive majority of the papal commission.

These include: the substantiation of the encyclical from natural law is not convincing; its concept of nature is naïve, static, narrow and completely unhistorical; the historicity of man is overlooked and man is dissected in the light of an abstract consideration of his essence; the restriction of the concepts of nature and natural law to physical and biological laws is a retrograde step, back to the long obsolete Aristotelian-stoic-medieval ideas of natural law; the distinction between "natural" and "artificial" is arbitrary and, in connection with hormone preparations for inhibiting ovulation, becomes a matter for the microscope and a question of milligrams. Possible misuse—according to the ancient Roman saying, *abusus non tollit usus*—does not abolish reasonable use. The rhythm method of Ogino-Kraus, with its complicated system of taking temperatures and following the calendar, is

anything but natural and in particular cases might even be
contrary to nature. The artificiality of a method is not an
argument against its permissibility (the Pope has declared
heart transplants permissible) and unconditional respect for
nature gives the latter a sacred character that contradicts
the modern conception of man's responsibility. What happens
between two persons is reduced to a biological event and
the essential difference between animal-biological and hu-
man-responsible sexuality is overlooked. "Total consideration"
of man particularly demands birth control, even by technical
means. The document moralizes about the contemporary situation (particularly the enormous overpopulation of the earth),
but fails to understand it and plays it down. Evaluation of
the sexual factor is still subconsciously handicapped by the
unchristian, manichaean heritage; and the whole encyclical
and its language are evidently completely remote from concrete experience. So the arguments might continue.

Under these circumstances, it is not surprising that the
opinion of the Tübingen canonist, Professor Johannes Neumann, is widely shared:

> If, because of a world-picture belonging to the past, an
> anachronistic theology and an inadequate—because un-
> scriptural—notion of faith, the so-called ecclesiastical teach-
> ing office does not proclaim the glad tidings of Jesus
> crucified and risen, but boasts of being "teacher of the
> nations" and puts forward a "doctrine" made up of an
> inappropriate medley of platonic-artistotelian-thomistic
> ideas, then it is going beyond its mandate, then it can
> claim neither obedience nor credibility. This is precisely
> what is so deplorable about this encyclical: that, in its
> foundations—not in the good intention which may also
> have played a part in its composition—both philosophical
> and theological, to say nothing at all of the empirical
> sciences like medicine and sociology, it was already refuted
> before it was published at all.[2]

At a time when people would prefer to annul the Galileo-process, we are now in danger of creating a second Galileo-case:

It seemes grotesque to think of taking up again the Galileo-case, in order to bring about his rehabilitation, as is said to have been suggested lately, when we are faced with this encyclical and the philosophical and natural law "Weltanschauung"—if you want to call it that—behind it. It is not the Galileo-case, shameful enough but originating in the same way of thinking as this encyclical, that should be dealt with today—the Church is 350 years too late for that—but rather the question of the total meaning of marriage and of accepted and responsible parenthood. It is this Galileo-case of today—that is, the question of the personal meaning of marriage—which ought to be decided today and today be given a helpful answer. Only in this way—that is, by directing people in the spirit of Christ while doing justice to the facts, the situation and man—can the Church today expect to be heard again and taken seriously by Christians, especially by Catholics, but also by all men "of good will."[3]

By contrast with its unequivocally negative, basic attitude on the main point and the weight of the objections, the "progressive elements" of the encyclical, commended by theologians and bishops thinking in terms of apologetics, pale into insignificance. For one thing, these progressive elements are taken for granted by the greater part of the Church: for instance, when Paul VI, in contrast to Pius XII, refrains from calling for complete continence; or when "responsible parenthood" is made the starting point of the argument; or when the marital union is no longer considered—as in the Code of Canon Law—as a remedy for concupiscence. For another thing, with the change of attitude on the part of the teaching office, these "progressive elements" are used to intensify the negative argument of the encyclical, as for in-

stance when sexual love is now no longer subordinated to
procreation as the primary end of marriage, but only in
order precisely to bring out the "inseparable connection" of
the two ends as an argument for rejecting contraception.

In its essentially negative character then the encyclical is
and remains a bitter pill, even though it is offered with
modern coloring and is sugar-coated. That is why there has
been scarcely any progress in the discussion of the content
of the encyclical since its appearance. In reality, both sides
merely repeat the old, familiar things: opinions formed long
ago were plainly not changed by the encyclical and—as is
clear from the reactions of different episcopal conferences—
the camp of the unconditional supporters in the Catholic
Church is breaking up. It is depressing when a Catholic
theologian has to observe:

> The world at large will not find much of interest to criticize
> in the problems dealt with by the encyclical; there is no
> going back on knowledge once acquired; in this respect
> the Pope's arguments are not interesting, even as a con-
> tribution to the discussion . . . In the immediate future
> there will have to be an intensive study of the question of
> the papal teaching office. Hence theologians will now have
> to show how far the functions of the papal teaching office
> extend and how the authoritarian abuse of power begins
> as soon as theoretically fallible doctrinal opinions of a
> Pope are manipulated in practice as infallible decisions.
> And possibly the wrong decision of Paul VI on the question
> of birth control, with its serious consequences, will thus
> provoke the theological clarification of many questions
> about the papal primacy which have remained open since
> Vatican I. It is to be hoped that in this way the Petrine
> office of a supreme teacher and pastor—which Catholics
> think is willed by Jesus as Founder of the Church—will
> thereby be liberated finally from its last authoritarian-
> absolutist outgrowths and reduced to its biblical stature.[4]

3. The question of authority

What really interests us then in this encyclical is not the
question of birth control, but that of the teaching office. Since
the encyclical's appearance a number of doubts have been
raised about its authority, but often with far too superficial
arguments.

First, there are those who say that the pope can make
authentic doctrinal decisions only in properly dogmatic and
not in specifically moral questions; and the question of birth
control is a specifically moral question. Certainly, by far the
greater part of both papal and conciliar decisions lies within
the field of dogma and the question of birth control belongs
to the field of moral theology. But this assertion may be
countered by another question. If we recognize the pope's
competence in the one field, why not also in the other?
Can dogma and morals be separated? Has not dogma moral
consequences and morality dogmatic presuppositions? Is not
the Catholic morality of marriage based precisely on dogmatic arguments?

Others say, the pope is competent only to interpret the
moral requirements of Christian revelation itself and not
the deductions from a so-called natural law. It must be
admitted that the encyclical does not produce a single
biblical argument for its negative thesis and the Bible has little
more than an ornamental function in it as a whole. But here
we may raise a further question. How are the requirements
of Christian revelation and those of natural law (if we want
to make use of this problematical expression) to be adequately
distinguished from one another? Doesn't the Bible also contain "natural law"? And isn't the Decalogue for the most
part both in one? And could not the prohibition of birth
control be linked—if necessary—with the dignity of marriage as
this is asserted in Scripture?

There is a third view. According to Vatican II the pope is

bound to govern the Church collegially. But the encyclical was issued by the Pope in an uncollegial solo effort. This is true and the authority of the encyclical is seriously compromised by the fact that the Pope decided against the overwhelming majority of the commission which he himself had set up, composed of specialist theologians, bishops, doctors, demographers, and other experts. They had worked on and discussed the matter for years, and yet he neither took the official report of this commission seriously nor convincingly refuted it. Further, he prevented a discussion and a decision on the question at the Council by a peremptory intervention and also, after some initial hesitation, avoided a later consultation of the world-episcopate and even of the synod of bishops. Finally, he reached a decision when the Church herself was in a state of doubt and, consequently was promptly plunged again into a state of doubt. As a result of such a procedure, the credibility of the encyclical was seriously placed in question from the very beginning by the Pope himself.

Nevertheless, here too, a further question may be raised. Did not the episcopate itself at the Council—admittedly hoping for a positive outcome—more or less passively, without serious reason, allow the Pope simply to reserve to himself both this decision and the similarly weighty decision on the reform of the Curia? Did this not allow the Pope to decide these things "alone," in the absolutist style that had become customary from the period of the high middle ages (in fact a super-commission had been secretly formed which, by its curial make-up, guaranteed the desired result from the very beginning)? Were not the problematic decisions of Vatican I on the papal primacy simply repeated at Vatican II, without safeguarding the Church through effective control against a possible absolutist misuse of papal power? Had not the Pope been assured that in principle he might also act alone? Had not the question, already raised by the ancient and medieval tradition, as to whether even the Bishop of Rome might separate from the Church and thus become a schismatic, been sedulously avoided in the conciliar discussion? In all these circumstances, is it still permissible to complain about illegitimate, uncollegial procedure on the part of the Pope? At this point ought not much more fundamental questions on Church government and the teaching office to have been raised?

We should therefore not enter on this discussion only with light theological weapons. The arguments cited above are at best of secondary value. And there is another argument frequently heard that must be rejected even more forcefully: namely, that Paul VI is an arch-reactionary who wanted a negative decision from the very beginning. This argument, even if not malicious, displays ignorance and a failure to understand the Montini-Pope and his pastoral intentions. In reality, he had wanted a positive answer. Admittedly, it had to be a responsible decision. And it is to his credit that he took his responsibility so seriously and wrestled with the problem for years before arriving at his decision. It is true that he could have reached this decision more easily, at less expense to himself and his authority. If he had simply been arch-conservative by nature, he would only have needed to confirm the negative decision of Pius XI. He could also simply have been silent. But he repeatedly insisted that the question would have to be investigated and left open the possibility of a new orientation. He insisted that the traditional teaching remained valid, "at least as long as we do not feel obliged in conscience to alter it" (Address to the College of Cardinals, June 23, 1964).[5]

Admittedly, this attitude got him into a tight corner when the theologians drew his attention to the fact that the disclosure by the Pope himself merely of the possibility of a change, the appointment of a commission for the investigation of the whole complex of questions, and the intensive theological discussion that had broken out meanwhile in theology and Church, clearly proved one thing: the prohibi-

tion of contraceptive methods was a dubious obligation and,
according to universal Catholic moral theology, came under
the old Roman principle, *lex dubia non obligat,* a doubtful
law is not binding.

Priests and faithful, here, there, and everywhere, began
increasingly to appeal to this principle. This led the Pope,
in an address to the Italian national congress for gynecology
and midwifery on October 28, 1966,[6] to dispute the claim
that the teaching office of the Church—in what he here too
admitted to be this "far-reaching and delicate question"—
"is at present in a state of doubt"; it was only in a "state of
study" (not *in statu dubii,* but *in statu studii*). On this account people have accused the Pope of lying; also because,
in his address to the German *Katholikentag* in Essen in
1968, he asserted that "the overwhelming majority of the
Church" had accepted the encyclical "with assent and obedience."[7] The most outstanding Catholic theologian in England
gave this papal statement of 1966 as the immediate occasion
for his final departure from the Catholic Church in view of
her general dishonesty (*Observer,* London, January 1, 1967).[8]

It would however be unjust to the Pope to allow this discussion to develop simply into a question of personal
morality. It is not a question of personal dishonesty, but a
quite definite view of the teaching and the teaching office of
the Church which leads the Pope to act in this way, as he
points out in the address of 1966 when he says he is "conscious
of the obligations of our apostolic office." At the same time, it
is to his credit that he did not make the exercise of his
teaching office any easier by concerning himself with the
question in an intensely personal way, as he explained in
moving words in his defense of the encyclical on July 31, 1968.
There too he honestly admitted his doubts:

> How often have we had the impression of being almost
> overwhelmed by this mass of documentation! How many
> times, humanly speaking, have we felt the inadequacy of
> our poor person when faced with the formidable apostolic

obligation of having to make a statement on this matter!
How many times have we trembled in the face of the
dilemma between an easy surrender to current views and
and a decision that modern society would find difficult
to accept, and which might prove too arbitrary a burden
for married life!⁹

"*E più facile studiare che decidiere*" (it is easier to study
than to decide), he had said in his first interview as Pope,
with the same disarming frankness, as he glanced at the many
papers on his desk.¹⁰ To this extent, there is a striking distinction between him and some of his predecessors, who
always found it easier to decide than to study theological
questions (Pius IX, for instance, in connection with the
Syllabus, or even Pius XII in connection with the encyclical,
Humani Generis).

At the same time, however, the question arises as to
whether the Pope—with the very best intentions—in his
office of *pastoral* proclamation, which, as John XXIII showed,
can have a supremely positive function in the Church, is not
taking on excessive burdens when—in notoriously controver-
sial theological questions—he wants to study like a theologian,
that is, as a representative of the *scientific* teaching office,
and then to decide for the whole Church.

In any case, we must be acutely aware of the profoundly
tragic situation that the very Pope who—according to his
opening address at the second session of the Council—wanted
to be moderately progressive felt obliged more and more to
act in a reactionary way; that precisely the Pope who made
a variety of compromises of a personal and material character
in his desire to satisfy all in the Church should have become
a partisan as rarely a pope before him has done; that the
Pope who wanted to do more for the unity of the Catholic
Church and of Christianity has exposed that Church to the
greatest tensile test of this century; and that finally the Pope
who wanted to be systematically the successor of John
XXIII *and* Pius XII, by his whole attitude, threatens to lose

to an alarming extent the good will that John XXIII and the Council earned for the Catholic Church, because in him Pius, put on the same plane as John, *was bound* to prove the stronger.

It is very sad to have to say this. It need not have been so. The French theologian, Jean-Marie Paupert says:

> Now however the Pope has blatantly and definitively taken the other side, the side of conserving structures which have served their time. *Humanae Vitae* forms only one element in this decision, to which it is by no means difficult to append further elements: the papal encyclical on priestly celibacy (June 1967), the declaration about the body of St. Peter (June 1968), the Credo of Paul VI (June 30, 1968), and the massive abuse heaped on the Dutch Catechism. I believe and I am deeply touched by this, but must nevertheless say quite distinctly that we can be certain—in view of the encyclical, *Humanae Vitae*—that the door opened for the first time by the Council has been closed again even before the Church could take the path to which this door gave free access.[11]

4. Teaching office and conscience

Only someone who knew the Montini-Pope badly anyway would fail to see how much of all this touches him very closely and burdens his pontificate almost unbearably. And even though objectively we can and frequently must be of an opinion different from that of the Pope, we should not deny at least sincere sympathy to the man who has taken on himself this mighty burden and, above all, we should show respect for his conscientious decision. The Freiburg pastoral theologian Professor Alois Müller, puts it well:

> In this new and difficult situation of the Church today respect for the Pope does not cease, but in fact begins. But we must refuse to see this respect fulfilled by an immature obedience contrary to our own opinion. We must take the Pope seriously in his need and in his limitations.

We must bear responsibility in the Church so that his responsibility does not become too heavy. Even in opposition, we must do him the service of leading the Church to new insights which again give him confidence in faith, in communion with his brothers in the episcopal office and with the whole people of God.[12]

Respect for the Pope's conscientious decision therefore means on the other hand respect for the conscientious decision of all those who cannot agree with the Pope. The other side of the problematic must also be seen in all its acuteness, as Hanno Heibling explains:

For not only freedom from state-compulsion, but also freedom from ecclesiastical tutelage, must be assured, if the Christian family is to reach responsible self-development, which the Pope himself describes as the purpose of his guidance. As long as this freedom is lacking in things which have an essential part in the existence of individuals, as long as conscientious decision is not made the measure of the life of married couples and their children, the dignity of the person lacks that autonomy in which alone it can completely prove itself. This does not necessarily mean that the Church should leave a development to take its own course when she knows its dangers. On the contrary, pastoral care also would come to its supreme and certainly most demanding task when it could offer its help in the light of free consideration of individual problems of life and questions of conscience. But the Pope does not let it come even to such a test: by his encyclical he subjects the pastor to a strict rule. We cannot deny his courage to bind. It is the courage to loose that he does not seem able to find.[13]

In regard to the individual's freedom of conscience, we must recall the theological principles which were invoked immediately after the appearance of the encyclical and on which an international consensus of theology is more and more taking shape. Those who, after serious and mature reflection, before themselves, their marriage partners, and God, come to the conclusion that—for the maintenance of their love and the endurance and happiness of their marriage—they have to act in a way different from that which the encyclical lays down, are bound—according to the traditional teaching, also of the popes—to follow their conscience. They will therefore not accuse themselves of sin when they have acted according to the best of their knowledge and in all conscience, but, calmly and secure in their conviction, will share in the life of the Church and her sacraments.

An allusion to Catholic tradition may not be out of place here.[14] It is the view of classical theology and canon law that even the threat of excommunication may not hold back a Christian from following the dictates of his conscience. If a Christian or theologian were to find himself confronted with such a tragic conflict, the very fact of his being a devout Christian would oblige him to bear the excommunication in faith, however difficult this might be for him in view of his loyalty to the Church. Appealing to the words of Paul, constantly and rightly quoted in such cases, "every act done in bad faith is a sin" (Rom. 14:23), Innocent III gave the answer: "What is not from faith is sin and whatever is done contrary to conscience leads to hell . . . since the person must not here obey the judge against God, but rather humbly bear the excommunication."[15]

The Church historian, Sebastian Merkle, giving an account of these views in an article on Savonarola, observes: "Consequently then even St Thomas, the greatest doctor of the Order of Preachers, and with him a number of other scholastics, taught that someone excommunicated as a result of erroneous presuppositions ought rather to die under the censure than obey an order which, according to his knowledge of the objective situation, was mistaken. 'For this would be contrary to the truth (*contra veritatem vitae*) *which is not to be sacrificed even on account of a possible scandal.*'"[16] And even at the time of the Counter-Reformation, when

Church leaders were much more rigid on this question, Cardinal Bellarmine, for all his emphasis on the authority of the Pope, had to admit: "As the Pope may be resisted if he makes a bodily attack on someone, so too if he attacks souls, if he sows confusion in the state, and most of all if he attempts to destroy the Church: passively resisting, by not carrying out his orders; actively too, by preventing him from getting his will."[17]

But, in spite of all emphasis on freedom of conscience, we may not give way to the convenient fallacy that a reference to the subjective conscience settles the question. The objective problematic must also be resolved.

5. The neuralgic point

The question that now becomes urgent is how did things come to such a state? Concretely, in regard to the encyclical it may be asked (and the same question might be raised in regard to the Papal Credo): why did the Pope decide for the conservative teaching? A closer look with particular attention to the statements of the Pope himself should provide an answer.

It is a unique event in the history of papal encyclicals when a real storm of rejection breaks out within the Catholic Church, and causes a pope, immediately after the publication of the encyclical, to defend it publicly. In his apologia the Pope does not adduce any further objective arguments, but only the subjective motives for his decision: "The first feeling was of the very heavy responsibility we bore . . . We have never been more conscious of the burden of our office as on this occasion."[18] Why? In the first place, the Pope explains:

We had to give an answer to the Church and to the whole of mankind; we had to evaluate, bearing in mind both the duty and the freedom of our apostolic office, a doctrinal tradition that is not only centuries old but also recent, that of our three immediate predecessors.[19]

In regard to this, Johannes Neumann observes:

> In the way of an objective and relevant decision of Rome
> there stood an invincible obstacle: the encyclical of Pius
> XI, *Casti Connubii*, of 1930. The assertions of this encycli-
> cal, which itself invoked an immutable natural law, evi-
> dently prevented the present Pope from deciding with
> the necessary frankness and freedom of heart and mind.[20]

According to his own testimony, the Pope plainly did not
consider more closely the original biblical message. Presumably he was convinced that no arguments against contraception could be drawn from that source. Especially is this true
today when the former stock biblical example—that of Onan,
refusing to give children to his brother's widow—is regarded
universally by theologians and popes as having nothing to do
with our question. But the Pope drew no conclusions from
the surprising silence of the original documents of faith, in
which generally sins of all kinds are clearly listed by name.
Plainly, something else was more important for him.

What turned the scales in favor of the Pope's negative
answer? "Natural law," on which the whole argument is built?
True, but it is just "natural law" at this very point that has
been disputed, at least since the Council, in the whole Church
right up to the papal commission. Therefore, what turned
the scales was not "natural law" as such, but a particular
ecclesiastical interpretation of this natural law. Which? According to the words of the Pope cited above, that interpretation which is given *in the traditional teaching of the Church
and particularly of the most recent popes.*

About twenty-five times in this short encyclical there are
references to the "teaching of the Church" and the "magisterium," while "gospel" appears only twice and then as "law
of the gospel" (as if Paul had not contrasted "law" and
"gospel"). About thirty times, in different ways, there is talk
of the "law" that the Church upholds and proposes, while
freedom of the will and civic freedom are mentioned, but

not the "freedom of the children of God" (as if Paul had not taught that Christ liberated us from the law into this freedom). Papal statements are quoted forty times, those of the Second Vatican Council thirteen times (by the same Pope who forbade the same council to take a decision on this question), while Scripture is quoted sixteen times but in a moralizing connection and never in any instance in order to substantiate the main thesis.

All these are clear signs that in this document the law counts for more than Christian freedom, the ecclesiastical teaching office for more than the gospel of Jesus Christ, papal tradition for more than Scripture. They are signs therefore of how much the teaching office of the Catholic Church still suffers under moralizing legalism, unrealistic ideologizing, and papal triumphalism. It would not otherwise have required the most diverse pressures in the approved way through the nunciatures and the religious orders or the secret letter of the Cardinal Secretary of State, Cicognani, to the bishops of the world, (published in *The Times* of London, September 4, 1968) by which, in the involved style of totalitarian party central offices, but equally unmistakable in its meaning, subordinates were required to bring to bear all their spiritual power in order "to put forward again in all its purity the constant teaching of the Church," in other words, to make it prevail. The letter goes on:

And now, he (the Pope) turns to all priests, secular and religious, and especially those with responsibility as general and provincial superiors of religious orders, to exhort them to put forward to Christians this delicate point of Church doctrine, to explain it and to vindicate the profound reasons behind it. The Pope counts on them and on their devotion to the chair of Peter, their love for the Church, and their care for the true good of souls.

Like them, he is informed of the ideas and practices prevalent in contemporary society, and he is well aware of the efforts that will be needed to educate men's minds on this

point. He knows what sacrifices—sometimes heroic ones—
are involved in the application of Catholic principles in
conjugal morality. It is his desire that the bishops, the
priests, the Christian centres participating in the various
Catholic movements and organizations become with joy-
ful submissiveness the apostles of the teaching of Holy
Mother Church and be able to find the convincing language which will ensure its acceptance. . . .

Finally, it is essential, in the confessional as well as by
preaching, through the press and the other means of social
communication, that every pastoral effort be made so that
no doubt whatever remains among the faithful nor among
outside opinion on the position of the Church on this grave
question.[21]

Is it surprising then that many people inside and outside
the Catholic Church drew comparisons with what happened
in Czechoslovakia in 1968? And is it then also surprising
that unenlightened bishops in "their devotion to the chair
of Peter" felt encouraged publicly to insult theologians and to
suspend from their duties the most zealous of their priests
and by that very fact to create crises in their Churches?

With all due respect to the traditional teaching of the
Church and the most recent popes, why was such an immense effort using every means put forth, risking tremendous stakes on the outcome of this particular struggle? And
here is the neuralgic point: the question of *error* in the traditional teaching of the Church and of the most recent popes.
This emerges unequivocally from the Pope's own statements.
He wanted to make "a personal examination of this serious
question [birth control] . . . above all because [within the
commission] certain criteria of solutions had emerged which
departed from the moral teaching on marriage proposed
with constant firmness by the teaching authority of the
Church."[22] It is quite clear: the permissibility of contraception
could have been conceded only under the one condition

completely unacceptable to Pope and Curia, of disavowing the traditional teaching of the Church and particularly of the last three popes, of admitting an error in this teaching of the Church.

6. Why the Pope was not convinced

The theologians of the progressive majority of the commission were in fact prepared to admit an error on the part of the teaching office:

Not a few theologians and faithful fear that a change in the official teaching could damage the confidence of Catholics in the teaching authority of the Church. For they ask how the assistance of the Holy Spirit could permit such an error for so many centuries, and one that has had so many consequences, especially in recent centuries. But the criteria for discerning what the Spirit could or could not permit in the Church can scarcely be determined *a priori*. In point of fact, we know that there have been errors in the teaching of the magisterium and of tradition. With regard to intercourse one should note that for so many centuries in the Church, with the active concurrence of the popes, it was all but unanimously taught that marital intercourse was illicit unless accompanied by the intention to procreate—or at least (because of the words of 1 Cor. 7) to offer an outlet for the other partner; and yet no theologians hold to this teaching today, nor is it the official position.[23]

The (sole) official comment (accepted by nine votes to three, with 3 abstentions) was less clear on this point about the possibility of a change in the teaching on birth control; but it was clear enough for Cardinal Ottaviani, president of the commission and head of the small but valiant curial minority, to refuse even to deliver to the Pope this official standpoint of the commission, decided by a fair vote after endless discussion (out of fifteen bishops only two had answered the question, "Is birth control intrinsically evil?" with an unequivocal "Yes"). Cardinal Döpfner as vice-president was thereupon asked to deliver it and did so. The Pope still waited several months. But—in spite of the intervention of some cardinals and also of the German episcopate in the meantime—he decided for Ottaviani and the conservative minority. Undoubtedly, an important victory for curial theology—if it does not turn out to be a pyrrhic victory.

The great question remains, although it is seldom raised: Why was the progressive majority unable to convince the Pope (whose good intentions we have constantly emphasized)? Our answer is this: since the progressive majority, consisted largely of moral theologians it did not take sufficiently seriously the arguments of the conservative Roman minority, which were drawn *ultimately* not from moral theology (in regard to contraception), but from fundamental theology (in regard to the authority of the teaching office).

This can be substantiated by closer examination. In order to justify a new moral theological argument to the teaching office of the Church, the progressive majority had attached particular importance to two points: A. There is a question of a *new historical situation,* which permits a new argumentation. B. It is *not* a question of a doctrine *infallibly* decided in Pius XI's encyclical and thus creating fundamental dogmatic difficulties against a new statement. The conservative minority attacked both arguments violently: rightly, it seems to us. This view of ours is supported by the conservative theologians' statement, which was later proposed as the "minority report" in opposition to the official statement of the commission. This report is particularly illuminating and significant in presenting the theological arguments of the conservative minority.

A. The progressives had urged that a new historical situation would permit a new doctrinal statement. Since 1930 (the encyclical, *Casti Connubii*) great changes had taken place in the world, psychologically, sociologically, medicinally (not least the pill).

The conservatives by no means deny all the changes. But their decisive objection is that, in terms of theological principle, the situation has not changed. And they have a convincing argument: essentially the same reasons for contraception were brought forward in 1930 by the Anglican bishops' conference, the Lambeth conference (the commission too was unanimous that the present problem was not merely about the pill). And it was precisely against these arguments that the encyclical *Casti Connubii* was directed at that time. Thus, basically the same reasons as those brought forward today had also been presented at that time *and* rejected by the ecclesiastical teaching office. So the "minority report" explains:

> For, as a matter of fact, the teaching of *Casti Connubii* was solemnly proposed in opposition to the doctrine of the Lambeth Conference of 1930, by the Church "to whom God has entrusted the defense of the integrity and purity of morals . . . in token of her divine ambassadorship . . . and through Our mouth." . . . Some who fight for a change say that the teaching of the Church was not false for those times. Now, however, it must be changed because of changed historical conditions. But this seems to be something that one cannot propose, for the Anglican Church was teaching precisely that and for the very reasons which the Catholic Church solemnly denied, but which it would now admit. Certainly such a manner of speaking would be unintelligible to the people and would seem to be a specious pretext.[24]

In other words, the theory of the development of dogma abundantly used and abused in Catholic theology since the nineteenth century—under the influence of Newman and the Catholic Tübingen school, especially Johann Adam Möhler—here breaks down completely. If the progressive theologians had been able to present Paul VI with a formula making a positive teaching today appear merely to be the

"development" of the negative teaching of Pius XI in 1930—
that is, according to which Paul VI today would only say
more clearly (explicitly) what Pius XI also said unclearly
(implicitly)—then we do not doubt for a moment that
Paul VI would have spoken out *for* contraception. For the
continuity of Catholic teaching and especially of the last
three popes would have been assured; no error would have
had to be admitted, but only an incompleteness, a provision-
ality, or something of the kind; and with continuity the
authority also of the teaching office would have been secured
or once again triumphantly confirmed.

But this was the very thing that plainly could not work.
In fact, even with all the tricks of theological dialectic, it
could not be made credible that the *prohibition* of contraception by Pius XI in 1930 was implicitly, inclusively, unclearly the *permission* of contraception by Paul VI in 1968. In
brief: between Pius XI and Paul VI there would then be no
evolution, but simply contradiction. And, for the sake of the
continuity of Catholic teaching and the authority of the
teaching office, this is exactly what Paul VI was under no
circumstances ready to concede. And it must be admitted in
his favor that the progressive majority of the commission
offered him no help to overcome this decisive obstacle, at
least on the lines of traditional Roman dogmatics.

B. The progressives had established that the encyclical
Casti Connubii, of Pius XI, in the final analysis is not an
infallible doctrinal statement. And to this extent, if necessary, an error of the teaching office could be admitted without putting its authority in mortal peril. Errors had indeed
at times crept in to the teaching office, even in the field of
marital morality.

The conservatives do not at all deny all the errors attributed
to the ecclesiastical teaching office. But the examples brought
forward, they object, are comparatively slight and qualita-
tively different: the Galileo condemnation was concerned
with a peripheral question (world picture); the condem-

nation of the Eastern Patriarch Photius, which was withdrawn by Paul VI after 900 years, was only an excess in the mode of procedure. But to have to make a similar admission in regard to the present question would mean admitting an extremely serious error in matters of morals (*in moribus*):

> If contraception were declared not intrinsically evil, in honesty it would have to be acknowledged that the Holy Spirit in 1930 (*Casti Connubii*), in 1951 (Address of Pius XII to midwives) and 1958 (Address to the society of haematologists in the year of Pius XII's death), assisted Protestant churches, and that for half a century Pius XI, Pius XII and a great part of the Catholic hierarchy did not protect against a very serious error, one most pernicious to souls; for it would thus be suggested that they condemned most imprudently, under the pain of eternal punishment, thousands upon thousands of human acts which are now approved. Indeed, it must be neither denied nor ignored that these acts would be approved for the same fundamental reasons which Protestantism alleged and which they (Catholics) condemned or at least did not recognize.[25]

Nor do the conservatives contest the fact that the encyclical of Pius XI was not as such an infallible doctrinal statement. But they maintain that this discussion only diverts attention from the essential point of dispute: the truth of the immorality of contraception, as it is supported and guaranteed—and this is decisive—by the consensus of the teaching office as a whole, of popes and bishops, at least in recent decades up to the time (so "chaotic" for the Romans) of Vatican II.

The documentation produced by the conservative minority, who controlled the archives of the Holy Office (accessible to no one else), is in fact overwhelming. It consists of solemn statements of popes, of bishops' conferences on every continent, of many outstanding cardinals and bishops as also of the universal teaching of theologians: the aim being to

prove that, according to the universal consensus of the ecclesiastical teaching office at least in the present century (it
is nothing new for spiritual means of compulsion to be used
in maintaining it), it is a question of a universal teaching of
the ecclesiastical teaching office, binding under pain of grave
sin:

> Our question is a question of the *truth* of this proposition:
> contraception is always seriously evil. The truth of this
> teaching stems from the fact that it has been proposed
> with such constancy, with such universality, with such
> obligatory force, always and everywhere, as something to
> be held and followed by the faithful. Technical and juridi-
> cal investigation into the irreformability and infallibility of
> *Casti Connubii* (as if once this obstacle had been removed,
> the true doctrine could be found and taught) distracts
> from the central question and even prejudices the ques-
> tion.[26]

In other words, the curial group did not use a particular
encyclical or papal address as an argument; they did not
appeal, that is, to what is known as the *extra*ordinary teaching office (*magisterium extra ordinarium*). They appealed
to the ordinary consensus in teaching of pope and bishops,
that is, to what is known as the *ordinary*, everyday teaching
office (*magisterium ordinarium*).

There are many things (for example, in the strict sense
the existence of God or—in morals—the prohibition of killing
the innocent) which have never been defined by the extraordinary teaching office of the pope or of an ecumenical
council and which nevertheless count quite universally as
truths of Catholic faith. In the language of the Roman textbooks: something can be *de fide catholica*—that is, belonging
to the Catholic faith—on the authority of the ordinary teaching office, without for that reason being *de fide definita*,
that is, without being defined by a solemn pronouncement

on faith of the extraordinary teaching office (definition by a pope or council).

Thus, even according to Roman theory, the prohibition of contraception has not been defined as an infallible truth of faith either by a pope or by a council. And yet, because—as we have shown—it had always or at least for half a century before the Council been taught unanimously by the ordinary teaching office of the pope and the bishops, it belongs to the universal, infallible Catholic faith. In view of this it is comparatively unimportant whether the intention was to "endow the papal statement with formal infallibility" (as the group of authoritarian conservatives thought), against the progressives (in theory or practice), or on the other hand to avoid an *ex cathedra* statement (as the pastorally minded conservatives thought). For even this more moderate group was "very concerned to secure the continuity of the teachings of Pius XII in order 'to ensure the exercise of authority in the Church.'" "In their eyes, while maintaining *unchangeable principles*, there had to be a search for possible 'openings.' Hence an *ex cathedra* statement was to be avoided, the therapeutic use of contraceptive methods not forbidden (but left open to a decision as the occasion arose) and the moral sanction not underlined again."[27]

For the rest, one can only be sincerely shocked at the obscure, almost ghostly proceedings within the Vatican after the close of the official work of the commission in "a veritable labyrinth of editorial committees and individual reporting, frequently little or not at all informed about one another's existence."[28] "It may be asked where—in all this—any freedom remained to the Pope, who strikes one in the whole picture as a spider in the net."[29]

We can see now the real reason why the progressive majority of the commission were not able to convince the Pope. To judge from their own progressive report and the progressive official reaction of the commission, they had

plainly not grasped sufficiently the full weight of the argument
of the conservative group: the moral inadmissibility of contraception has been taught as a matter of course and even
emphatically by all bishops everywhere in the world, in
moral unity, unanimously, for centuries and then—against
opposition—in the present century up to the Council (and the
confusion which arose in this connection), as Catholic moral
teaching to be observed on pain of eternal damnation: it is
therefore to be understood in the light of the ordinary
magisterium of pope and bishops as a factually *infallible*
truth of morals, even though it has not been *defined* as such.

This was the argument which finally convinced the Pope
(for the theory of development plainly broke down here).
He could not be expected—so he must rightly have said to
himself in the light of this conclusion—to abandon as an
error a moral truth constantly and unanimously taught by
the ordinary magisterium and therefore in fact infallible. We
can now well understand his continual recourse to the constant teaching of the Church and particularly of the most
recent popes; we understand very well his sharp rejection of
any kind of deviation from this teaching. And we understand
now also numerous other small details:

A. Why Ottaviani refused even to put before the Pope
the reaction of the commission, which he must in fact have
regarded as heretical, and why in the Curia resistance did
not weaken but increased more and more clearly in strength;

B. Why in the Vatican at first, instead of an encyclical,
only a "declaration" (*declaratio*) had been planned on this
teaching, the authority of which was absolutely firm on other
grounds;

C. Why Paul VI himself carefully avoided describing
his encyclical as not infallible, but rather presented it as
the teaching of Christ and declared himself and his encyclical
to be "like her (the Church's) divine founder, a 'sign of
contradiction'"[30];

D. Why the Pope, as with an infallible doctrinal statement,

invoking the Holy Spirit, demands full and absolute obedience:

> loyal internal and external obedience to the teaching authority of the Church. That obedience, as you know well, obliges not only because of the reasons adduced, but rather because of the light of the Holy Spirit, which is given in a particular way to the pastors [note the plural, indicating the magisterium of the whole episcopate] of the Church in order that they may illustrate the truth. You know, too, that it is of the utmost importance, for peace of consciences and for the unity of the Christian people, that in the field of morals as well as in that of dogma, all should attend to the magisterium of the Church, and all should speak the same language. Hence, with all our heart we renew to you the heartfelt plea of the great Apostle Paul: "I appeal to you, brethren, by the name of Our Lord Jesus Christ, that all of you agree and that there be no dissensions among you, but that you be united in the same mind and the same judgment." To diminish in no way the saving teaching of Christ constitutes an eminent form of charity for souls.[31]

And to priests the Pope says:

> We are full of confidence as we speak to you, beloved sons, because we hold it as certain that while the Holy Spirit of God is present to the magisterium proclaiming sound doctrine, he also illumines from within the hearts of the faithful and invites their assent.[32]

Finally, in the closing words:

> Great indeed is the work of education, of progress and of love to which we call you, upon the foundation of the Church's teaching, of which the successor of Peter is, together with his brothers in the episcopate, the depositary and interpreter[33];

E. Why the answer of the official Vatican commentator, Monsignor Lambruschini, to a question raised in the press conference, that the encyclical is an authentic but not infallible document, roused very great indignation among certain curial circles (according to the Roman view, it would have been permissible to say at most, if it was desired to formulate the answer delicately: the intrinsically fallible document of a doctrine already infallible on other grounds) and why not a word of this observation—undoubtedly more important than most of the others that Lambruschini had made—was reported in the *Osservatore Romano* (this is said to be the reason why Lambruschini was so soon afterward promoted [or removed] to be Archbishop of Perugia);

F. Why one of the oldest and closest theologian-friends of the present Pope, the Swiss neoscholastic theologian, Cardinal Charles Journet, published on the front page of the *Osservatore Romano* of October 3, 1968 a long article under the slogan, "It is absurd for a son of the Church to oppose the infallibility of his own personal conscience to the authority of the encyclical." Summoning up all the Roman theology of the primacy, Journet tries to prove that the Pope here is exercising his ordinary supreme teaching authority in order, faithful to the constant teaching of his predecessors, to bring out more precisely the meaning of the first article of the creed, on God the Creator, and thus to close a controversy which had raised doubts about a traditional teaching approved for centuries by the teaching office. The arguments brought forward in the encyclical would in fact prepare but not substantiate the conclusion, which concerns a fundamental point of morality. This conclusion is substantiated rather in the light of the Holy Spirit, with which the pastors of the Church are endowed in a special way in order to illustrate the truth. The Pope did this after examining a tradition, not only centuries-old, but also recent, namely that of the last three popes.

Journet, quite logically, goes so far as to envisage a possible future infallible decision: "One thing is certain: the ordinary teaching office of the Pope was here exercised in its fullness. The theologian who reflects on the seriousness of the matter, on the sublime light into which it was brought for clarification, and finally on the exactitude and certainty with which the answer was given, might even think that he was presented here—and this is our personal opinion—with a point of moral teaching which could be further defined and thus in the future be confirmed by a consensus of divine faith."[34] And here the slogan is repeated, how absurd it would be—even apart from such a decision—for a son of the Church to set against the encyclical the infallibility of his own conscience;

G. Why finally, with all desirable clarity and with reference to Journet, the former curial general secretary of the Council and present president of the commission for the reform of canon law, Cardinal Pericle Felici, wrote an article in the *Osservatore Romano* which would seem sensational only to non-Roman readers and in which he said: "in regard to the teaching expressed in the encyclical *Humanae Vitae* in a clear, evident and moreover official-authentic fashion, a state of doubt cannot be asserted because of the fact that the teaching has not been defined *ex cathedra* . . . In fact, since they are not confronted with an *ex cathedra* definition, some conclude that the teaching is not infallible and thus that there is a possibility of change. With reference to this problem, it must be kept in mind that a truth can be sure and certain and therefore binding, even without the charism of an *ex cathedra* definition, as in fact is the case with the encyclical *Humanae Vitae*, in which the Pope as supreme teacher in the Church proclaims a truth that has constantly been taught by the Church's teaching office and corresponds to revealed doctrine."[35] This is completely unambiguously, in its whole "continuity, coherence and firmness," the Roman—even though not without more ado Catholic—teaching on the infallibility of the ordinary magisterium. We must now take note of this position if we want to diagnose the crisis correctly.

There is then in fact a dilemma here: the conservative minority had the formal aspect of the doctrine (infallibility) in its favor, but it had the material aspect of the doctrine (permissibility of contraception) against it; but the progressive majority had the material aspect (permissibility of contraception) in its favor, the formal aspect (infallibility) against it. The Pope decided for the infallibility of the teaching against all the objective arguments of the experts whom he himself had called in. And at what a cost! Unfortunately, it must be said, at unforeseeable cost to Church and Pope and to their credibility. And even now, a considerable time after the decision, a large part of the Church and of the episcopate is quite unable to accept the responsibility of completely agreeing with the Pope.

The consensus which the Pope had in mind on this question is today further away than ever. On the contrary, in the curial ghetto, he is in danger of being isolated particularly from the most dynamic elements and members of the Church. The conclusion is forced upon us that the dilemma will never be solved simply by adopting one of the alternatives: consistency of teaching or possibility of change.

We cannot rigidly maintain the continuity, traditionality, universality, authority, infallibility of the teaching on birth control, when the content of that teaching is no longer accepted in its entirety by the whole Church in the consensus of faith and when consequently the Pope is disavowed on his own principles.

But how is it possible to solve the dilemma by asserting the possibility of change and therefore the permissibility of contraception, even supported by the weight of theological opinion and the greater part of the Church today, if it means abandoning the whole continuity of Catholic teaching and the authority of a pastoral office of teaching and proclamation? We might put the question concretely in this way: how could the commission have convinced the Pope of the opposite in regard to the contents? One thing is certain: only if it had not avoided the formal problem of infallibility. It would then have had to take the bull by the horns: the problem of the infallibility of the ecclesiastical teaching office today may no longer be presupposed as clarified in principle.

But is it true that the problem of infallibility has really not been clarified once and for all? Can the Pope appeal for his view of infallibility, not to textbook theology, but also to Vatican I and II? This is what must now be investigated.

II. FIRM FOUNDATIONS

1. The textbook arguments

There was a time when Catholic theologians tried to come to terms with difficult points of Church teaching by interpreting them as broadly as possible. Propositions were stretched, twisted, dialectically shaken up, until they came to mean first one thing, then another or in some circumstances the very opposite. This led occasionally to downright equivocation or even to a complete perversion and distortion of the original meaning of the proposition, and thus to an unintended scientific dishonesty.[1]

At the same time, however, this method did not prevent the same propositions from being used again if necessary by the teaching office, in the old, rigorous sense, without allowing for the theologians' interpreting skills. At any rate, if we had taken more seriously all that was to be found on the Church's infallibility in the textbooks of fundamental theology and dogmatics, and then perhaps also criticized and corrected more seriously, we might have managed better with our typical question of birth control. In brief: even though this does not make it easier for us, we shall follow the opposite procedure here and take the statements both of textbook theology and of the councils as seriously and literally as possible, in order then of course also to raise our critical questions.

We need only open at random any manual of dogmatics in the Roman-neoscholastic tradition to note at once that Pope Paul VI's view of the tradition of binding ecclesiastical teaching is supported by textbook theology. What do we read there? That not only is the pope infallible when speaking *ex cathedra,* nor an ecumenical council infallible when giving a binding definition of doctrine on faith or morals, but the totality of the episcopate scattered throughout the world—by contrast with the individual bishop—is also infallible, when together with the pope it agrees on a truth of faith or morals to be held by all the faithful. It is maintained in the textbooks as a dogma of faith (*de fide!*): "The totality of the Bishops is infallible, when they, either assembled in general council or scattered over the earth, propose a teaching of faith or morals as one to be held by all the faithful" (*De fide*).[2]

By contrast with the extraordinary teaching office of an ecumenical council or of a pope defining *ex cathedra,* it is a question here of the "ordinary," day to day teaching office (*magisterium ordinarium*): "The Bishops exercise their infallible teaching power in an *ordinary* manner when they, in their dioceses, in moral unity with the Pope, unanimously promulgate the same teachings on faith and morals."[3] And how can such an agreement on a particular point of doctrine be established? "The agreement of the Bishops in doctrine may be determined from the catechisms issued by them, from their pastoral letters, from the prayer books approved by them, and from the resolutions of particular synods. A morally general agreement suffices, but in this the express or tacit assent of the Pope, as the supreme head of the Episcopate, is essential."[4]

A truth of faith or morals is then infallible by the very fact of being proclaimed by the episcopate in universal agreement as binding, and not only when it is formally declared to be infallible. And who could deny that such agreement on the question of birth control existed for centuries right up to the time of Vatican II, and had been defended in numerous official statements by bishops' conferences and individual bishops. Particularly has this been so from the beginning of the present century, as the question became more and more disputed outside the Catholic Church and Catholic theologians too as isolated individuals tried diffidently to raise some questions? Thus the conservative minority of the papal commission can observe:

> History provides fullest evidence (cf. especially the excellent work of Professor John T. Noonan, *Contraception*, Harvard University Press, 1965) that the answer of the Church has always and everywhere been the same, from the beginning up to the present decade. One can find no period of history, no document of the church, no theological school, scarcely one Catholic theologian, who ever denied that contraception was always seriously evil. The teaching of the Church in this matter is absolutely constant. Until the present century this teaching was peacefully possessed by all other Christians, whether Orthodox or Anglican or Protestant. The Orthodox retain this as common teaching today. The theological history of the use of matrimony is very complicated . . . On the contrary, the theological history of contraception, comparatively speaking, is sufficiently simple, at least with regard to the central question: Is contraception always seriously evil? For in answer to this question there has never been any variation and scarcely any evolution in the teaching. The ways of formulating and explaining this teaching have evolved, but not the doctrine itself. Therefore it is not a question of a teaching proposed in 1930 which because of new physiological facts and new theological perspectives ought to be changed. It is a question rather of a teaching which until the present decade was constantly and authentically taught by the Church.[5]

What is to be said then against such arguments? There are only two possibilities: either, like the minority of the commission and the Pope, treat such teaching as infallible and irreversible and adhere to it despite all difficulties and objections, even, if necessary, sacrificing one's intellect; OR simply question this whole theory of infallibility. The progressive majority was not able to prevail because it did not recognize this dilemma as clearly as its curial opponents.

If we look at the proofs of the above very far-reaching statements in neoscholastic textbook theology, we find the following sequence of arguments.[6] Infallibility is defined as the impossibility of falling into error. According to the Council of Trent (DS 1768) and Vatican I (DS 3061) the bishops are successors of the apostles. As such they are pastors and teachers of the faithful (DS 3050) and thus also bearers of the infallibility assured to the ecclesiastical teaching office: an active infallibility in teaching (*infallibilitas in docendo*), which is the cause of the passive infallibility of the faithful in believing and assenting (*infallibilitas in credendo*).

If we go back further and ask about this infallibility assured to the ecclesiastical teaching office, we find on the one hand a reference to Vatican I (DS 3074) and on the other a proof—admittedly only indirect—from Scripture: because Christ promised to remain with the apostles (Mt. 28:20) or that his Spirit would remain, the Spirit of truth (Jn. 14:16f.), the purity and integrity of the proclamation of faith by the apostles and their successors is assured for ever (cf. Lk. 10:16). If the objection were to be raised that there is nothing about infallibility in any of these texts, the answer is ready at once: "This presupposes [!] that the Apostles and their successors in their promulgation of faith are removed from the danger of error."[7] Similarly "St. Paul sees in the Church 'the pillar and the ground of the truth' (1 Tim. 3:15). The infallibility of the promulgation of faith is a presupposition[!] of the unity and of the indestructibility of the Church."[8]

Of "infallibility" therefore, in the sense of an impossibility of falling into error, there is as little mention in the Scripture texts as in the rare patristic quotations of Irenaeus, Tertullian (the heretic) and Cyprian (the opponent of the Bishop of

Rome). 'The whole question is therefore, whether the *pre-supposition* here is rightly made or whether the same Scripture texts permit also another presupposition. For the moment, further critical questions may be deferred.

Meanwhile we should not omit to mention how wide is the scope of papal and episcopal infallibility as understood or again deduced by textbook theology: it extends not only to formally revealed truths of Christian teaching on faith or morals, but also to all truths and facts closely connected with revealed doctrine, that is, theological conclusions, historical facts (*facta dogmatica*), truths of natural reason, canonization of saints. Since even the canonization of saints is supposed to be covered by infallibility, it is not surprising that birth control too could be the object of ecclesiastical infallibility.

Many a person will perhaps be tempted lightheartedly to thrust all these arguments of the textbooks aside as preconciliar. (Was perhaps the recent "deposition" of saints supposed to be infallible?) But it is not as easy as all that.

2. Vatican II and infallibility

Anyone who has studied the documents of Vatican II must have noticed that the wind blowing in the third chapter of the Constitution on the Church, *Lumen Gentium*, is different from that in the two previous chapters.[9] The language here is no longer, as in the chapters on the Mystery of the Church and the People of God, mainly biblical, pastoral, ecumenical, but mainly—even though occasionally with a little unction—juridical, institutional, disciplinary, Roman.

The third chapter, on "the hierarchical structure of the Church, with special reference to the episcopate," is introduced with a massive confirmation of Vatican I and its statements on the primacy and infallibility of the pope (art. 18). But for the rest, in its presentation of the Church's constitution, Vatican II sought quite deliberately and sys-

tematically to create a balance to Vatican I (which had
never been closed) and the latter's emphasis on the papal
prerogatives. This was brought out by a very detailed account
of the episcopate (arts. 19–27), while the position of priests
(art. 28) and deacons (art. 29) was given only very brief
and scanty attention, without even a thorough exegetical-
historical clarification of the advantage the bishop is supposed
to have over the priest, apart from jurisdiction over a larger
area of the Church.

The reflections on the episcopate start off with a section
on the appointment of the twelve apostles (art. 19) and
the bishops as successors of the apostles (art. 20). Then
follow three sections on episcopal ordination as a sacrament
(the fact that one becomes a bishop by ordination seemed
important to offset the Roman claim to nominate bishops
or at least confirm their appointment: art. 21), on the
episcopal college and the pope as its head (here is the
section on collegiality and co-responsibility of bishops in
the supreme government of the whole Church, which was
fiercely opposed by the Curia: art. 22), and on the mutual
relationships of bishops in the college (here is a section on
the local Church which is fundamental to the new image of
the Church: art 23). Finally the office and function of
bishops is described (art. 24) and in a threefold perspective:
as teaching office (art. 25), as sanctifying office (art. 26),
as governing office (art. 27).

For our question the section on the teaching office, particularly the second paragraph on the teaching office of
bishops, is decisive. This paragraph however presupposes
the observations of the first paragraph on the ordinary teaching office of the *individual* bishop, although—significantly—
there is no mention here of infallibility.[10] At the beginning
of the whole article is the fundamental statement that the
eminent task of the bishop is the proclamation of the gospel.
The reason given for this is that the bishops are messengers

of the faith, leading new disciples to Christ, and authentic teachers equipped with the authority of Christ. It is striking that all these statements about the bishops (as also the corresponding statements about the Pope) are in the indicative ("bishops are, preach" etc.), as if this were obvious, while the subsequent statements about the faithful are in the strict imperative: "In matters of faith and morals, the bishops speak in the name of Christ and the faithful are to accept their teaching and adhere to it with a· religious assent of soul. This religious submission or will and of mind must be shown in a special way to the authentic teaching authority of the Roman Pontiff, even when he is not speaking ex cathedra" (art. 25).

The fact cannot be overlooked, on the one hand, that a very great deal is asserted here. Can the simple statement of one bishop—who is acknowledged to be fallible—command in this way, unconditionally, a religious submission of will and mind (in the schools question for instance, when a bishop declares it to be a matter of faith or morals)? How in such unguarded and unconditional utterances is the misuse of episcopal teaching authority—of which there are innumerable examples—to be excluded? Appropriate suggestions for textual improvements were rejected as superfluous by the theological commission of the Council, which referred questioners to the textbooks.

On the other hand, however, very little is asserted. When it is presupposed—and expressly stated at the beginning of the next section—that "the individual bishops do not enjoy the prerogative of infallibility" (art. 25), the question nevertheless arises: and why not in fact? Why is the individual bishop as successor of the apostles—who, according to this theory, were infallible as individuals—not also infallible as individual bishop? Are we now suddenly to be afraid of certain consequences of this theory? But if we are afraid of this, why are we not afraid in other respects? There seems to be a lack of clarity here. But let us leave this and come to the central statement of the Council on infallibility. Here it is in full:

Although the individual bishops do not enjoy the prerogative of infallibility, they can nevertheless proclaim Christian doctrine infallibly. This is so, even when they are dispersed around the world, provided that while maintaining the bond of unity among themselves and with Peter's successor, and while teaching authentically on a matter of faith or morals, they concur in a single viewpoint as the one which must be held conclusively. This authority is even more clearly verified when, gathered together in an ecumenical council, they are the teachers and judges of faith and morals for the universal Church. Their definitions must then be adhered to with the submission of faith (art. 25.3).

Is it not obvious what happened? Vatican II adopted completely the teaching of textbook theology on the infallibility of the episcopate as a whole, in regard both to the extraordinary and the ordinary teaching office. In regard to the ordinary teaching office of the bishops scattered throughout the world, the conditions are clearly indicated. Teaching is infallible when

A. there exists the communio, the communion, the agreement of the bishops with each other and with the pope,

B. an authentic, that is, not merely private but official teaching is present, and in fact

C. in matters of faith or morals, so far as this

D. is taught as definitively to be maintained.

An interim question arises: do not all these conditions hold for the traditional teaching on the immorality of contraception? It must also be observed here that such an infallible teaching by the episcopate does not by any means have to be put forward *as* infallible. We can speak of a doctrine as infallible when it is put forward by the episcopate as "defin-

itively to be maintained" (*definitive tenenda*), as is quite
clearly the case in the question of contraception which has
been constantly condemned with an allusion to eternal
damnation. It is in fact not even a question of doctrine
"definitively to be believed," but only "definitively to be
maintained." On which Karl Rahner rightly comments: "The
text says 'to be held', not 'to be believed', because according
to the general view, a definition by the Church is possible
under certain circumstances with regard to truths not strictly
revealed, and it is only the latter which can be *believed*
(*credenda*) by 'divine faith' on the immediate authority of
God who reveals himself."[11]

This last qualification is perhaps the most important if we
compare the definitive text of 1964 with the first draft in
1962 of the conciliar preparatory commission. In fact, what
was said at that time was absolutely the same: the episcopal
college is infallible, not only in a general council, but also
"when the individual bishops, each in his own diocese, together with the Roman Pontiff, as witnesses of the faith,
share the same opinion (doctrine, statement, *sententia*) when
transmitting revealed doctrine. Whatever therefore is held
by the bishops everywhere in the world, together with the
pope himself, on matters of faith and morals, and taught by
the ordinary teaching office, even if there is no solemn
definition, must be maintained as irrevocably true and—if
put forward as divinely revealed—must be believed by divine
and Catholic faith."[12]

In the final version a definition is given of the material
extent of the infallible teaching authority of the episcopate
(and of the Pope): "This infallibility with which the divine
Redeemer willed his Church to be endowed in defining a
doctrine of faith or morals extends as far as extends the
deposit of divine revelation, which must be religiously
guarded and faithfully expounded" (art. 25). To those who
are unfamiliar with Roman theology infallibility here might
seem to be restricted to the truth of revelation properly so

called. Not at all. On the scope of infallibility the words at
the end, which appear to be of secondary importance, prove
to be primary.

What is meant by "religiously guarding" the deposit of
divine revelation? "The words, *sancte custodiendum,* imply
that the object of infallible authority includes truths which
form a safeguard for the deposit of revelation strictly speaking, even though these truths are not formally revealed
(implicitly or explicitly)."[13] And what is there that cannot
be part of the safeguarding of the deposit of revelation
properly so-called? On the basis of such a definition the
Roman teaching office has never hesitated to take up a position "authentically" on almost all questions in any way relevant—from particular questions of exegesis and history to
those of natural science, politics, economics, culture, schools,
and thus of course to that of birth control—in all of which
the limits of "infallible" were often fluid.

And what is meant by "faithfully expounding" the deposit
of revelation? "The words 'to be faithfully expounded' indicate
briefly that there is a historical development of dogma itself,
and not merely of theology."[14] On the basis of this second
qualification the Roman teaching office seems to be permitted
to explicate "authentically" and—as in the case of the two
new Marian dogmas—even to define infallibly all kinds of
things on which not a word was said either in Scripture or in
early tradition.

We can see that even in this brief, sober statement it is
not a question of abstract theory, but of the very concrete
substantiation or justification of a very concrete practice.
The positive aspect, however, of the statement quoted may
lie in the fact that the infallibility in question is entirely that
with which the Redeemer willed to endow, not simply the
bishops or the pope, but the *Church.* But how then are
episcopal and papal infallibility connected with the Church's
infallibility? Which is fundamental? And if we are in fact
talking about an infallibility of the Church, and not only of

the bishops, to what extent then have all priests and laity —who are the Church—a share in this infallibility? Would they all be endowed—as textbook theology says—only with a passive infallibility, in hearing, believing, obeying? Or, as Vatican II seems to suggest, would the infallibility of the bishops actively produce the infallibility of the Church?

Unfortunately there is nothing to be found here on this important question. But, although Vatican I and the infallibility of the pope defined there had been solemnly confirmed at the beginning of the whole chapter III, there follows once again in article 25 an extensive section on papal infallibility: to adapt a well-known slogan, we might say of the Roman mentality, *de Romano Pontifice nunquam satis*. All anti-Gallican formularies of Vatican I are hammered in again, as if under the influence of an unacknowledged fear. The only difference is that in one sentence this infallibility is extended to the episcopal college, admittedly with the qualification "when that body exercises supreme teaching authority with the successor of Peter" (art. 25). Cases of conflict between pope and episcopal college, which have constantly occurred at dramatic moments in Church history, are passed over in silence. Instead, the last sentence of this section, again solemnly formulated in the indicative, speaks of a never failing assent (a fact that will be noted subsequently with special interest in view of the dissent arising as a result of the encyclical *Humane Vitae*): "to the resultant definitions the assent of the Church can never be wanting, on account of the activity of the same Holy Spirit, whereby the whole flock of Christ is preserved and progresses in unity of faith" (art. 25). But, we feel urged to ask, what is wrong when this assent does not come about in a particular case? We can hardly blame it on the Holy Spirit.

The fourth section of our article 5 describes briefly the way in which infallible truth is discovered. Again it is not postulated, but simply stated as self-evident: "But when either the Roman Pontiff or the body of bishops together with him defines a judgment, they pronounce it in accord with revelation itself. All are obliged to maintain and be ruled by this revelation, which, as written or preserved by tradition, is transmitted in its entirety through the legitimate succession of bishops and especially through the care of the Roman Pontiff himself. Under the guiding light of the Spirit of truth, revelation is thus religiously preserved and faithfully expounded in the Church" (art. 25).

It might almost seem from this that in the last resort the teaching office of the pope and bishops is in fact the ultimate, self-sufficient authority on what is revelation. Are perhaps the accusations confirmed here that some raise against the Catholic Church and theology: that Scripture is played down by tradition and tradition again played down by the present-day teaching office, which decides what is tradition and therefore also what is Scripture?

According to the text it seems nevertheless that all—therefore, apparently, also pope and bishops—are bound to be guided by revelation. The real ambiguity arises however from the inconvenient fact that, four hundred years after Trent, Vatican II still could not see its way to define neatly and clearly the relationship between Scripture and tradition, which theologians have carefully investigated particularly in the present century. In historical perspective the Scriptures of the Old and New Testament, although by no means all written by the apostles, are the sole testimonies that have been recognized and acknowledged by the Church as sound, original tradition (that is, as "canonical" Scriptures).

What was there to be found then of "divine" tradition outside the New Testament? What purports to be original tradition outside the New Testament (Gospels, Acts, Letters of the Apostles), although partly stemming from the second century, was rejected by the early Church as apocryphal tradition. Even to the superficial reader of that time it was easily recognized as spurious because of its inferiority when compared to canonical literature; today it is generally recognized to be useless as a historical source. The books of the New (and Old) Testament thus rightly remained definitive. All subsequent ecclesiastical tradition comments on, explicates, applies, and transposes this original tradition, although with varying success. It is this that has to remain vitally obligatory, binding, normative: Scripture, that is, as *norma normans* of an ecclesiastical tradition which may then also be taken seriously precisely as *norma normata.*

Thus Scripture—metaphorically speaking—turns out to be a sort of main tap which, if it were ever turned off, would mean that all the springs of ecclesiastical tradition in the house would dry up. In the Constitution on Revelation, however, at Vatican II an attempt was made to take this seriously only in the additional, final chapter on the Bible in the life of the Church. Completely under the influence of unhistorical, counterreformation views and the obvious interests of ecclesiastical policy, the curial preparatory commission had upheld a two source theory of Scripture *and* tradition. Unfortunately, nothing more than a compromise was reached. The theological commission of the Council under pressure from the curial minority finally agreed to leave open the determination of the relationship: hence the text, "written *or* (*vel*) handed on." It was felt that progress had been made, although in fact it was scarcely progress, instead of separating Scripture and tradition, to bring them as close as possible together and let them flow into one—almost as in modern fittings hot and cold water flow together into one outlet. This, as we know, permits us to mix the two in the proportions we want: very practical in everyday life, but disastrous for theology. What we do not get from Scripture, we get from tradition, but the teaching office of the Church decides on the proportions of each at a particular moment; what is supposed to be the *ultimate* criterion for the teaching office itself, we do not know.

Chapter II of the Constitution on Revelation, on the transmission of divine revelation, presented by the commission expressly as a compromise, covers up the problem with a leveling-out quasi-trinitarian formula and a praise of harmony which sounds very melodious in Latin, and passes over the *norma normans* by an appeal to the divine decree: "It is clear, therefore, that sacred tradition, sacred Scripture, and the teaching authority of the Church, in accord with God's most wise design, are so linked and joined together that one cannot stand without the others, and that all together and each in its own way under the action of the one Holy Spirit contribute effectively to the salvation of souls" (art. 10).

Vatican II however suffered from the first day to the last from the fact that the question of what really is the ultimate, supreme norm for the renewal of the Church remained undecided. Once again the beneficiaries were that group which, for understandable reasons, was able to prevent a decision in favor of the New Testament: the Roman Curia, its teaching office and canon law.

In the Constitution on the Church there follows—again in an ambiguous indicative—a statement on the human efforts of the teaching office to acquire knowledge: "The Roman Pontiff and the bishops, in view of their office and the importance of the matter, strive painstakingly and by appropriate means to inquire properly into that revelation and to give apt expression to its contents" (art. 25). Karl Rahner rightly observes: "This statement is put very briefly and formally, clearly for fear that more details about the ethcial norms to be observed by the magisterium in finding the truth and forming their judgment could be understood as canonical law, whose fulfilment could be subject to investigation by another legal authority."[14a]

The problem thus arises: is the activity of the teaching office in trying to make so many decisions at all subject to control or is it completely uncontrolled? In other words, can it make use or not make use at its own choice and discretion of "appropriate means" (perhaps an all-too-political expression when we recall certain repressive measures adopted in the past) to determine the content of revelation? Article 25 closes, however, with the statement, disappointing perhaps for some, but consoling for the others: "But they (the Roman Pontiff and the bishops) do not receive a new public revelation as pertaining to the deposit of divine faith" (art. 25).°

3. Critical counterquestions

The schema of the curial preparatory commission for the Constitution on the Church devoted two whole chapters out of eleven to the teaching office and obedience and wanted expressly to forbid discussion of theologians, even concerning fallible doctrinal statements of the Church; compared to this, the final text represents a considerable shortening and a gratifying extension to more important matters: particularly to the concept of the Church as the People of God, the community of believers, the universal priesthood and the charismatic dimension of the Church, the significance of the local Church, and of ecclesiastical office as service.

Nevertheless, as already pointed out, the Constitution on the Church, like the Constitution on Revelation, contains chapters and passages on very different theological levels. Chapter III particularly, on the hierarchical structure of the Church, in spite of the progress already noted, looks backward rather than forward. It should also be noted that this chapter is not in fact based on the New Testament—in article 25 the Bible is quoted only three times and then not for the main statements—but on Vatican I, particularly the exposition of Bishop Gasser, spokesman for the deputation on faith.

For the basic thesis on the infallibility of the episcopate scattered throughout the world, together with a text of Vatican I on the ordinary magisterium—which, however, contains no mention of infallibility (DS 3011)—there is produced as documentary evidence merely a note (!) to a schema (!)

° Translated from the Latin. The Abbott translation is not clear at this point.

on the Church which had never been passed by Vatican I
(!), but had itself been taken over from Cardinal Bellarmine (!) and commented on by the Council-theologian,
Kleutgen (!).[15] Were they hoping at Vatican II to be able in
this way to domesticate the infallibility of the pope through
the infallibility of the episcopate? The documents cited
ought to have sounded suspicious, as also the letter quoted
from the Syllabus-Pope, Pius IX, to the Archbishop of Munich-
Freising on the congresses of German theologians (DS 2879).

Both from the Constitution itself and the documents of
Vatican II it is clear that the question of the infallibility of
the episcopate was neither seriously discussed nor seriously
examined at the Council, but simply taken over from textbook theology shaped by Vatican I. But questions which
crop up are not answered if they are simply ignored and not
faced. They take their revenge by returning, when everything
seems to be clarified, only to produce further doubts. And if
we want to use history as the basis of our argument, the
questions that history itself raises are particularly dangerous.
As an ancient Roman saying has it, *Facta infecta fieri nequeunt* (What has happened cannot be made not to have
happened). But this saying, particularly useful in jurispru-
dence, can also be reversed, to the advantage of theology:
Infecta facta fieri nequeunt (What has not happened cannot
be made to have happened).

We may leave aside here both the numerous infelicities
of article 25, to which we already alluded, and the substantiation of papal infallibility from Vatican I, on which the
whole article is based. In order to balance Vatican I's definition of papal infallibility, Vatican II emphasizes the collegiality of the bishops with the pope and asserts the infallibility of the universal episcopate. This is done with the
best intentions, but the arguments are partly drawn from
presuppositions which today can no longer be regarded as
historically sound. The whole substantiation of episcopal
infallibility depends on the presupposition that the bishops in

a definite, direct, and exclusive way are the successors of the
apostles and that the apostles claimed infallibility for themselves. A study of history as it really happened raises questions which should be discussed here.

A. It is scarcely possible to prove that the apostles as a
college and still less—as textbook theology presupposes—
the apostles as individuals claimed an infallibility in the textbook sense (impossibility of error). There is no need to
waste words here on the fundamental importance of the
apostles for the founding of the Church, which is universally
acknowledged. Yet even the connection of the apostles with
the twelve ("twelve apostles") is a later construction; the
college of twelve—as representing the twelve-tribe-people and
as basic witnesses of the resurrection—slips completely into
the background even in the Acts of the Apostles; as such it
dies out. What does remain fundamental is the apostolate itself (which in any case is not restricted to the twelve):
the apostles as the primary witnesses sent out by the Lord
himself are the preachers of the gospel and thus the founders
and first leaders of the Church.

But the real apostles are described neither as heroes nor
as geniuses, but as weak and fragile human beings who
carry their treasures in earthly vessels (cf. 2 Cor. 4:7) and
can do nothing of themselves (Jn. 15:5). The synoptic gospels illustrate more than is to the liking of some people today the statements of Paul and John in this connection, with
concrete evidence of the weakness and unintelligence, the
human failings and faults, of Jesus' chosen disciples—before
and after the resurrection. Particularly is Peter, the first of
the apostles, an example of how error does not render the
apostolic mission impossible, although it certainly impedes
that mission, (each of the three classical texts on the special
importance of Peter is accompanied by the ominous shadow
of a particular failure). All this is by no means scandalous
for the believer, but rather consoling. The apostles too remained human and as such—as becomes clear particularly in

Paul—in need of the intercession, comfort and support of their fellow Christians. Yes, the Church "has the apostles (and prophets) for its foundations" (Eph. 2:20; cf. 1 Cor. 12:28; Rev. 21:14). But there is no mention of any kind of personal or collegial infallibility, of incapacity of error.[16]

B. It would likewise be impossible to prove that the bishops in the direct and exclusive sense are the successors of the apostles (and still less of the college of the twelve). Certainly we need not raise any objections if the bishops today regard themselves as being in the special succession of their apostolic ministry, in so far as—like the apostles—they found churches and rule churches. But it is easy to make too much of this statement in its theoretical and practical interpretation. For:

(1) As the immediate, primary witnesses and primary messengers of Christ, the apostles could not *a priori* be replaced or represented by any successors; they (together with the prophets) and not the bishops are and remain the foundation of the Church.

(2) Even though there can be no new apostles, the mandate and function of the apostles remain: that is, apostolic mission and apostolic ministry. Apostolic mission and apostolic ministry, however, are primarily carried on further by the *whole* Church. *Every* Christian is in the succession of the apostles in so far as he strives for harmony with the apostolic testimony (succession in the apostolic faith and confession) and for the connection with the apostolic ministry (succession in apostolic service and life). In this sense the whole Church is and ought to be the apostolic Church.[17]

(3) It is true that there was church leadership from the very beginning, whether through the apostles or through other charismatic ministries. But it must be traced back, not to "divine institution," but to a long and complex historical development,

(a) that the episkopoi (presbyters) prevailed against the prophets, teachers and other charismatic ministries as the chief and finally sole leaders of the community (from the "collegiality" of *all* the faithful there emerges gradually a collegiality of certain groups of ministries *over against* the community, so that a division of "clergy" and "laity" becomes marked);

(b) that the monarchical episcopate of an individual episkopos, by contrast with a plurality of episkopoi (presbyters), increasingly penetrates the communities (from the collegiality of the different episkopoi or presbyters there now emerges the collegiality of the one episkopos with his presbyterium and his deacons, so that the division of "clergy" and "laity" finally prevails);

(c) that, with the spread of the Church from the towns to the country, the episkopos as president of a congregation now becomes president of a whole area of the Church, of a diocese, etc., a bishop in the modern sense (together with the collegiality of episkopoi and presbyterium, the collegiality of individual monarchical bishops with each other becomes increasingly important and then, even though only in the West, with the Bishop of Rome).[18]

C. On the basis of what has just been explained, it would be impossible to prove that the bishops have more advantage over the presbyters than simply the supervision (jurisdiction) of a greater area of the Church. A canonical and disciplinary demarcation is possible and reasonable; a theological-dogmatic is unjustified and impossible. Originally, episkopoi and presbyters were either otherwise or not at all distinguished from one another, as we have just shown. The tripartite division of offices (episkopoi-presbyters-deacons) is not to be found in the New Testament, but in Ignatius of Antioch, and is therefore a development which took place first in the region of Syria. It is not clear that there is any fundamental difference between the ordination of a bishop—on the sacramentality of which up to a point there was so much discussion at Vatican II—and that of a presbyter. Nor is there any more evidence of a difference in regard to the authority transmitted by ordination: while the Council of Trent ascribes authority to confirm and ordain exclusively to the bishop, under pain of excommunication (DS 1777), according to Vatican II the presbyter also can be the ordinary minister of Confirmation (cf. art. 26) and the question of authority to ordain is expressly left open.[19]

D. Nor on the basis of the development briefly outlined here, would it be possible to prove that the bishops are the sole (or sole "authentic") teachers in the Church. According to the New Testament, all are called to proclaim the word. And although the leadership of the community, which fell to the episkopoi and presbyters in the course of historical development, has to be exercised primarily through the word, this cannot in any case mean the absorption of the other charisms and ministries of proclamation. In 1 Corinthians 12, Paul defends himself expressly against individuals craving to monopolize everything and emphasizes *alongside* the apostles two other groups: "second to prophets, third to teachers" (1 Cor. 12:28), to whom in the Didache the episkopoi and deacons still seem to take second place for the celebration of the Eucharist. Along with a special succession of the apostles there is also a special succession of prophets and teachers: we shall not discuss here what this means when translated into modern terms, but it will be taken up again later in connection with the obscure concept of the teaching office.[20]

Someone who sees the importance of these questions with all their consequences might ask whether those assembled at Vatican II were not at all aware of them. To this we may answer: they did perceive these questions, at least peripherally, but in practice put them aside. Nevertheless, the apodictic definition of Trent was corrected, that the "*hierarchy,* instituted by divine ordination, *consists* of bishops, presbyters and deacons" (DS 1776; cf. 1768), so that now "the ecclesiastical *ministry* (not hierarchy=sacred dominion) *is exercised* (not consists) on different levels by those who *from antiquity* (not by divine ordination, that is, from the beginning) have been *called* (not are or must be) bishops, priests, and deacons" (art. 28). But, seen as a whole, precisely this chapter III on "the hierarchical structure of the Church" offers merely a theological-pastoral description of the present division of offices, oriented to the status quo.

What is missing then is an exposition of the essential structure of the ecclesiastical ministry and its historical development, solidly substantiated exegetically and historically in the light of its origin and thus at the same time critically constructive. "Whatever may be the historical origin of presbyters, deacons or other ministries and also the exact meaning of the terms used to describe them in the New Testament, it is asserted . . .": this note of the theological commission on the central statement just quoted from article 28[21] could be placed appropriately as a subtitle above the whole of Chapter III.

But why then were these truly important questions not investigated? There are a number of reasons:

A. It is really too much to expect any council to try to practise theology in the proper sense of the term and not "only" proclamation.[22]

B. In particular, a conciliar commission would inevitably be faced with too great a burden if it wanted to work out, not only some important guidelines for the modern understanding of the Church, but also a comprehensive Constitution on the Church.

C. Critical exegesis, although primarily competent for the questions above raised and also for many many others, was in practice scarcely represented or at least not in sufficient force in the theological commission of Vatican II.

D. Like all council documents, the Constitution on the Church particularly was a compromise between a fundamentally progressive conciliar majority and a reactionary curial minority.

E. The curial minority dominating the machinery of the

Council saw to it, with the Pope's help, that a fundamentally new version of a scheme prepared in the posttridentine spirit would be possible only within very definite limits, and made sure that certain traditional opinions and formulas would be taken over into the new draft and that certain important questions and problems would not be dealt with. In these circumstances, it proved to be simpler to introduce "new" features into the Constitution than seriously to examine what had long been dogmatically fixed. This holds also for the questions of the episcopate and of infallibility.

As a result, it has become clear that, even if we seriously recognize the positive new orientation of the Constitution on the Church and its fruitful new approaches and if moreover, in spite of all critical questions, we completely affirm in theory and practice the historical legitimacy and pastoral appropriateness of a presbyterial-episcopal Church,[23] we shall have to say: the statements about an infallibility of the college of bishops, based on the traditional, unhistorical theory of a direct and exclusive apostolic succession of the bishops, exegetically, historically, theologically, have feet of clay. That is to say, unless the substantiation were to be supplied by the basic source to which Vatican II, in article 25 on the infallibility of pope and bishops, constantly refers: Vatican I.

Vatican I then and its substantiation of papal infallibility will have to be investigated. A not unimportant question may serve as a transition from the second to the first Vatican Council: would Vatican II have defined infallibility if this had not already been defined by Vatican I? Scarcely. Two reasons can be put forward against it:

A. Vatican II showed an aversion to *doctrinalism*. Under the influence of John XXIII, who was not a Pius IX nor a Pius XII, the Council was aligned, not in a doctrinaire way like the preparatory commission, but pastorally. New dogmas were undesirable in principle and even formulations which sounded like dogmatizing were eliminated. Instead of fixation, the Council strove as far as possible for renewal in practice and in theory.

B. Vatican II showed an aversion for *centralism.* Many bishops had had more than enough of the constant excessive demands of the Roman central authority. Triumphalism, juridicism, centralism, were the passwords of the righteous struggle for more collegiality, solidarity, community, dialogue in the Church. It was again John XXIII who had revealed a new ideal of an unpretentious, ecumenically and humanly disposed Petrine *ministry* to the brethren and attached so little importance to the infallibility attributed to him that he could say on one occasion with a smile: "I'm not infallible; I'm infallible only when I speak *ex cathedra.* But I'll never speak *ex cathedra.*" And John XXIII never did speak *ex cathedra.*

Oddly enough too, the very council that had so much to say in its Constitution on the Church theoretically about the infallibility of the episcopate and also of the ecumenical council, following John XXIII and to the scandal of many an heir of Vatican I, did not formally claim this infallibility on a single occasion. Indeed, Vatican II was in reality so little interested in this infallibility that it never seriously discussed it. In the last resort, can we perhaps manage in the Church without such infallibility? On a bright spring day we are inclined to forget a murky autumn—until it returns. Vatican II must not make us forget Vatican I, if we do not want constantly to have the same problems and cares particularly in regard to infallibility.

4. Vatican I's interest in infallibility

If Vatican II was so surprisingly uninterested in infallible definitions, why was Vatican I on the contrary so surprisingly passionately interested in an infallible definition of infallibility? It is not our intention here to write or even merely to sketch a history of Vatican I or simply of its infallibility debate.[24] To do so thoroughly we should have to go back very much further.

We should have to depict how the policy and theology of the Church of the Roman imperial capital and of the two chief apostles, Peter and Paul, met with opposition and countermovements, faced temporary stagnation and harsh reverses. Nevertheless, from the time of the early Bishops of Rome—Victor and Stephen, Damasus, Siricius, Innocent, and particularly Leo—and then again in a new advance in the ninth century with Nicholas and John VIII, and finally systematically and decisively under the influence of the forged Isidorian Decretals from the Gregorian reform in the eleventh century, Roman policy and theology were directed toward a Church of unity tightly and juridically organized under a monarchical, Roman, universal episcopate. We should have to explain further how—because of this process—in the same period of the Gregorian reform the unity of the Eastern and Western Churches was substantially and finally broken; how then in the West the Church began in earnest to be centralized, juridicized, and romanized, and reached an unsurpassable peak in the thirteenth century with the religious-political universal monarchy of the popes; how later in the Avignon exile and the period of the Reform councils the political—religious decline became blatant, although the Renaissance papacy acted in a more absolutist and unecclesial way than ever. Finally, it would have to be explained how in the end the unity of the Western Church was shattered on this absolutism and thus the state of Christendom was radically changed; how Rome at the time of the Counter-Reformation did not dismantle but single-mindedly consolidated, admittedly in more spiritual forms, the bastions of power in the remnant of empire, against all opposition external and internal, even after the French Revolution, until well into the nineteenth century.

If all this could be set out, it would become clear why, in Catholic books on Church history, even in the present century, Vatican I (and the Code of Canon Law of 1918) could be lauded as the glorious peak of a thousand—indeed, almost two thousand—years of history of the Church of Christ. In this history it could undoubtedly be shown clearly enough how much Roman ecclesiastical policy and theology, from the time of the migration of the peoples, did for the unity and freedom of the (Western) Church, as this was understood in Rome: positive aspects which, however, cannot blot out the negative aspects of this history with their devastating consequences for the unity and credibility of the Church as a whole. It is however less easy to understand why Catholic historians and theologians displayed so little anxiety about the legitimacy of the whole process. And, what is more decisive, the majority at the First Vatican Council were not concerned about its legitimacy. Why?

We shall never understand the definition of papal infallibility merely by analyzing the text of the Council's Constitution in Denzinger's *Enchiridion*, nor even by studying the documents of Vatican I in Mansi's great collection. The definition of papal infallibility was largely decided before the Council itself voted for it. Would papal infallibility ever have been defined in 1870 if the majority of the council fathers had not grown up in the period of the political restoration and of the antienlightenment and antirationalist romanticism of the first half of the century: a time when people in Europe, after the confusion and excesses of the great revolution and of Napoleonic times, had an irresistible longing for peace and order, for the good, old times—in fact, for the Christian middle ages—and when nobody better than the Pope could offer the religious foundation for the maintenance of the political-religious status quo or the restoration of the status quo ante? The greater number of the leading Catholic churchmen in the different countries were regarded as supporters of political-social reaction; some were closely connected with the fashionable philosophical trend of traditionalism (at that time an honorable title).

And would papal infallibility have been defined in 1870 if the whole work of the Restoration had not been threatened in its foundations during the second half of that century by liberalism (and its opponent, socialism, which resembled it in many respects), rapidly establishing itself with advancing industrialization, which, with its belief in progress and freedom in economic life, politics, science and culture, seemed to be abolishing all religious authority and tradition? Clericalism and anticlericalism were stirring each other up. The rationalism of the Enlightenment had returned in the form of anti-idealist and antiromantic positivism and of the rising empirical sciences of nature and history. The way in which ecclesiastical authorities not only supported the established political system, but also maintained the traditional "biblical" world picture, frequently drove politicians and scientists to violent aggressiveness toward all that had to do with religion.

Because of this historical constellation, this constrained situation, into which a Church leadership, no longer understanding the signs of the times and constantly arriving too late, had been largely maneuvered, it was almost inevitable that Vatican I—so wholly different from Vatican II—would be conceived from the very beginning, not as a council of hope but of fear, not of internal reform and renewal but of reaction and encapsulation toward the outer world, not of aggiornamento but of defense and polemics. It was wholly in the spirit of that *Syllabus errorum*, of that list of errors of 1864, with which Pius IX had condemned more or less the whole of modern developments under the headings of naturalism, socialism, indifferentism, Gallicanism, freemasonry, etc. and had provoked tremendous resentment among progressive, cultured Europeans.

Nevertheless, these two more general factors—the desire to maintain the old order and hostility toward the new—do not of themselves provide sufficient motive for the interest of Vatican I in a definition of infallibility which—so completely differently from former conciliar definitions—had not been occasioned by any special heresy at all, but was urged by the Church leadership itself. In order to understand what happened, at least two further factors must be mentioned.

The infallibility of the pope would not have been defined in 1870 if the "Roman Question" had not been considered by the pope and Curia as the most immediately pressing problem. Certainly there were other reasons for anxiety: in France the political-ideological controversies about revolution and antirevolution, between ecclesiastical hierarchy and anticlericals, between republicans and supporters of Napoleon III, who extended a protective hand over the Church of France and—for the time being—also over the papal states; in Germany the theological controversies between the university theologians, committed to contemporary scientific methods, and the neoscholastic theologians and seminary teachers, trained in Rome and supported by Rome, which led finally at the Council itself to a polarization of Catholic theology between the theology of the German universities (its leader, Ignaz Döllinger, was not invited) on the one hand and the neoscholasticism of the Roman Jesuit university, the Gregorian (Perrone, Schrader, Passaglia), on the other. Nevertheless, in Rome the Roman question overshadowed all others.

Would the papal states, restored in 1849, but by the intervention of the Piedmontese government in 1860 restricted to Rome and its neighborhood—known everywhere for their monsignorial mismanagement and social backwardness—have to be given up or could they hold out in the long run, solely with French support, in the face of the Italian unity movement which meant to make Rome its capital. In the Vatican the situation was viewed with the utmost anxiety. But would anyone venture to proceed against a pope whose universal primacy and personal infallibility had been solemnly and definitively proclaimed *urbi et orbi* in an ecumenical council? This was almost the sole ray of hope for those who fought—appealing to Matthew 16:18—for the maintenance of the papal states.

Nor would the infallibility of the pope have been defined in 1870 if this pope himself had not pressed more and more blatantly as time passed for a definition of papal infallibility as his deepest wish. Greeted at his election in 1846 as liberal and reformer, Pius IX, after his political failures and his exile in 1848, became more and more a political and theological reactionary. He not only listed and condemned the so-called errors of the time, without a trace of self-consciousness, but at the same time demanded the subordination of the state and scientific research to the authority of the Catholic Church—demands and condemnations which made it difficult even for Vatican II to produce much, for instance, about freedom of religion and conscience. Against the Italian unity movement too he flung his persistent *non possumus*, with constantly renewed pathetic protests, which roused the ultramontane press and numerous bishops and faithful particularly in France to a violent campaign against Italy.

Although Pius IX in this way brought the Italian Catholics into unnecessary severe conflicts of conscience, he won tremendous sympathy for his person and his office in the role of a man persecuted by unchristian powers. The dogmatic bond of Catholics to the pope now acquired a sentimental touch. A completely new phenomenon arose: a highly emotional "veneration of the pope," which was considerably strengthened by the now customary papal audiences and mass pilgrimages to Rome. Pius IX, a philanthropic, very eloquent, strongly radiant personality, but dangerously emotional, superficially trained in theology, and completely unfamiliar with modern scientific methods, badly advised moreover by zealous but mediocre, unrealistic and dogmatically minded associates, saw the crisis of the papal states simply as an episode in the universal history of the struggle between God and Satan and hoped to overcome it with an almost mystical confidence in the victory of divine providence.

It is only in the light of this basic attitude that the pope's desire for a dogmatic definition of his own primacy and infallibility can be understood. Only in the light of the veneration offered to him as pope can it be understood how far a definition of infallibility struck a favorable response on the part of large circles of clergy and people, and how far the process of indoctrination and administrative centralization within the Church, rapidly and systematically urged on by Rome after some initial nervous hesitation, no longer met with opposition. This was true not only of the Syllabus, the condemnation of German theologians, the placing of all works with a Gallican or Febronian tendency on the Index, but also of the increasing Roman influence on episcopal elections and interference of nuncios in the internal affairs of the Churches, the summons to the bishops to strengthen their contacts with Rome, the deliberate promotion of priests who were propagating the Roman ideas often against their own bishops, the constantly renewed instruction of the faithful on the doctrine of the papal primacy . . .

So the way was well prepared when the Pope, to strengthen his own position and to draw up the Church as an army in battle array under Rome's command, to the world's surprise, after an interval of three hundred years, convened an ecumenical council to Rome. It was simply impossible to think of any other place. In any case, the ultramontane press campaign, worked up to a frenzied pitch, and encouraged by the Roman Curia, which almost overreached itself in its demands for the romanizing of the whole Church in doctrine, liturgy, discipline, and customs, provoked a new growth of the supposedly dead "Gallican" opposition on the part of some bishops, theologians, and laymen in Germany and France. Consequently, the Vatican Council did not get underway as rapidly and as smoothly as the organizers and their most zealous partisans had hoped.

Meanwhile, it should be observed in our brief outline that the problematical historical background of the definition of infallibility belongs not merely to the prehistory of the definition, but to the history of the definition itself. But it is not sufficient to expose this background critically and frankly —as Catholic historians do today—while at the same time refraining from any critical reflection on the definition itself. The historical problematic revealed here does not affect merely the "opportuneness" of the definition of infallibility— as it was often innocuously formulated in the past—but its very truth.

5. *The definition of papal infallibility*

Our whole attention must now be concentrated on the definition of infallibility itself and its substantiation by Vatican I, which is in fact also the basis of all statements of Vatican II on infallibility. The debates at Vatican I—exciting as their often poignant history may be—interest us here only in so far as they give expression to the motives and the shaping of the definition itself.[25]

a. The definition of papal infallibility presupposes the definition of papal *primacy*. Both were included in the dogmatic constitution *Pastor Aeternus*, of July 18, 1870—against the objections of the minority, the chapters on the pope were put first, boldly reversing the order of the original schema on the Church—and the primacy substantiated in three stages: as petrine, perpetual, and Roman. The mood which led to the definition of primacy and infallibility becomes immediately clear in the introduction:

> With daily increasing hatred, on all sides, the gates of hell are rising, to overturn the Church if it were possible, against its divinely established foundation. Therefore we judge it necessary for the protection, safety and increase of the Catholic flock, with the approval of the sacred council, to propose the doctrine of the institution, perpetuity and na-

ture of the sacred apostolic primacy, in which the strength
and solidity of the whole Church consists, to be believed
and held by all the faithful, according to the ancient and
constant faith of the universal Church and to proscribe
and condemn the contrary errors so pernicious to the
Lord's flock (DS 3052).

Chapter 1 deals with the institution of the apostolic primacy
in Peter. After appealing to John 1:42; Matthew 16:16ff. and
John 21:15ff., it declares excommunicate anyone who says
that "blessed Peter the Apostle is not constituted by Christ
our Lord as prince of all the apostles and visible head of the
whole Church militant, or that he received directly and
immediately from the same Lord Jesus Christ a primacy
only of honor and not of true and proper jurisdiction" (DS
3055). Chapter 2 is concerned with the continuation of the
Petrine primacy in the Roman pontiffs. After appealing to a
speech of the Roman legate at the Council of Ephesus in
431 and a still later sermon of Leo the Great, together with
a sentence each from Irenaeus and Ambrose (dealing however not with the Bishop, but with the Church of Rome) it
declares excommunicate anyone who says that "it is not by
the institution of Christ our Lord himself or by divine law
that blessed Peter has perpetual successors in the primacy
over the universal Church, or that the Roman pontiff is not
the successor of blessed Peter in the same primacy" (DS
3058).

Chapter 3 defines the content and nature of the primacy of
the Roman pontiff. After a general appeal to former Roman and conciliar witnesses and after repeating a statement
from the decree for the Greeks, at the Council of Florence in
1439, there is a more precise description of the primacy of
jurisdiction and explanations of the subordinate jurisdiction
of the bishops, of the free and direct communication of the
pope with all the faithful and of the constant possibility of
recourse to his final judgment, from which there is no appeal.

Then, finally, it declares excommunicate anyone who says that "the Roman Pontiff has the office only of inspection or of direction, but not full and supreme power of jurisdiction over the universal Church, not only in matters pertaining to faith and morals, but also in those pertaining to the discipline and government of the Church spread throughout the whole world; or that he has only a principal part and not the whole plenitude of this supreme power; or that this power of his is not ordinary and immediate, both over all and individual Churches and likewise over all and individual pastors and faithful" (DS 3064).

There is no need to go into great detail at this point particularly since our theme is not the primacy, but infallibility. Some brief comments will suffice.

(1) Although the deputation on faith of Vatican I, overwhelmingly one-sided in composition and wholly under the influence of the Curia, because of anti-Gallican fears, had opposed any formulation of the limits to the papal primacy in the Constitution itself, it is clear from the documents that their spokesman at the council admitted such limits, to which the pope is morally bound: limits in general set by Christ and the apostles; limits derived from natural law and divine law; limits in particular arising from the existence of bishops and their ordinary exercise of office; limits to the pope's own exercise of office, in so far as it must not be used in an arbitrary and reckless way, but for the building up and not for the destruction of the Church.[26]

(2) The history of the Church, of theology, and of canon law, make clear that the question of the papal primacy is understood in all its implications only when the possibility —discussed and affirmed from the middle ages onward, but tendentiously omitted at Vatican I and II—of a schismatic or heretical pope is considered: the possibility, that is, of a pope who himself abandons communion with the Church by his arbitrary rule or otherwise and therefore loses his office and may perhaps have to be judged by a representative organ of

the Church (council, episcopal synod, college of cardinals).[27]

(3) The whole course of the argument of Vatican I in regard to the existence of a petrine primacy of *jurisdiction*, still more of a *continuation* of the petrine primacy, and most of all a continuation in the *Roman pontiff*, presents mãny serious difficulties from the standpoint of contemporary (even, to some extent, of nineteenth century) exegesis and history, which no Catholic theologian has been able to resolve up to now. They make the possibility of a convincing proof of a historical succession of the bishops of Rome in a primacy of Peter seem extremely dubious.[28]

(4) Although it may be impossible to provide an exegetical-historical proof of a succession, this does not mean that the primacy of one individual in the Church is contrary to Scripture, or even that it cannot be in accordance with Scripture: so far, that is, as it is a question of a succession (possible in principle also in a charismatic fashion) in the Spirit, in the petrine mission and function, in the petrine testimony and spirit. We are speaking of a succession in a really living primacy of service which would be more than merely a primacy of honor or merely a primacy of jurisdiction; rather would it be a pastoral primacy in the spirit of the gospel, in the sense of Matthew 16:18; Luke 22:32; John 21:15–17, following the examples, not of Leo the Great, Innocent III, Pius IX, or Pius XII, but of Gregory the Great and John XXIII.[29]

b. By comparison with the definition of the primacy, which was intentionally stated without qualifications or distinctions, the definition of papal *infallibility* in *Pastor aeternus* was distinguished by its clear formulation of the conditions. This may be counted as a success for the ultimately unsuccessful opposition at the council. There is no doubt that the formula finally passed in a chapter supplementary to the three chapters on the primacy—to which the original constitution on the Church had been reduced—was far more modest than the original ideas probably of the Pope and certainly of the extreme ultramontanes. This may be shown by examining some characteristic testimonies of the leading propagandists of a definition of infallibility, who had such a tremendous influence on the clergy and the Catholic laity.

For the protagonist of infallibility in England, W. G. Ward, convert and editor of the *Dublin Review,* "all direct doctrinal instructions of all encyclicals, of all letters to individual bishops and allocutions, published by the Popes, are *ex cathedra* pronouncements and *ipso facto* infallible."[30] The editor of the *Univers,* the layman Louis Veuillot, nimble and not particularly scrupulous, but unquestionably the most influential publicist of papal infallibility in France, wrote: "We all know certainly only one thing, that is that no man knows anything except the Man with whom God is for ever, the Man who carries the thought of God. We must unswervingly follow his inspired directions." Or, during the council: "Does the Church believe, or does she not believe, that her Head is inspired directly by God, that is to say, infallible in his decisions regarding faith and morals?"[31] Veuillot did not hesitate in the *Univers* to apply hymns like "Veni Sancte Spiritus" to Pius IX in person and to paraphrase the hymn "Rerum Deus tenax vigor," as "Rerum PIUS tenax vigor." Even the Roman Jesuit organ, edited by theologians, *La Civiltà Cattolica,* printed such statements as "the infallibility of the Pope is the infallibility of Jesus Christ Himself"; "When the Pope thinks, it is God who is thinking in him."[32] The famous or notorious article which appeared in this periodical of February 6, 1869—as "French Correspondence"—thrust the definition of the "dogmatic infallibility of the pope" (as also of the assumption of Mary), which was to be unanimously acclaimed by the Council, into the foreground of the discussion and thus caused enormous excitement.[33]

Among the council fathers, too, some singular theories about the pope were circulating. Some spoke of the pope as "Vice-God of mankind" and Mermillod, auxiliary bishop of

Geneva, spoke of the "three incarnations of the Son of God": in the Virgin's womb, in the Eucharist, and in the old man of the Vatican.[34] And, what was more, the strong leader and whipper-up of the infallibilist majority, who was not averse to employing intrigue in his cause, Archbishop Manning of Westminster (the sole convert at the council, as he boasted), had already in 1865 suggested a formula which spoke without qualification of the infallibility of every papal utterance on faith and morals: "A public utterance by the Supreme Pontiff on faith, morals or what are known as dogmatic facts, or on truths connected with questions of faith or morals, is infallible."[35]

All these preliminary statements should be compared with the formula, defining papal infallibility as dogma given by God, in the supplementary chapter 4 on the infallible teaching office of the Roman pontiff in the Constitution, *Pastor aeternus*, on July 18, 1870, again asserting the typical motive: "But since, particularly at this time when the salutary efficacy of the Apostolic office is needed more than ever, there are not a few who impugn his authority, we think it absolutely necessary solemnly to assert the prerogative which the only-begotten Son of God deigned to link with the supreme pastoral office" (DS 3072). The definition of papal infallibility follows, according to the text, prepared by the Pope himself "with the approval of the council":

The Roman pontiff when he speaks *ex cathedra*, that is, when exercising the office of pastor and teacher of all Christians, he defines with his supreme apostolic authority a doctrine concerning faith or morals to be held by the universal Church, through the divine assistance promised to him in blessed Peter, is possessed of that infallibility with which the divine Redeemer willed his Church to be endowed in defining faith and morals: and therefore such definitions of the Roman pontiff are irreformable of themselves (and not from the consent of the Church) (DS 3074).

This definitive formula, perhaps the eighth or the ninth after the original text of the supplementary chapter, was clear and unambiguous for supporters and opponents. One should read with this the almost four-hour statement of the spokesman for the deputation on faith, Bishop Vincent Gasser, which is generally regarded as the official commentary on the definition of infallibility.[36] When then is the Roman pontiff infallible? When he speaks *ex cathedra,* that is, in virtue of his supreme teaching authority. For this, according to the formula itself, the following conditions must be fulfilled:

(1) The Roman pontiff must be defining—that is, finally deciding in declaratory form—not as a private person nor even merely as pope, but as supreme pastor and teacher of Christendom, in virtue of his supreme apostolic authority: only in this way is he the subject or—perhaps better—the *organ* of ecclesiastical infallibility.

(2) Not any kind of teaching, but only a doctrine of faith or morals can be the *object* of an infallible definition: which however includes not only formally revealed truth (*credenda*), but also all truth connected with this (and therefore *tenenda*).

(3) The Roman pontiff speaks infallibly, not because of a new revelation or of an inspiration (which holds only for Scripture), but because of a divine assistance: thus it is not a continual assistance of the Holy Spirit, but one which operates on each occasion, merely protecting from error and therefore "negative," that is the *cause* of papal infallibility.

(4) What is presupposed is not an infallibility granted exclusively to the Roman pontiff, but the infallibility of the Church, with which—that is—the Redeemer himself willed his Church to be equipped in final decisions in doctrines of faith and morals: the Church appears here as the (primary?) *subject* of infallibility, the pope being its organ.

Added to the definition is the statement: "If—which may God avert—anyone should presume to contradict this definition of ours, let him be anathema" (DS 3075). As we know, this anathema had concrete results: not only the excommunication of the leading Catholic theologian of Germany (and perhaps of Europe), Ignaz Döllinger, but a new schism in the Church, the splitting off of the Old or Christian-Catholic Church in Germany, Austria, Switzerland, and the Netherlands. Did that have to be? A schism—even perhaps a greater one—was to be expected. The Pope and the council majority were prepared to risk everything for the sake of this definition. In this respect, including the treatment of the minority (in this case, conservative), Vatican II took a different course.

6. Pope against Church?

The relationship in principle between the infallibility of the Church and the infallibility of the pope remains undefined in the formula of Vatican I. And subsequently, up to Vatican II and beyond this, there were discussions as to whether there are two subjects of infallibility or only one: the pope alone or the pope with the episcopate or council. But this is a dispute about non-essentials. Even the spokesman for the deputation on faith, Gasser, had no hesitation in rejecting theories which made it seem "as if all the infallibility of the Church were seated in the Pope and from the Pope derived and communicated to the Church."[37]

For him and for the majority, thinking in Roman and pragmatic terms, such abstract-theoretical questions were not important. The main thing was the realistic-practical decision: that the pope, of himself, at any time, without necessarily bringing in the Church or the episcopate, can claim ecclesiastical infallibility and with finality decide alone any question of theory or practice that is important for the Church. So that not the smallest opening would remain for any kind of Gallican solutions, at the last moment—it is supposed, through the efforts of Manning and of Senestrey, Bishop of

Regensburg—a restrictive clause was incorporated in the last sentence of the definition: "therefore such definitions of the Roman pontiff are irreformable (*irreformabiles*) of themselves, *and not from the consent of the Church* (*non autem ex consensu Ecclesiae*)" (DS 3074).

This could be misunderstood by some, but for all those acquainted with the terminology it was all too intelligible and quite clearly meant that, for the complete validity of an infallible definition by the pope, no consent of the Church —previously, simultaneously or subsequently—is necessary; in particular—as the "Gallicans" and some of the minority of the council fathers had thought—no consultation, co-operation, or ratification of the episcopate is necessary. The meaning of this restrictive clause was well understood. It provided the final stimulus for the premature departure of the most outstanding representatives of the minority, among them—in addition to the Archbishops of Milan and St. Louis (Missouri) —the representatives of the most important metropolitan sees in France, Germany, Austria, and Hungary; their successors were to constitute the core of what became the progressive majority at Vatican II. Meanwhile, for all their struggle for collegiality and for giving the pope his place within the people of God at Vatican II, they only repeated and did not correct the notorious *non autem ex consensu Ecclesiae*.

Did this mean that all problems were thereby solved? Neither the papal infallibilists nor the Gallican anti-infallibilists could have got to the root of the question at that time. But let us look more closely at the matter.

In the report of the deputation on faith, among many other things, Gasser had already put forward two important qualifications in regard to papal infallibility which seem to be more clearly conciliatory to the minority than the definition itself:

First, it is made clear that what is claimed for the pope is *not an absolute infallibility:* "I answer and declare honestly: papal infallibility is in no sense absolute, because absolute in-

,fallibility belongs to God alone, the first and essential truth, who can nowhere and never deceive or be deceived."[38] On the contrary, the pope's infallibility, given to him for definite purposes, is restricted in three ways: *restricta est ratione subiecti . . . ratione obiecti . . . ratione actus . . .*[39]

At the same time it is clear that the pope is *not to be separated from the Church:* "we do not thereby separate the Pope from his ordinated conjunction with the Church. For he is infallible only when as leader of all Christians, that is, as representing the universal Church, he judges and defines what is to be believed or rejected by all."[40] "He can no more be separated from the Church than the foundation can be separated from the building it is meant to sustain."[41] The infallibility of the pope is oriented to the pastoral ministry of the Church as a whole: "Apart from this relationship to the whole Church, Peter does not possess in his successors this charism of truth by the certain promise of Christ."[42]

It is possible then to cite interpretations from Vatican I which would also have pleased the majority at Vatican II. Certain progressive theologians were inclined to bank heavily on such qualifications. But all this scarcely changes anything in the basic problem: the problem is still papal absolutism, as it has taken shape since the eleventh century and as it was exercised not only in the middle ages and the Renaissance, but also in modern times at the expense of the Church and the unity of Christendom.

Even the Second Vatican Council, with all its solemn and pious talk and decrees on collegiality, did not really succeed in getting at this papal absolutism. It was of course possible at Vatican II to make use of the now progressive majority much more correctly and democratically and yet no less effectively than the very unscrupulous (conservative) majority or their whippers-up did for their part at Vatican I; the postconciliar Church now has to bear the consequences of those compromising surrenders to the curial minority. The fact that infallibility as defined at Vatican I was asserted with the utmost formality also of the episcopate, does not represent any counterweight (since the episcopate is wholly dependent on the pope) and even renders the problematic more acute, as we saw in connection with the ordinary magisterium. Even the qualifications of Vatican II do not prevent the pope in any way from issuing infallible and of course still less fallible proclamations, whenever and wherever he wishes, exactly as Vatican I wanted and decided. For if we are aware, without any wishful thinking (mostly indeed unfulfilled) of what Vatican I decided and what Vatican II half-heartedly confirmed, then it becomes clear that Paul VI in regard to *Humanae Vitae* and other matters, together with textbook theology and Vatican II, had also obviously Vatican I wholly on his side. Indeed, he could have proceeded still more imperturbably, with still less consideration for episcopate, theology, commissions and public opinion in the Church. For what does the sober reality, dogmatically and juridically secured, look like?[43]

Even according to Vatican I the pope is supposed to use his infallible teaching office in relation to the Church, for the building up and for the good of the Church as a whole.[44] But he and he alone (together with his court of course) can decide from one case to the next what is for the good of the Church. Even according to Vatican I the pope is supposed to proceed carefully and after reflection.[45] But no one in the Church can prevent him from acting willfully and arbitrarily. Even according to Vatican I the pope is expected to use the appropriate means (councils, synods, advice from bishops, cardinals, theologians, and others) in preparing a definition (and of course also for other doctrinal pronouncements), in order to investigate the truth correctly and formulate it appropriately.[46] But he alone judges, free of any controls, whether, when and how, according to the importance of the matter, he will make use of these "means." Even according to Vatican I the co-operation of the episcopate particularly on a definition is not excluded (and the episcopate was used

·only too readily, when there was likely to be no dissent, as in 1854 and again in 1950).[47] But the pope and the pope alone decides whether he will make use of this co-operation and how far he will follow it.

Presumably even the sun king, Louis XIV of France, would have had no objections to such theoretical-abstract restrictions on his power. It must be recognized without any illusions that, according to Vatican I (and II), no one can prevent the pope from proceeding arbitrarily and autocratically in questions of doctrine—fallible or infallible. Of course he is tied at the same time to revelation and the faith of the Church: this fact is always emphasized. But the Pope makes his own decision, and with the means that seem to him appropriate, on what this revelation is meant to say and what is the true faith of the Church. This holds for all matters of faith and morals and everything that Roman opinion includes under this heading (and how much "faith and morals" can be made to include we know from recent and very recent Church history). But the teaching of Vatican I really amounts to this: if he wants, the pope can do everything, even without the Church.

This was precisely the important thing for the infallibilist majority. Any reasonable compromise broke down at this point: the papal power to decide had to be established unconditionally. For this very reason the clause, "and not from the consent of the Church," was introduced as an absolutely final assurance. Here then in fact the ways divide, as Bishop Gasser, the spokesman for the commission, correctly stated. For him the consent of the Church could be described as "opportune" or even "relatively necessary," or in any way at all except as "absolutely necessary": "It is on this point, of strict or absolute necessity, that the whole difference between us lies; not the opportuneness or relative necessity of such a procedure, which is to be left to the judgment of the Pope .according to the circumstances."[48]

Nor has Vatican II made any difference to the fact that

the pope in the last resort has dogma and law (one and the same thing in good Roman practice) on his side. And what matters for the Romans in the last resort is dogma and law, not morals and conscience, which remain the pope's personal affair. Indeed Gasser gently answered the demands of various council fathers for an indication of further conditions for the exercise of infallible teaching authority ("good faith," "carefulness," etc.), that such conditions would certainly be binding on the pope's conscience, but for that very reason had no place in a definition: "they are to be ascribed more to the moral than the dogmatic sphere."[49]

Gasser would have been able to say this sort of thing also about all-too-abstract speeches on dialogue and collegiality, as long as things were not expressed more clearly and concretely. In Rome there were some who did not hesitate to say in fact that, even if the pope sinned in the act of defining (for bad motives perhaps), he would always be right with the definition itself. His sin therefore, as a question of morals and conscience, concerned only his confessor; but his definition concerned the Church. The sun king too had a confessor for his morals and conscience, without being in the least hindered thereby in his absolutist rule.

Pope and Curia can easily deal with abstract, conciliar doctrinal statements on collegiality and the like. This is evident, *after* Vatican II and its decisions, not only from the Pope's high-handed encyclicals and decrees, but also from the first two episcopal synods, supposed to be "collegial," but in fact completely manipulated by the Curia and so completely ineffective. Still more ominous was the Roman secret draft of a "basic law of the Catholic Church" (*lex fundamentalis Ecclesiae*), crammed with formularies of Vatican II, but conceived in a completely absolutist sense, which, if it were ever to be accepted, could bury once and for all the progress made at Vatican II.

Can anything be done about all this? Well, if we want to beat them at their own game, we would have to use all the tricks of canon law to provide collegiality in the Church also with juridical security, as the Romans have been doing so thoroughly for centuries for the papal primacy. Only in this way would the absolutist monarch—the only one from the old order who has survived the French Revolution —become at least a constitutional monarch, and the Roman Empire something like a Catholic Commonwealth.

In this connection we can also no longer avoid the question —passed over in silence at Vatican I and II, for tactical reasons or because of ignorance or fear, but always likely to arise—of a conflict between pope and Church and the possibility, constantly discussed in Catholic tradition, of a heretical or schismatic pope. For what has already been noted in connection with the papal primacy of jurisdiction is likewise possible with doctrinal decisions, and there are popes enough from antiquity up to the present time who have subsequently been disavowed by the Church in doctrinal questions. It therefore needs to be asked from the very beginning (and even Vatican I permits such a question), whether the pope can proceed, although perhaps *without*, also *against* the Church.

If the pope can define even without the *consensus Ecclesiae*, can he do so—for example, in an infallible definition of the immorality of birth control, which is quite possible in the view of the Roman extremists—also *against* the *consensus Ecclesiae?* Even Vatican I did not venture to suggest anything like this, although there are Roman theologians who, if the pope were to stand up against the whole Church, would attribute orthodoxy to the pope alone and charge the Church as a whole with heterodoxy. According to the classical Catholic tradition, even of the middle ages and the Counter-Reformation, it is certain that a pope who tried to excommunicate the whole Church or proceeded with a definition against the consensus of the Church would have to be treated, if not as a heretic, then at least as a schismatic,

because "he will not maintain with the whole body of the
Church the unity and connection which he must maintain."⁵⁰

7. Critical counterquestions

But what has been said up to now is not sufficient. There
are more fundamental questions to be raised. Since, according to the Roman theory, the pope's primacy of teaching
results from his primacy of jurisdiction, the same unresolved
difficulties which burden the primacy of jurisdiction are involved also in the primacy of teaching⁵¹: difficulties against
a primacy of teaching on the part of Peter, difficulties even
more against the necessity of a continuation of such a primacy, and most of all difficulties against a continuation in
the Roman pontiffs.

The Constitution of Vatican I on papal infallibility might
be expected to be of help here. But the chapter on infallibility does not provide any more than does the chapter
on the primacy a substantiation of this far-reaching definition
in terms adequate for the present state of theology. And
the theologian can certainly not be content with the juridical
information that the decree is valid, even apart from its
substantiation. Since—as Vatican I itself says—no new revelation and no new inspiration are bestowed on the pope,
then neither are they granted to the Council; and since
Vatican I describes its infallible definition of infallibility as
divinely revealed dogma, then it must indeed be found—
according to the view of the Council itself—in the testimonies
of this revelation. Hence the Council too cites such testimonies. But we are involved here—if it were possible—in
even greater embarrassment than in connection with the
primacy. It can only assist the Church today if this is stated
frankly and honestly.

a. It is immediately striking that in the whole chapter
on infallibility, apart from an indirect quotation of Matthew

16:18, Scripture is quoted only once: "I have prayed for you, Simon, that your faith may not fail, and once you have recovered, you in your turn must strengthen your brothers" (Lk. 22:32).

Let it be said at once that even Christians outside the Catholic Church would be very glad if anyone in Christendom were to undertake this Petrine ministry in an evangelical spirit and outlook: strengthening, consoling, encouraging his brothers in virtue of a strong faith; John XXIII—he always has to be mentioned because he is the only unambiguous example in recent times—did this, but—as we said—without any appeal to infallibility, indeed while expressly refraining from infallible utterances. Hence the question is not about a living succession in the Petrine ministry to the faith of the brethren, but about the historical and formally legal succession of a papal teaching office with a claim to infallibility. For this there would have to be proved what hitherto —even with all the aids of scholastic speculation and logical reasoning—has not been convincingly proved:

(1) that in Luke 22:32 (and in Matthew 16:18 and John 21:15) it is a question of a teaching office and moreover of an infallible teaching office: there is not a word here about infallibility; even someone whose faith doesn't "cease" (this is the literal translation) has no need at all to be immune from error in individual cases; and finally even someone by no means infallible (Peter, for instance) can strengthen his brothers in faith.

(2) that in Luke 22:32 (and in Matthew 16:18 and John 21:15), not only Peter, but also any kind of successors are addressed: again there is no mention of successors here.

(3) that the Bishop of Rome is meant to be such a successor: which presents very many more difficulties in relation to an infallible teaching office than in relation to a primacy of jurisdiction.

It would be interesting to see a serious attempt to deal with these questions (I haven't found one at any rate in the Roman textbooks). Rather it would seem that up to now no Catholic theologian has succeeded in convincing Christians outside the Catholic Church, in whom—at least after Vatican II—we can no longer presuppose merely ignorance or evil will. And experience shows that it is better not to ask for arguments from average Catholics or often from average theologians.[52]

Still less encouraging is the way in which, even in recent (although mostly still preconciliar) Catholic commentaries, Scripture is treated even by exegetes who are regarded as critical. On Luke 22:32, J. Schmid,[53] for example, writes at first completely unambiguously: "Jesus' saying does not look further than the situation immediately after the passion or beyond the circle of the disciples." Such an interpretation of course is contrary to that of Vatican I. But the Catholic author continues: "As soon however as one"—whether he includes himself, he prudently leaves open—"links Matthew 16:18 with this"—by what right and on what hermeneutical principles is not stated—"and recognizes"—apparently less an act of insight than of faith—"that here an office is promised to Peter which holds not merely for his person and time"—which is just as questionable in regard to Matthew 16:18 as in regard to Luke 22:32. What follows? "One [!] must [!] also recognize [!] that the function of giving the 'brothers' stability in faith holds also for all those in whom Peter lives on [!] as head of the Church [!]." If "one" already regards such "exegetical" arguments as acceptable, one will also not be surprised when the exegete incorporates—in brackets—the dogmatic support for his arguments: "Vatican Council, Session 4, Chapter 4."

Meanwhile only the naïve reader can have overlooked the fact that, apart from all the other oddities, the protective aid of the exegete does not meet the case. The important thing for "Vatican Council, Session 4, Chapter 4" is precisely what has not emerged, in spite of all, from this

singular exegesis: that Luke 22:32 has to do not only
with "stability in faith," but with "infallible definitions."

In this connection it may be recalled that the text of
Matthew 16:18f., so important for the modern Roman pontiffs,
which now adorns St. Peter's Basilica in large black letters
on a gold background, does not occur on a single occasion
in its full wording in the whole Christian literature of the
first couple of centuries; that the text is quoted for the first
time in the second century, by Tertullian, and then not with
reference to Rome, but to Peter; that only in the middle
of the third century did a bishop of Rome—Stephen II, an
early type of Roman authoritarianism, making use particularly
of excommunication, who calumniated the great Cyprian
as pseudo-apostle and pseudo-Christian—claimed the better
tradition by appealing to the pre-eminence of Peter; but
that only from the fourth century onward was Matthew
16:18f. used (particularly by the Roman pontiffs, Damasus
and Leo) to support a claim to primacy, and even then
without any formal claim to infallibility. And finally, in all
Eastern exegesis of Matthew 16:18 until into the eighth
century and beyond, it was considered at best as a reference
to Peter's personal primacy, without any serious thought of
a Roman primacy. And, with reference to Matthew 16:18 or
Luke 22:32, neither in East nor West is there ever a claim
raised for the infallibility of the Roman pontiff.

b. Hence it is clear why the definition of infallibility
in particular at Vatican I is supported by such sparse *testimonies of tradition*. At the beginning of the chapter on
infallibility, it is asserted in a general way in favor of a
primacy of teaching on the part of the Roman pontiff (included in his primacy of jurisdiction) that "this Holy See
has always held, the perpetual usage of the Church confirms and the ecumenical councils have declared (that the
pope's supreme teaching authority is included in his primacy
of jurisdiction)" (DS 3065). In this respect, if we are to
avoid a vicious circle, we must keep in mind from the very

beginning the fact that no ecclesiastical tradition may be accepted without examination, but must be judged critically in the light of the original Christian message: whether, that is, this tradition was a development according to the gospel, against the gospel or outside the gospel (*secundum, contra, praeter evangelium*). Facticity or even juridical legality by no means signifies legitimacy in the theological sense, seen in the light of the gospel. But for an infallible teaching primacy there are doubts even in regard to facticity.

Obviously no one will question the frequently salutary and helpful role of the Roman Church. This Church of the imperial capital, both ancient and mighty, distinguished by her extensive activity of love, bearing witness to the faith in a variety of persecutions, is rightly regarded as a haven of orthodoxy. She was tested in the struggle against Gnostics, Marcionites, and Montanists; the idea of the apostolic succession and tradition had taken root here at an early date; and in regard both to the baptismal creed and the New Testament canon, Rome's influence had been momentous. In matters of doctrine the Roman Church prudently adopted a middle, mediating position, in which subsequently she was supported especially by Alexandria. The fact that the reputation of the community was transferred to its bishop is not therefore surprising.

In spite of all this, however, there was no talk of a primacy of teaching, still less of an infallibility of the Roman pontiff or even merely of the Roman Church. The Roman claim became questionable as soon as it began to be established in an authoritarian way, more and more juridically understood as time went on, without regard for the special character and autonomy of the other Churches in teaching, liturgy or church order. We see examples of this sort of thing when, toward the end of the second century, within this federation of episcopal Churches, Victor, Bishop of Rome, excommunicated all Asia Minor for the sake of a new Roman date of Easter (opposed by the bishops of the West—especially Irenaeus—and of the East); or when, in the middle of the third century, Bishop Stephen again wanted to excommunicate large areas of the Church because of their different valuation of baptism by heretics (opposed by Cyprian, the Churches of Africa and the great Churches of the East).

Neither Victor nor Stephen was able to establish the claim to a primacy in succession to Peter. Only from Constantinian times—the Western rump synod of Sardica (Sofia) in 343 being particularly notable in this respect—under Roman influence did a monarchical structure come to be realized more and more in the Western Church. Thus Bishop Damasus was the first to claim the title of Sedes Apostolica exclusively for the Roman See; Bishop Siricius (contemporary of the far more important Ambrose, Bishop of Milan) was the first to call himself "pope," began peremptorily to call his own statutes "apostolic," adopted the official imperial style, and energetically extended his official powers on all sides; Bishop Innocent I wanted to have every important matter, after it had been discussed at a synod, put before the Roman pontiff for a decision, and tried to establish liturgical centralization with the aid of historical fictions, and so on. The wider extension of power of the Roman Sancta Sedes—especially in connection with the papal states and the forged "Donation of Constantine," with the monstrous but influential forgery of the Isidorian Decretals, and finally with the Gregorian Reform—is well known.

It was only from the time of the Gregorian Reform in the high middle ages that the Roman power began, in a strictly juridical and centralizing way, to exercise an influence on doctrine. Certainly Rome's influence had been important in the Arian struggle and Leo had won a great victory at Chalcedon. But at the same time the most important bishops and theologians even of the Western Church, Ambrose and Augustine, had not deduced from the words to Peter in Matthew 16:18 any prerogative of the Bishop of Rome as successor of Peter, but on the whole thought on the same lines as Cyprian. And when the Roman pontiffs from Damasus to Leo attempted to deduce from that saying legal conclusions for a Roman jurisdiction over other Churches, they were raising claims which for the time being largely remained Roman postulates, neither accepted nor realized in the whole Church. And the great Roman and jurist Leo, who was the first to adorn himself with the title of the pagan high priest, Pontifex Maximus, and, appealing to the Petrine text, demanded obedience and even the subordination of the ecumenical council, had to watch the same Council of Chalcedon conceding the same position of supremacy to his great antagonist in Constantinople as Patriarch of the Eastern Church.

Even though the ecumenical councils—where, apart from Chalcedon, the bishops of Rome exercised scarcely any influence—would not pass any decisions on faith without or against the pope—Patriarch of the Western Church and first Patriarch of the Imperial Church—nevertheless they made their decisions in virtue of their own plenitude of power, for they had not been called by the Roman pontiff, nor led, nor necessarily confirmed by him. And how little the Roman claim to orthodoxy was understood as "infallibility" was shown in a drastic way by the excommunication at the fifth ecumenical council at Constantinople in 553 of Pope Vigilius, who thereupon gave way; even more striking was the famous condemnation of Pope Honorius I at the sixth ecumenical council at Constantinople in 681, a condemnation repeated both by the Trullan synod of 692 and by the seventh and eighth ecumenical councils; and moreover accepted also by the successor of Honorius, Pope Leo II, and again confirmed by subsequent popes.

Until into the twelfth century, outside Rome, the importance of the Roman Church for doctrine was not understood as teaching authority properly so-called in the juridical sense. This has recently been brought out by Yves Congar in his amazingly rich work on the ecclesiology of the high middle ages. Summarizing the whole state of research on this matter, he explains:

> The teaching authority explicitly acknowledged in the pope is more of a religious quality which Rome owes to the fact that it is the place of the martyrdom and the grave of Peter and Paul. Peter is the faith, Paul the preacher of the faith. We are fond of asserting that the Roman Church has never erred in faith. She appears here as a model, being the Church of Peter who was the first to profess his faith in Christ and thus set an example . . . This is not to admit what we call inappropriately the infallibility of the pope or—more exactly —the infallibility of the judgments that he can make in the final instance as universal and supreme pastor. Doctrinal pronouncements of popes have occasionally been contested.[54]

And Congar appeals here to the work of J. Langen who had gathered together all the facts and texts that he could find, in order to prove that from the seventh to the twelfth centuries the pope was not regarded as infallible.[55]

The great upheaval however in connection with the Gregorian Reform, when the condemnation of those popes had been forgotten, affected also the idea of the teaching authority. The monstrous forgeries of the Pseudo-Isidore Decretals of the ninth century (115 wholly forged documents of the bishops of Rome from the first centuries, from Clement of Rome onward; 125 documents with interpolations) were now employed to buttress the claim of the teaching authority of the pope.[56] These forgeries destroyed all sense of the historical development of institutions and created the impression that the Church in the earliest times had already been ruled in detail by papal decrees: an image of the Church and law of the Church that appears to be concentrated wholly on the Roman authority. For questions of doctrine the following claims from the forgeries were of particular im-

portance: that the holding of any council, even of a provincial council, is linked with the authority of the pope and
that all more important matters in the Church are subject
to the judgment of the pope. The pope appears as of himself the source of normativity for the whole Church: "Pseudo-
Isidore ascribes to the teaching office and the disciplinary
authority of the pope an autonomous character which is
not bound by the norms of tradition. He ascribes to Pope
Lucius, a contemporary of Cyprian, the statement that the
Roman Church, 'Mother of all the Churches of Christ,' has
never erred."[57]

In the second half of the eleventh century Gregory VII
relied on these and similar statements for his monarchical
conception of the Church, which in fact represented a new
Church constitution; then in the first half of the thirteenth
century Gratian, founder of the science of canon law, produced his law book, which was basic for all later times—
including the 1918 Code of Canon Law—and in which 324
passages from popes of the first four centuries are cited,
313 of them proved forgeries. From now on Matthew 16:18
is used in Rome precisely in this monarchic-absolutist sense
with reference to the Roman Church and the Roman pontiff,
with all the juridical consequences which the great papal
legislators of the twelfth and thirteenth centuries were able
to deduce from this primacy and able to establish in a
highly practical way with the aid of papal synods, papal
legates, and the mendicant orders, who were likewise in-
dependent of the local Church leadership (bishops and parish
priests).

Both the Western-Germanic and particularly the Eastern
Empire were weak at this time, and the Eastern Church
as a result of these developments had turned away completely from Rome; at this time the schism with the East
became final. Now therefore there was no longer any obstacle
in the way of the development of papal authority. Gregory
VII, it is true, in the *Dictatus Papae*, had asserted only of the

Roman *Church* that it can never err in faith and his assertion of a personal holiness of the pope granted him in virtue of Peter's merits failed to be accepted; presumably it could all too easily have been turned against the legitimacy of a pope. Even the curially minded canonists upheld the teaching that a pope can become a heretic and then be judged by the Church. Nevertheless, in the thirteenth century papal power not only attained its peak in world politics and canon law, but prevailed also in theology, which was inclined to move more slowly.

It was St. Thomas Aquinas, himself a member of a centrally governed mendicant order, who incorporated the new political-juridical development in the second half of the thirteenth century into the dogmatic system. For all the indisputable merits of Aquinas in regard to theology as a whole, this point must be made clear. In his opusculum, *Contra errores Graecorum,* which he wrote in 1263, commissioned by the Curia, for Pope Urban IV and the negotiations for union with the Emperor, Michael VIII Palaeologus, he presents to the weak Greeks the arguments for the Roman rights in an exorbitant way, and this had its effect also on the West. In connection with the sublime questions of trinitarian doctrine, in several chapters toward the end of the work, which positively wallow in quotations from forgeries, it is "shown" "that the Roman Pontiff is first and greatest of all bishops," "that the same Pontiff presides over the whole Church," "that he has the fullness of power in the Church," "that in the same power conferred by Christ on Peter the Roman Pontiff is the successor of Peter."[58] In regard to papal teaching authority Aquinas demonstrates "that it is for the pope to decide what belongs to faith." All these chapters culminate in the statement apparently given a dogmatic formulation for the first time by Thomas and then bluntly defined by Boniface VIII in the Bull, *Unam Sanctam:* "that to be subject to the Roman Pontiff is necessary for salvation."[59] In this article too, which is fundamental for the papal teaching authority, Aquinas relies on forged quotations from Cyril's *Liber thesaurorum*, which he took from an anonymous *Libellus de processione Spiritus Sancti:* "It is explicable that Thomas quoted from the *Libellus* just those sentences which were suitable for the substantiation of his statements on the primacy; from what has been said however it is clear that they are mostly sentences which have either been forged or interpolated through forgeries."[60]

These theses resting on forgeries Thomas then takes over in the *Summa Theologiae*, where they really do begin to make history. Basic for our context is the article on whether it is for the pope to ordain a profession of faith.[61] As usual, Thomas lists a number of objections to his thesis, then in the *sed contra* briefly states his argument from authority in favor of the thesis. He takes as his major premise the historically correct statement: "The publication of a profession of faith takes place in a general council." His minor premise is documented only from a text in the Decretals, which again is based on the Pseudo-Isidore forgeries already mentioned and in no way corresponds to the historical truth:[62] "But a council of this kind can be called only by the authority of the Supreme Pontiff." The conclusion then follows (*because* the publication is by a council, it is by papal authority): "Therefore the publication of a profession of faith pertains to the authority of the Supreme Pontiff." The answer in detail runs:

A new publication of a profession of faith is necessary to avoid errors that are arising. The publication therefore comes under the authority which has to define formally what matters are of faith, so that they may be held by all with unshakable faith. But this belongs to the authority of the Supreme Pontiff, "to whom the Church's greater and more difficult questions are referred" (here again a decretal text is quoted which is based on Pseudo-Isidore). Hence too our Lord says to Peter (Lk 22.32), since he had appointed him Supreme Pontiff: "I have prayed for you, Simon . . ." And the reason for this is that there must be one faith of the whole Church according to 1 Corinthians 1:10: "All say the same thing, let there be no divisions among you." This could not be maintained unless a question arising on faith were decided by him who presides over the whole Church, so that his judgment may be firmly held by the whole Church. Hence a new publication of a profession of faith pertains solely to the authority of the Supreme Pontiff: as also everything else that pertains to the whole Church, such as convoking a general council and other things of the same kind.

There is no doubt that Aquinas, basing himself—we may assume, in good faith—on the forgeries, in this way laid the foundations for the doctrine of infallibility of Vatican I. This is not to say that it was at once generally accepted. A short time afterward, the Avignon exile, the Western Schism with its two and then three popes contradicting one another, and finally the conciliar period, made exaggerations of the papal teaching power seem as utopian as exaggerations of the ecclesiastical-secular power of jurisdiction. All the same, after the Council of Constance, Cardinal Torquemada revived on thomistic foundations the papalist ecclesiology we have described (he admitted, however, the possibility of a heretical pope), followed later—when the Curia had again gained the upper hand—by Luther's contemporaries, Cardinal Cajetan and Jacobazzi.

In the fifteenth century, however, and at the time of the outbreak of the Reformation—this must be said if we are to understand Luther—there was no unanimous opinion in the Church about the papal primacy (and its relationship to the council) or about the teaching authority of the pope. Even the Council of Trent, fearing a reawakening of conciliarism, did not venture to make any decisions on these questions. Cardinal Bellarmine, however, took up again the tradition, Aquinas-Torquemada-Cajetan, and then in the nine-

teenth century, when the time had become ripe for a definition, became with Aquinas a principal witness for the
infallibility of the pope. Marginally, it may be noted that
the condemnation of Pope Honorius by several councils and
popes was unknown to Aquinas; but, after its discovery,
was brazenly declared by Torquemada to be an error of
the Greeks and still more brazenly by A. Pigge and Bellarmine in the Reformation period to be a forgery by the
Greeks of the conciliar documents (even Melchior Cano, the
theologian of the Council of Trent, protested sharply against
this hypothesis of forgery); finally, this condemnation of a
pope was indeed acknowledged by the infallibilists at Vatican
I as an historical fact, but now—in virtue of what has become a customary anachronistic distinction and subterfuge
—Honorius' decision was interpreted as not being an *ex
cathedra* declaration.[63]

In the light of this brief outline of the history of papal
infallibility, it will be understood why Vatican I was content to substantiate the definition with brief, general statements: "this the Holy See has always held" and "this the
perpetual usage of the Church confirms." The *historical
reality* looks different. The papalist overcharging of the teaching authority in theory and practice may be based both on
what today have been proved to be forgeries and the decretals based on these and also again on the theologians
"proving" these decretals, but certainly not on Scripture nor
on the common ecumenical tradition of the Church of the
first millennium. They have a substantial share of the responsibility for maintaining the schism with the Churches
of the East, which have never accepted such a development,
and with the Churches of the Reformation, which have
opposed this development in the name of the freedom of
the gospel and of the Christian man.[64]

If still another illustration is needed for the problematic
of the development we have indicated, we may take—so
to speak—as reverse check the conciliar texts quoted in favor

of papal infallibility in the fourth chapter of the constitution *Pastor Aeternus:* none of the three astonishingly lengthy texts stems from a universally recognized general council.

Certainly we cannot blame Vatican I for not quoting in particular the Council of Chalcedon with its famous Canon 28 which conferred on New-Rome (Constantinople) the same civic dignity as Old-Rome; here in fact is heard another, non-Roman tradition.° But on the other hand, against the background of the whole historical development in the second millennium, what do the quotations from the Council of Lyons (1274) and Florence (1439) prove? They were Roman acknowledgments of the Roman primacy, composed by Romans, which one tried to impose on Greeks who were being greatly oppressed politically by the Arabs—an attempt which was ultimately unsuccessful. At the same time, in spite of all the emphasis on the Roman teaching authority, there is not a word about infallibility in either the Lyons or the Florentine texts. The same holds for the fourth council of Constantinople (869-70), which is cited as the first testimony by Vatican I: not a word on infallibility nor anything about the Bishop of Rome, but only about the Roman See. Nor is this council included among the universally recognized general councils. On the contrary, held during the dispute between the Patriarch Ignatius and the Patriarch Photius, it was formally annulled some years later, its original documents were lost, and in all the Byzantine collections it is completely ignored. Even in the West it had no sort of importance until in the second half of the eleventh century—again significantly in connection with the Gregorian Reform and the final break with Constantinople —the council began to be quoted as the eighth ecumenical council.[65]

c. When we look at the argument for the dogma of in-

° Heinrich Denzinger, otherwise painfully exact in nosing out quotations for primacy and infallibility from documents which are often of very secondary importance, passes over in silence as in so many cases also this canon of an ecumenical council which does not fit into his system.

fallibility from Scripture and tradition, plainly as scanty as it is brittle, we may wonder how the overwhelming majority of the bishops could have given their assent to this definition. We have also examined the *motives* closely.

Undoubtedly numerous extratheological motives played their part. We have already spoken of the mentality of most of the bishops, marked by the ideas of the restoration, romanticism, and traditionalism, and—linked with this—the aversion to modern liberal and democratic ideas, which enabled them to support a strengthened hierarchical order, built entirely on the pope. We spoke of the novel, sentimental veneration for Pius IX, which could not deny him anything that he seriously wanted and which saw in the definition of his prerogatives a compensation for the insults he had suffered. More might be said of the desire of many bishops finally to liquidate "Gallicanism," which was felt to be a weakening of the single Catholic front; and also of the pressure of the Curia, which undoubtedly played a part especially with those bishops who were financially dependent on it. But all this is still inadequate to explain the motivation.

What motives then were finally decisive for the definition of papal infallibility? In fact papal infallibility was already taken for granted by the majority of the bishops before it was defined. For the most part they came from the traditionally Catholic countries; to these were added Easterns trained in Rome and almost all the missionary bishops, as well as some from countries where the struggle against liberalism or Protestantism was particularly acute. For all of them, with little thought of the enormous exegetical, historical and systematic difficulties in the way of a definition, the matter was clear from the very beginning. Roger Aubert, who has given a very exact analysis of the different motives, correctly states:

> Even if they did not approve all the centralizing measures of the Curia, these prelates hardly saw anything

unsuitable about a solemn acknowledgment by the Council
of papal infallibility, which was admitted at least in practice by all their faithful and clergy and which seemed
to them an obvious theological truth. They saw in the
Gallican and Febronian theses a backward step, a departure from the ancient tradition attested by some Scripture texts which seemed to them quite clear and by the
totality of the great scholastic teachers from St. Thomas
to Bellarmine. They considered it normal therefore to take
advantage of the assembling of the Council to cut short
the revival of what they regarded as completely sterile
controversies on this matter.[66]

On the other hand, however, the fact cannot be overlooked that motives were varied and the state of affairs
by no means clear on the part even of the minority—especially German, Austro-Hungarian, and about thirty French
and twenty Italian bishops, as well as some Eastern bishops.
For these, too, education and the political situation in their
own countries played a part: they feared a renewed condemnation of modern ideas and the reactions of their govern-
ments. But pastoral and ecumenical motives were more important: it was feared—and, unfortunately, as things turned
out, very rightly—that there might be a schism and an
imperiling of ecumenical efforts, perhaps a new aggressiveness
on the part of Protestant circles. The main reasons however were theological, and Aubert again sets them out very
clearly, of course—and this cannot be passed over in complete silence—with the usual depreciatory labels attached
(here noted with a question mark), concealing the fact
that behind a number of these tendencies there lay the
oldest and best Catholic tradition:

In the first place were the theological motives. A Gallican [?] or semi-Gallican [?] conception of the Church's
magisterium on the part of a number of bishops who
would not admit that the pope in certain cases can decide

a point of doctrine independently of any ratification by the episcopal body. The influence of the tradition of Bossuet, an episcopalian [?] mentality derived from the Febronian [?] theologians of the eighteenth century, historical difficulties such as the condemnation of Pope Honorius in 681, an archaizing [?] theological mentality concentrating too much [?] on the sources and with little sense of dogmatic development [?], had led them to conclude either that the pope did not enjoy the privilege of personal infallibility or at least that the question was obscure and it was premature to want to settle it. Still more frequent seems to have been the very legitimate, although occasionally somewhat excessive [?], preoccupation of safeguarding the second element of the divine structure of the ecclesiastical hierarchy: the episcopate.[67]

And yet Aubert—with many other authors—is not entirely wrong in having recourse to labels like "Gallicanism," "episcopalian," "Febronianism," etc. For from a theological perspective too it cannot be overlooked that the minority itself remained largely fixed in the traditional ways of looking at questions. This was due not least to the fact that the council minority, in view of the diversity of motives and positions, concentrated on the question which would provide the broadest basis for the opposition to attack a definition of infallibility: the question of opportuneness. This question of opportuneness thrust the essential question too much into the background. People avoided tackling the question of infallibility from the center.

But one thing must have become clear in the course of this whole chapter: the traditional doctrine of ecclesiastical infallibility, however precisely described in the textbooks, at Vatican I and II, rests on foundations which for a modern theology and perhaps even for that time could not be described as secure and unassailable.

III. THE CENTRAL PROBLEM

1. Negative demarcations

If the foundations of neoscholastic doctrine on infallibility are so fragile and its expression, both in connection with the pope (Vatican I) and in connection with the episcopate (Vatican II), creates so many unsolved and perhaps insoluble problems, would not the simplest and best solution be to abandon altogether the whole doctrine of ecclesiastical infallibility? But what then—we shall hear the counterquestion —is to be made of those biblical promises on which this doctrine of infallibility claims to be based? The promises—according to the original testimony—are given to the Church, not to any purely secular communities or structures and have come down to us in a variety of traditions. We have been told that the Lord will remain with his disciples until the end of the world, that the gates of hell will not overcome the Church, that the Spirit of truth will lead the disciples into all truth, that the Church is the pillar and ground of truth.

In this chapter particularly we must not attempt a hasty solution, either of the left or of the right, but rather try to reveal more exactly the state of the question and ascertain where the fundamental difficulty lies. This will be done in the light of ideas developed in previous chapters; at the same time our conclusions will be confirmed and clarified with the the aid of more recent publications, some of which have appeared in connection with the centenary in 1970 of Vatican I and its definition of papal infallibility. It will then soon become clear that a great deal has been accomplished by way of qualifying and correcting the Vatican definition. But the central question has still not been examined sufficiently closely. What really constitutes the *central problem* within the problematic of ecclesiastical infallibility if we set aside the inadequate, questionable and tenuous arguments considered in the previous chapter? We shall first make a negative demarcation, in order then to give a positive answer.

a. Lack of freedom at Vatican I?

(1) The majority of the council were very largely influenced by the ideas of political-religious restoration, of anti-enlightenment traditionalism, and of absolutist papalism; they were also subject to the authoritarian pressure of Pius IX. Today, a hundred years later, these things are frankly and boldly admitted by Catholic authors and the depressing climate of that council compared unfavorably with Vatican II. Here are some recent Catholic testimonies on the subject.

On the way in which Vatican I was *ideologically conditioned and restricted*, Victor Conzemius, the Luxembourg church historian and editor of the correspondence between Ignaz von Döllinger and Lord Acton, writes:

> In the age of the restoration the papacy became the indispensable support of backward-looking legitimist-monarchist thinking. Moreover new possibilities were offered for the development of spiritual, papal authority. For secularization meant that the national Churches of France, Austria, Germany and Italy, were largely relieved of secular tasks. Clinging to Rome, they now looked for support against a state policy that attempted partly to thrust the Church out of public life, partly to domesticate bureaucratically her newly won freedom. Rome gave reliable support both to national Churches struggling for their freedom as Churches and also to the missionary Churches rapidly developing in the nineteenth century in America and Asia.

As a *quid pro quo* these Churches became more closely tied to the Roman central administration. In addition, Rome for a time gave real scope also to progressive Catholic forces agitating against state-tutelage of the Church in the police-state of the restoration period. The papacy was extraordinarily favoured by an ideological trend which led directly to a strengthening of its moral prestige. Two Frenchmen, de Maistre and Lammenais, both "converts" who had found their way back to the Church after many years of estrangement, were the heralds of this movement. For de Maistre and Lammenais the Catholic Church was the main support of European social order: anyone who attacked her, was doing violence to the foundations of society.[1]

Important for the historical understanding of this ideology is the brief summary of the ideas of the two fathers of papal ultramontanism, which Rome was to spread by every means among faithful and clergy in the second half of the century:

Typical for de Maistre is the logical argument with which he seeks to win the French king, Charles X, for his ideas: "No public morality and no national character without religion, no European religion without Christianity, no Christianity without Catholicism, no Catholicism without the pope, no pope without the supremacy which belongs to him." From his pen there flow lapidary formulations like these: "Without the Roman Pontiff there is no Christianity" or "Christianity rests exclusively on the Roman Pontiff." De Maistre does not substantiate his thesis. He simply continues in an apodictic manner to hammer in the parallelism between ecclesiastical and secular society. "There can be no human society without government, no government without sovereignty and no sovereignty without infallibility." De Maistre here achieves a kind of cosmic identification of Church and society. Both are subject to the same system of law, to the same ethos. He seems to have a kind of monomania, compelling him to insist on the principle of authority. The flight to authority, which he transforms into a kind of oracle, seems to him the only solution to the social crisis of his time. It is important to remember that this Savoyard count wrote very deliberately as an opponent of the French Revolution, while living under a feudalistic-authoritarian rule in Russia, where he was ambassador at the Czar's court. His doctrines, which were taken up reluctantly in Rome itself, at once gained followers. Lammenais, the great sower of ideas formative of the future, became their popularizer. He softened their harshness, directly related them to the life of the Church and thus made them extraordinarily comprehensible.[2]

In the atmosphere of doom of the years before the loss of the papal states, when Peter's pence as a voluntary offering for pope and Curia was revived, abundant finance from all Europe flowed into the Roman coffers and young Catholics —especially the Dutch—competed with each other to be accepted into the papal army. Pius IX had become a symbol of the Catholic will to survive:

> This was the climate in which it began to seem as if the strengthening of papal authority was the alpha and omega of ecclesiastical wisdom. From the standpoint of the history of ideas, it is interesting that, at a time when material authority was gradually dissolving personal authority, the Church not only clung to the authority of the person, but gave to it a new consecration with dogmatic trimmings. People were confirmed in this mental attitude by the general attack on Christianity.[3]

Of the *climate* at the council itself the conciliar historian, Hubert Jedin, observes:

> The climate in which the council took place was full of tension. But it was not the joyous, expectant tension in

which people awaited the "ecumenical" council after Pope
John's first announcement; the fears outweighed the ex-
pectations, particularly among the intellectual leaders of
the German-speaking countries and of France. A short time
before, Pope Pius IX in the Syllabus had declared war
on modern thinking and modern ideas of the state.[4]

And Walter Kasper, the dogmatic theologian, puts it still
more clearly with regard to the effects of this climate—so
different from that of Vatican II—on the definition of the
council itself:

> The differences between the two councils find expression
> also in a very different conciliar climate. Sharp practice
> and truly fanatical tendencies led at Vatican I to some ex-
> tent to extremely pointed and ill-considered statements
> on the primacy and infallibility of the pope. At the same
> time a considerable minority of bishops was simply passed
> over. Even before the closing of the council most of them
> had left Rome embittered. For life within the Church, for
> the growing together of the separated Churches, as well as
> for relationships with the modern world, problems had
> thus been created which simply could not be cleared up
> even by Vatican II. The primacy of the pope, defined by
> Vatican I as centre, sign and principle of unity, had in fact
> become a ground of separation between the Churches and
> the occasion of many psychological schisms within the
> Church. The problems raised by Vatican I are therefore
> not yet by any means settled.[5]

Finally, on *Pius IX's influence* on the council, W. Kasper again
says:

> The council of the last century was called by Pius IX in
> order to condemn the errors of modern times, just as the
> Council of Trent in the sixteenth century had rejected the
> heresies of the Reformers. The attempt was made to pre-
> sent the infallible authority of the pope as a remedy for

the crisis of modern society, which was even then beginning to take shape. John XXIII on the other hand, in his memorable opening address of October 11, 1962, rejected all prophets of doom who thought that everything developing in society and the Church was for the worse and that the world was on the brink of disaster. He recommended the Church not to use strict measures under present conditions but those of compassion and to open the windows wide on to the world.[6]

And, in regard to concrete events, H. Jedin writes:

It must be admitted that, in the highly dramatic struggle for the formulation of the definition of infallibility, Pius IX did not maintain that reserve on which his successor insisted during the Second Vatican Council in the discussion on the third chapter of the Constitution on the Church. It was due to him in fact that the chapter on the pope was withdrawn from the general draft on the Church in March 1870. During the debate, starting out from his personal ideas on the scope of infallibility, he tried to influence the participants in the council in favour of his view; and, for example, when Cardinal Guidi of Bologna in the general congregation of June 18 had made a suggestion to conciliate the minority, he reproached him bitterly the same evening and—obviously in an outburst of anger—let himself be carried away and used the expression, which was circulated at the council on the very next morning: "Tradition—that's me."[7]

All this has to be remembered—and we have already emphasized its importance in the previous chapter—in judging not only the council, but also the definitions themselves, which can be understood only in the light of this ideological conditioning and this conciliar climate.

(2) In spite of everything, however, the claim, frequently asserted, that the council was not free, although frequently

asserted cannot be maintained. Despite all the often scandalous manipulation of the council by the Curia, the pope, and the leaders of the majority, there was freedom of speech (and often more clear speaking than at Vatican II) and freedom of voting. The decisive factor was that the majority did not at all need to be forced into the definition, since this was completely in harmony with their way of thinking.

Conzemius answers the criticism that the council was not free:

> This is not true. Certainly the council's leaders, devoted to the Curia, occasionally exercised undue pressure. The Pope too, in occasional outbursts of his easily roused temper, exposed himself far too much as a partisan. The right to free expression of opinion was not thereby curtailed, the council's freedom not affected at its very core. The majority of the bishops did not at all need to be pressed on: as we explained, their categories of thought led directly to a strengthening of the papal prerogatives. The resolute protagonists of this trend too were not Italians or Spaniards, but Northerners: Manning, Archbishop of Westminster; Senestrey, Bishop of Regensburg; Mermillod, Auxiliary Bishop of Geneva.[8]

Apposite too is the comment of the Catholic publicist, Walter Dirks:

> The majority of the fathers—the same holds clearly for the ordinary faithful—did not simply yield to the pressure of a Pope as stubborn as he was single-minded, but they themselves believed with him in the important presupposition to the definition of the dogma: that the Christian Church —the heretical Reformers did not count—had always believed in the infallible teaching authority of Peter's successor. For dogmas, by their very notion, are not meant to create "new" truths, but to define more precisely what has been believed always and by all.[9]

b. The primacy question?

(1) Agreement about a Petrine ministry in the Church or on the question of the primacy would not be a priori impossible. The most recent dialogue—as for instance with the Old Catholic Church, separated from the Catholic Church as a result of the definition of Vatican I—is particularly revealing here.

Even in the "Utrecht Declaration" of September 24, 1889, the international conference of Old Catholic bishops, while "rejecting the Vatican decrees of 18 July 1870 on infallibility and the universal episcopate," had no objection to acknowledging on the other hand a "'historical primacy,' such as several ecumenical councils and the Fathers of the early Church had attributed to the Bishop of Rome as *primus inter pares* (first among equals), with the agreement of the whole Church of the first millennium."[10]

The seven theses drawn up on September 13, 1969[11] by a conference of Old Catholic theologians, with the simultaneous agreement of the international conference of Old Catholic bishops, give a more precise form to the Utrecht Declaration (thesis 1) and affirm a "special position of Peter" in the New Testament, which "has a significative importance for the Church," so that "the missions entrusted to Peter must be realized also in the structure of the Church" (theses 2–4). Admittedly, without "touching the field of dogmatic conclusions" (cf. thesis 6), it can be observed on the other hand "that the function which Rome acquired in the history of the Church came about in the light of the acceptance of this mission," even though this was "often very very much obscured" (thesis 5). The conclusion is drawn in thesis 7: "Corresponding to the function which Peter exercised according to the testimony of Scripture, a 'petrine office' would have to be defined as a service to Christ, to his Church and to the world, through the obligation (not juridical com-

petence) in all decisive situations to take an initiative which
makes it possible for the totality of the Church to decide to
express its faith and manifest its unity visibly."

These gratifyingly unpolemical and promising theses, as
explained by the leading Old Catholic theologian, Werner
Küppers,[12] are regarded by Heinrich Bacht, the very capable
Catholic partner to the discussion, as offering "real chances
for an understanding."[13] In the light of his own studies,[14]
the present author can only agree. Likewise when Bacht
writes:

Contemporary Catholic theology is aware of the "hierarchy
of truths" (Decree on Ecumenism n.11); in this hierarchy,
however, the question of the papal primacy clearly takes
second place. Catholic theology is likewise aware that
elements of very diverse origin and dignity have come
together in the complex phenomenon "papacy" and that
their disentanglement is an urgent task. It is aware also
that by no means all the papal prerogatives mentioned at
Vatican I are of divine right; moreover, as a result of the
theology predominant at Vatican I, that the function of the
pope is unduly set apart from the totality of the Church
and that therefore the embedding of the question of the
primacy into the teaching on the Church as a whole is an
urgent need. Furthermore, long before Vatican II, the
"softening" of the one-sided juridical concept of the
Church's structures had begun. On the Catholic side too we
are well aware of the fact that the doctrine of the Church's
constitution found expression against the background of the
Gregorian Reform, with its excessive concentration on
the question of "power" and "authority." In addition, there
is a critical dissociation from the various "inadequacies"
and restrictions at the First Vatican Council (unfair agita-
tion on the part of the infallibilists, lack of ecumenical
responsibility, unnecessary exacerbation as a result of the
use of anathemas . . .).[15]

Bacht closes with an appeal for understanding: "May those who hold responsibility perceive the signs of the times."[16]

(2) A settlement of the question of the primacy does not mean that the question of infallibility is cleared up, but only that it is properly stated.

It is striking that the word "infallibility" does not occur either in the seven theses of the Old Catholic Church, or in Küppers' interpretation, or in Bacht's answer. This is scarcely an accident. The Old Catholic thesis 6, particularly, has to be linked with the question of infallibility: "In spite of the numerous fatal developments of the past which led to various schisms—among them that of Utrecht—at the First Vatican Council, in the light of an axiomatic preconception, an authoritarian way of thinking was made into a dogma which cannot be substantiated from Scripture and tradition." And W. Küppers might have had the question of infallibility particularly in mind when he observes in the theses a "complete reserve in regard to the field of 'dogmatic conclusions,' which is usually regarded as particularly relevant to the question of the papacy": "this reserve is based on an appreciation of the fact that the common presuppositions for dogmatic discussion have hitherto been lacking precisely at this point."[17] This much then is clear: even for the Old Catholics—to say nothing of the Orthodox and Protestants—an eventual settlement of the primacy still does not mean that the question of infallibility is settled. The latter certainly represents the most serious obstacle on the way to ecumenical understanding.

c. The rights of conscience?

(1) The rights of conscience remain even in regard to dogma. There is no need to repeat what was said here in chapter 1 with reference to the section in *Structures of the Church*. Fortunately, in the postconciliar period, the encyclical *Humanae Vitae* has helped Catholics considerably to go ahead with the urgently necessary task of forming

their consciences even in the face of solemn papal doctrinal utterances.

A recent, very clearly worded testimony to freedom as a factor in faith itself is provided by W. Kasper in his reflections on "The Church's Road from Vatican I to Vatican II": "Only when she (the Church) preserves her own freedom, can she serve the freedom of others. Her authority therefore must be the 'authority of freedom.' For faith is essentially an act of free assent; as an act that is also wholly and entirely human, it does not exclude, but includes intellectual responsibility. No one can or may delegate this responsibility in a 'blind' obedience—so to speak—to the official Church and her teaching office. Obedience of faith against one's own understanding would be an immoral act."[18] Likewise Walter Dirks: "For Catholics too the Pauline teaching, confirmed by St. Thomas Aquinas, holds, that whatever does not come 'from conscience,' from conviction, is sin. Among the presuppositions of the Catholic Church's system is its free and voluntary acceptance by faith and the upholding of this acceptance."[19]

(2) Recourse to conscience however does not settle the objective question either of papal or of episcopal infallibility. Certainly the practice has grown in recent times of having recourse to conscience and generally of finding excusing circumstances in subjective factors, when moral theology did not provide satisfactory answers to the objective questions themselves. Thus, particularly in face of the impasse of Catholic sexual morality, many a harsh objective burden could be made at least subjectively endurable (lack of knowledge or lack of free will excuses from grave sin in masturbation or birth control).

As self-defense for conscience and as a pastoral aid against an authoritarian teaching office, which prevents discussion by every means, this recourse to subjectivity is still justified. But it cannot become an excuse or pretext for not tackling theologically also the objective questions themselves. Confessional advice is not a substitute for serious theological criticism. This holds particularly for the question of infallibility. Individual Christians, theologians, bishops and bishops' conferences have made use of the appeal to conscience, for instance, in the case of the encyclical *Humanae Vitae*, and rightly so. But neither theologians nor Church leaders are thereby excused from coming to grips with the matter itself; and this means in the concrete case, over and above all questions of moral theology, the question of the authority of the teaching office. Even irrespective of all rights of conscience, is the claim of the teaching office ("ordinary" or "extraordinary," papal or episcopal) to infallibility valid or not? If this objective question had been pursued at an earlier stage, with the seriousness it required, many a conflict of conscience would have been avoided.

d. Opportuneness, conditions, and limits of the infallibility definition?

(1) Even if we share the view of the minority of those at Vatican I and deny the opportuneness of the definition of infallibility at that time, once the definition became a fact we must recognize that a clear understanding of its modalities and limitations is an essential preliminary to objective discussion.

For the centenary "jubilee" of Vatican I, Johann Finsterhölzl in his article, *Reflections on the Declaration of Papal Infallibility at Vatican I*[20] rightly brings out the fact that the council defined less than what supporters of the definition wanted and opponents feared. His remarks—centered on Gasser's report—on holders, scope, object and form of infallibility aim throughout "at the need to consider the Pope as organ of the Church, to recognize papal infallibility as the realization of the Church's infallibility, more clearly than was done at the time." "The Council," he says, "was far too nervous and failed to insist on the fact that the Pope himself

primarily belongs to the believing and hearing Church, which
is confronted by the demands of the Word of God and
its interpretation as brought out by tradition. Even an "assent"
to a dogmatic definition is not debarred, but on the contrary
required."[21]

(2) Settling the limits of papal infallibility, however, and
deciding the place of the pope in the Church in no way
solve the problem of ecclesiastical infallibility itself.

When, for instance, W. Dirks, under the title of "The
dogma of fallible popes," describes the "new" element in
the Vatican definition as "particularly the restriction, the
exact and very precise fixing of the limits and conditions,"
he is right. But then, appealing to the fact that this papal
infallibility has only been claimed twice in a hundred years
(1854 for Mary's immaculate conception; 1950 for her bodily
assumption into heaven), he concludes with the "thesis"
"that, in practice, in 1870 the fallibility of the pope also
became a dogma. All the theories of degrees of authority
do not alter the fact that the many encyclicals—sometimes
of very authoritarian popes—since 1870 can be described,
in the strict sense of the dogma, as fallible. The Pope of
Humanae Vitae has had to let this be said very forcefully."[22]

On this however it has to be observed that (1) in fact
(perhaps unfortunately) fallibility was just not *defined as
a dogma;* (2) a single infallible dogma—indeed, even the
possibility of such infallible dogmatic definitions—is sufficient
to raise the problem of infallibility in all its acuteness; (3)
the encyclical *Humanae Vitae*, in particular, shows clearly
that, because of the simultaneous infallibility of the ordinary
as well as the extraordinary teaching office, the restriction
of papal infallibility does not take us as far as we would
like to think.

It is also true, as Johann Finsterhölzl says, that "the truth
bestowed on the Church lives essentially on the fidelity of
God, who himself as truth turns to her."[23] But when he
jumps to the conclusion that the "infallibility of the Church,

as the First Vatican Council says, finds expression in solemn
definitions of the papal teaching office," he skips the decisive
question as to whether "the truth and fidelity of God himself"
finds "its historical realization in an excellent way" particularly
in such definitions and how this is proved. Or when he holds
that Vatican II, in the Constitution on the Church, article
25, gave "a precise interpretation" of the object and scope
of infallibility, he overlooks the fact that Vatican II—as
we showed—says no more and no less than Vatican I about
the object and scope of infallibility, but does now affirm
with the utmost formality the same infallibility of Vatican I
in regard to the episcopate. Or when the same author, with
an appeal to the statement of Gasser which we quoted,
thinks he can observe that "any attempt to ascribe divine
attributes to a man, in fact to the Pope, by referring to the
definition of papal infallibility, is thus excluded,"[24] he could
have read up in a "preconciliar" book the following comment:

> True, often, these discussions among Catholics distract
> people from the real difficulty of freedom from error and
> lead them to overestimate considerably the significance
> for ecumenical debate of the theological qualifications al-
> ready discussed. Let us have no illusions on this score:
> whether the pope alone or in union with the episcopate
> is free from error, whether he must make use of assistance
> or not, whether freedom from error extends only to matters
> of faith and morals or also to other areas, whether the
> pope as free from error in his definitions needs the consent
> of the Church or not, and so on, these are all very secondary
> questions for a Protestant Christian. To put it more sharply:
> for the problem to be raised in all its acuteness, it is
> sufficient if even one pope at any time at all is able to
> pronounce, with absolute certainty, as a pope *a priori*
> free from error, a single dogma binding on the Church:
> a man, who is not God—free from error? What holds for
> *one* man holds also for *several*, holds also for an ecumenical

council. In this respect the freedom from error of a council raises exactly the same problem as the infallibility of a pope.[25]

In the light of these distinctions we may conclude that we shall get no further in the discussion by striving merely for an interpretation of the Vatican definitions, albeit with a more refined apologetic and dialectic. This becomes boring, too, in the course of time. Instead, we must raise critical questions about the background of the definitions themselves: on the one hand, in regard to the plausibility of their substantiation, as we did in the previous chapter; on the other hand, as in the present chapter, in regard to the validity of their basic approach. Vatican I itself (together with Vatican II) forces such a radical questioning on us.

e. The term "infallibility"?

(1) It is largely admitted today that the term is open to misunderstanding. Gasser himself, the spokesman for the Vatican I commission, observed that the word *infallibilitas* was liable to be misunderstood, "because—for example—in the German language it could easily be confused with impeccability (*Fehlerlosigkeit*), sinlessness, immaculateness."[26] And in fact the fine distinctions of Vatican theology have never really made an impression on either the non-Catholic or the Catholic public.

Very recently Heinrich Fries has pointed out how the words "infallibility" and "irreformability" can be misunderstood:

Both words are open to misunderstanding and it may be asked why they continue to be used, although they are associated with ideas that are not really intended. "Infallibility" carries with it the idea of an absolute *non plus ultra*: in fact, it means that, when it is a question of the truth of Jesus Christ, the Church does not fall into error in making such a decision of faith. "Irreformable" carries with it the idea of an absolute fixation on the matter and its form of expression, but this is not exactly the meaning. "Irreformable" does indeed exclude an error of faith in the definition, but at the same time opens up the possibility of another, more complete version: not of course a version which would no longer be binding, but one meant to bring about a deeper understanding of what had been expressed in a dogma and which subordinates it to the word of God. But who can see all this in the word "irreformable"?[27]

(2) The objective question however would not be settled even by a better translation of *infallibilitas*. Since Vatican I understood *infallibilitas* in general as *immunitas ab errore*,[28] I previously suggested that the word "infallibility" should be replaced by "freedom from error," which does not have the same moral undertone of "impeccability"—at the same time clearly admitting that "not very much had thereby been clarified in theological terms."[29]

Bearing in mind the root of the word *infallibilitas* (*fallere*= put wrong, make a false step, lead into error, deceive, delude), I later translated *infallibilitas* more precisely and perhaps also more felicitously as "indeceivability" *(Untrüglichkeit)*, which certainly has a more general meaning. *Infallibilitas* can then be understood as a sharing in the truth of God himself who, according to Vatican I, "can neither deceive nor be deceived" *(Deus revelans, qui nec falli nec fallere potest*. DS 3008). *Infallibilitas* would then mean being free from what is deceptive, from lying and fraud.[30]

Yet even then the essential problem is not solved. For in Vatican I it is not simply that inerrancy or indeceivability is asserted of the Church. *Immunitas ab errore* means not only the Church but the pope, not only a *de facto* but a *de jure* immunity. The pope does not err, not merely in fact, in *ex cathedra* decisions; but in such decisions, in principle, *a priori,* he cannot err. This pointedness cannot be overlooked. It is indeed just this insistence on the principle that provokes reflection.

f. The truth, mandate and authority of the Church as such?

(1) The Church's truth cannot be assimilated to God's truth. For this reason we must examine expressly and of course critically from both sides the ecumenical import of our question (a factor which underlies all our discussions).

For the Evangelical systematic theologian, Karl Gerhard Steck, it is clear in retrospect after a hundred years "that the two Confessions had never been so estranged as they were at the time of the First Vatican Council."[31] He sees in Vatican I the conflict on Church and doctrine which had been started by Luther: "Each Confession emphasized one authority at the expense of the other: in the Reformation-Protestant sphere, doctrine—in other words, Scripture—was to have priority; in the Roman Catholic sphere, the Church. This was repeated very sharply in the pronouncements of 1870 with the emphasis on papal authority."[32] Nor is the conflict "in any way softened or settled by the doctrinal pronouncements of Vatican II."[33]

The Protestant speaks with praise of the fact that Vatican I, like Luther, finds "the ultimate reason for the assent of Christian faith in the acknowledgment of God's truth," but criticizes at the same time the "and": the fact that "other arguments, obligations or pronouncements"—namely, those of the Church—are associated with God's truth.[34] The Catholic theologian will have to agree with the Evangelical when the latter protests against the assimilation of the Church's truth to God's truth, with the result that the ambiguous historical reality of the Church is set up as an unequivocal sign of the credibility of Christian truth, faith is tied to the self-confident judgment of the Church even in regard to the disciplinary questions of entering or leaving the Church, and a system of ecclesiastical dominion is set up over souls and over biblical interpretation.

(2) God's truth however may be attested by the Church in a mandatory and authoritative manner. It is certainly a large undertaking "to base the certainty and binding character of the knowledge of faith solely on the authority of God revealing."[35] Is God the revealer then simply to be found in Scripture and is the word of revelation available there in some form other than it is in the human word of believing witnesses and communities? It seems then that God's truth, which "will be attested and prevail at all times," really needs the testimony of the Church as the community of those who believe and confess, and that no objection at all can be raised against "the authority of the Church," rightly understood, which is primarily attested precisely by Scripture.

In spite of his polemic against authority in the Church, K. G. Steck too has to admit: "The word of God is not as unambiguous as Luther and his followers thought. Protestantism lacks the unity which could be desired; without doctrinal authority neither the community of the New Testament nor that of later Christendom is conceivable or real. The Reformers themselves were by no means inclined to let the Church become a debating hall for all possible types of belief."[36]

All this, seen in its brutal reality, forms for the Catholic theologian the historical evidence for the fact that the alternative to the authoritarian Roman doctrinal system certainly cannot be a Protestantism which protests against all authority in the Church (it scarcely exists in Protestantism anyway). In the last lines of his article the Evangelical theologian himself has to admit indirectly that "reliance on the power of the gospel itself" does not merely not exclude, but can even justify an "authority of the Church." This means that here too we cannot get through alone with an exclusive Alone, but must acknowledge an And which remains—obviously in subordination and dependence—founded in that Alone.

From all this we may conclude that the problem is not the authority, power, truth of the Church as such, rightly understood; such an assumption is the result of what might be called a Protestant short-circuiting. The problem is rather that of an authoritarian ecclesiastical authority, an autonomously manipulated ecclesiastical power, a truth of revelation turned into church property: all for Luther concentrated in the affirmation of infallible, ecclesiastical doctrinal pronouncements. To that extent we would really have expected more pointed questions from an Evangelical theologian: questions perhaps in regard to a "charism of truth and never failing faith" (DS 3071), postulated for Peter and his successors, scarcely intelligible in the light of the pauline doctrine of charisms, which—surprisingly enough—has been active only twice in a hundred years. Or questions in regard to the eschatological finality and victoriousness of God's truth, which is in fact claimed all too hastily by modern Catholic theology for the infallibility of certain dogmas of the Church, without at the same time taking seriously the eschatologically provisional and fragmentary character of the Church's truth—even to the point of error and sin.

We may now close this section. It has certainly become clear that the more precisely we grasp a problem, the less we remain involved in secondary matters; the more we deny ourselves easy ways out and hasty solutions, the more hope there is of getting at the question and of being able to give a properly reasoned answer. We do not want to postpone our answer much longer; where then lies the central problem?

2. Positive determination

The central problem may be stated positively in this way: is the Church's infallibility dependent on infallible *propositions?* We are deliberately using the term derived from the

Latin *infallibilitas*, because its meaning remains somewhat indeterminate. The concept cannot be regarded as clarified nor our statement of the problem considered entirely satisfactory. We hope to bring out the more exact meaning in the further course of our discussion.

a. The faith of the Church is dependent on articles (propositions) of faith

This may be presupposed here, without going too closely into explanations. Christian faith is not a dumb faith. We know what we believe and confess what we know. There is no act of faith without a content of faith, however this is determined; no Christian *fides qua creditur* which is not in some way also *fides quae creditur*. And as far as this knowing and confessing faith finds expression, it is dependent on words and propositions of faith. And so far as Christian faith is in fact never merely the faith of abstract individuals, but faith in or in relation to a believing community, for communication within that community it is dependent on language, which is made up of words and sentences, therefore on propositions of faith in the broadest sense of the word.

There is more to our statement however than merely these general remarks. It means that a *community* of believers is dependent also on *common* propositions of faith or—to put it in a more practical way—at least has shown itself to be dependent on such common propositions of faith. In this sense then we speak of the faith of the Church (as community of believers), which is dependent on propositions of faith (common articles of faith, formulas of faith, formularies of faith). This can be explained in the concrete in three ways, the first two of which should be recognized as true, the third as false.

(1) The faith of the Church is dependent on summary professions of faith in Christ: on *abbreviating-recapitulating* propositions (professions of faith or creeds). This at any rate

was the Christian faith from the beginning, as the New Testament Scriptures testify. It is not for us to enter now into questions of detail: whether in the particular case it is a question mainly of the word of proclamation or of the response to this in a profession of faith; whether the concrete "living situation" (*Sitz im Leben*) of such propositions is more the act of worship, the catechesis or the church-order; whether the propositions in the particular case are more liturgical, kerygmatic, catechetical, juridical or edifying; whether it is a question more precisely of acclamations (common invocations: Amen, Alleluia, Hosanna, Maranatha=Come, Lord, Abba, Father, Lord Jesus), of doxologies (utterances of praise and thanksgiving, with the invocation of God's and then of Christ's name and with a later hymnal form), of blessings (in the sense of Jewish forms of greeting and beatitudes), of sacramental formulas (liturgical formularies for baptism and eucharist with fixed terminology) or of credal formulas in the strict sense or homologies.

The transitions between the individual forms and formulas were fluid from the very beginning: particularly those from the acclamation to the doxology and to the credal formula properly so-called, which may be specially connected with baptismal instruction and the baptismal liturgy.[37] In any case it cannot be disputed that such common, brief formulas of faith are already to be found in New Testament communities, centering on the Christ-event. The shortest of these formulas of faith are the numerous monomial expressions which link the proper name of Jesus with a particular honorific title drawn from the Jewish or hellenistic world: "Jesus is Messiah," "Jesus is Lord," "Jesus is God's Son" (among the earliest and best known is 1 Corinthians 12:3). At the same time we also find in the New Testament binomial credal forms relating to God and Christ (e.g., 1 Corinthians 8:6), and generally more extensive brief professions of faith, particularly in regard to the death and resurrection of Christ (e.g., 1 Corinthians 15:3–5; Romans 1:3f.), and finally professions of faith in triadic form completely isolated in liturgical pieces (Mt. 28:19; 2 Cor. 13:13).

The fact cannot be overlooked that such ancient (New Testament and later), brief formulas of faith have lasted in the churches until today. Furthermore, it cannot be disputed that such brief formulas, old or new, may also have a meaning today: whether it is—as from the beginning—in connection with baptism, catechesis, or otherwise with the life of the ecclesial community. Certainly the original formulas of faith and confession were not just fragments of a single Credo. For all their concentration on the Christ-event, on the significance of Jesus for the community of believers, they are too varied for this: in content and form, with this or that honorific title, according to this or that theme-series. And, not least, if new professions of faith are to be possible, perhaps more intelligible for a new age (which, of course, does not mean abolishing the old formulas), for the "edification" of the congregation, and perhaps also for ecumenical understanding between the separated churches, it must not be forgotten that these original professions of faith were by no means statements of dogma in the modern sense. They were not doctrinal laws. Spontaneous, variable, to a large extent they were not meant to be and could not be fixed, unsurpassable, indisputable propositions of a definitive and obligatory character, excluding new and different forms. Faith was not based on, but found expression in, such formulas: they were propositions of faith, not in a legalistic sense, but as a free expression of the faith of the congregation.

(2) The faith of the Church is dependent on polemical demarcations from what is unchristian: on *defensive-defining* propositions (definitions of faith or dogmas of faith). Propositions of this kind, too, have always existed, so far—that is—as the positive profession of faith in face of any expression of unbelief or superstition could suddenly acquire a defensive or polemical pointedness: *Jesus* is the Messiah, the Lord, the Son of God.

When Paul, for instance, on the one hand positively states, "no one can say 'Jesus is Lord' unless he is under the influence of the Holy Spirit," in the same breath he also formulates a negative demarcation, "for that reason I want you to understand that no one can be speaking under the influence of the Holy Spirit and say, 'Curse Jesus'" (1 Cor. 12:3). Presumably negative invocations like "Anathema" corresponded to positive acclamations, as in the light of the Old Testament curses corresponded to blessings (cf. 1 Cor. 16:22; 5:4–5). When in the course of time the gospel had to be marked off more and more against heresies, this became an occasion for the formulation of propositions of faith also in the negative (particularly clearly in 1 Jn. 2:22; 4:2–3). Persecution very often provided the testing situation for the profession of faith. In this connection it is again important to note that for Paul particularly it was obviously not primarily a question of the formula—positive or negative—but of affirming or denying Jesus: not of a faith in *propositions,* but of a proposition of *faith.* To this extent we have to be on our guard against wanting to find "dogmas," "dogmatic deposit," "dogmatic formulas," everywhere in the New Testament.

Nevertheless, in the postapostolic period immediately following the apostolic foundation period, when the churches could no longer fall back upon the original witnesses, it is understandable that tradition acquired a substantially greater importance: together with the apostolic (or believed to be apostolic) Scriptures and the Church's ministry, and naturally also the original professions of faith. These helped to prevent the youthful Church from losing contact with its origin and being dissolved into the all-absorbing world of syncretic hellenism. To this extent then propositions of faith acquired a far higher degree of binding force as de-finition, de-marcation and de-fense, re-jection, and in case of conflict even the character of a definitive and obligatory formula for the believing community, that is, of a dogma, but not on that account needing to be understood as a formula *a priori* free

from error and not open to correction, infallible and irreformable.

It cannot simply be assumed that the Church today may
not be in need of such defensive-defining formulas as a
demarcation against what is unchristian, against unbelief
and superstition. Under a totalitarian regime like that of
National-Socialism, where circumstances might lead to the
identification of a group in the Church with the political
power, there may be nothing else to do but draw up a delimiting profession of faith (for example, the Barmen Declaration of 1934). Here then is a *status confessionis*, which does
not permit endless discussions and distinctions but requires
a definitive Yes or No (for example, to Christ or to the
"Führer"). But such a *status confessionis* must not be too
readily assumed to exist. Three conditions must be fulfilled:

a. In the conflict of faith there must be involved a *causa
major*, where it is a question in one way or another of the
existence or non-existence of the Church (*articulus stantis et
cadentis Ecclesiae*).

b. Other means (discussion, exhortation, challenge) must
be exhausted, so that as an extreme measure—*in extremis*—
nothing remains except a dissociation in faith.

c. A definition may never be understood as a final judgment of damnation on men—which is for God alone to pronounce—but as a temporary measure with a view to the
restoration of the peace of the Church: a measure that may
not automatically be extended to the innocent descendants
of those concerned.[38]

The conclusion from all this is that, with these defensive-
defining propositions, even if they have a definitive and
obligatory—and, to that extent, dogmatic—character for a
particular situation, it is a question in the last resort of a ruling,
not on principle and for eternity, but of a practical ruling on
terminology conditioned by the situation.[39]

(3) Faith is *not* dependent on a deliberately planned
development of dogma, on *tendentious-explicating* proposi-

tions. This follows already from what we have just said. The Church is called upon constantly to proclaim the gospel afresh in continuously changing situations, but to make dogmatic definitions only in extraordinary emergencies. The early Church of both East and West, both the Orthodox Churches of early and modern times and also the medieval western Church, both the Reformation Churches and the Counter-Reformation Church, did not define what they *could have defined*, but what they *had to* define, "yielding to necessity, not following impulse." They defined, not the maximum possible, just for the pleasure of defining, but the necessary minimum, under external pressure. Seen in the light of this almost two-thousand-year-old, common Christian tradition, which is supported by the New Testament itself, it must be regarded as an aberration when a church—without being compelled to do so—produces dogmas, whether for reasons of ecclesiastical or theological policy (the two Vatican dogmas of the pope) or for reasons of piety and propaganda (the two Vatican dogmas of Mary). The aberration is all the greater when it deepens the division of Christendom.

As a result of the deliberate development of dogma, the faith will grow and be unfolded; it is a question of a "living tradition." These and similar arguments are used to defend definitions. We may answer:

a. Faith by no means grows and develops simply by the fact of defining. It may be doubted whether faith has really grown through the four exceptional dogmas, especially with the waning of extremist marian and papal piety and concentration on the "hierarchy of truths." But, even definitions which are justified, instead of having positive results for faith, may have thoroughly negative consequences: doctrinaire fossilization, new and worse misunderstandings, the arrogance of orthodoxy, theological unteachability, and increasing ignorance on the part of the *beati possidentes*.

b. It was a common Christian opinion of all Churches at all times that faith grows and is unfolded by a sound proclama-

tion of the gospel, by the right administration of the sacraments, by prayer, love, suffering, personal knowledge. It is
only since the nineteenth century that Roman theologians,
misunderstanding the idea of development introduced into
Catholic theology by the great Tübingen theologians (especially Johann Adam Möhler) on the one hand and John
Henry Newman on the other, interpreted this in an over-
intellectual and legalistic way and then demanded, instead
of the tried and tested methods of explicating the faith,
dogmatic explications of the faith and binding definitions.
At the same time they could have looked up Aquinas and
read that the truth of faith is sufficiently explicated (*suffi-
cienter explicata*) by the preaching of Christ and the apostles,
so that there is no need at all of any *explicatio* as such of
the faith, "but a clarification (*explanatio*) of the faith is
necessary because of errors that arise."[40] Fortunately, the
Roman craving for dogmatic definitions, which continued to
find expression in the preparatory work for Vatican II, has
been checked since then by John XXIII and the Council itself.

b. It has not been proved that faith is dependent on infallible propositions

By infallible propositions we mean—wholly in the sense of
Vatican I—statements which must be considered as guaranteed a priori to be free from error: sentences, propositions,
definitions, formularies, and formulas, which are not only *de
facto* not erroneous but in principle simply cannot be erroneous.

It is clear from the explanations given in the previous
section that we can wholly affirm the sense, the advantage,
and occasionally even the necessity of abbreviating, summary
propositions of faith (professions of faith or creeds), or even
of delimiting, defining propositions of faith (definitions of
faith or dogmas), without on that account having to affirm

infallible and immutable propositions of faith. In other words: to accept the *binding character* of propositions of faith does not mean having to accept also their *infallibility*. But the question naturally arises: is it not the Christian message itself that requires, at least in certain cases, the acceptance also of the infallibility of propositions of faith together with their binding character? This however cannot simply be presumed, but must be substantiated. And even a council needs to show reasons, for itself and for others, if it wants to assert the infallibility of certain propositions. Our close investigation of Vatican I and II has produced these results:

(1) The existence of propositions which are infallible in principle has not been convincingly substantiated either by Vatican I or Vatican II. Vatican II in its statements on infallibility is obviously completely dependent on Vatican I and is on very shaky ground when, for its own part, it attempts to broaden the conception of Vatican I with the aid of an unhistorical theory of an exclusive apostolic succession of bishops.[41] But Vatican I cites neither Scriptural testimonies which show the need for infallible propositions nor testimonies of a universal, ecumenical tradition which might subtantiate an infallibility of propositions.[42]

(2) Nor is neoscholastic textbook theology able to demonstrate from the testimonies of Scripture and the testimonies of the oldest ecumenical tradition the necessity or reality, or even merely the possibility, of propositions which must be a priori infallible. This theology merely asserts that the promises bestowed on the Church, according to Scripture, necessarily *presuppose* infallible propositions, although the other possibility does not seem to be conclusively ruled out: namely, that the promises bestowed on the Church would still hold even without presupposing infallible propositions.[43]

(3) It is just this possibility—that the promises given to the Church (and also to Peter) might hold without presupposing a priori infallible propositions—that was not discussed at all at Vatican I (and consequently not at Vatican II),

as is evident from the silence on this question both in the constitution *Pastor Aeternus* and also in the records of the council (particularly the Gasser report). In the same way as the Council of Trent presupposed the ptolemaic world picture, Vatican I presupposed a particular conception of truth and thus started out a priori from the by no means obvious presupposition that the promises given to the Church or in particular the "infallibility" of the Church simply could not be realized without infallible propositions. Did the council then err? It would be better to say that it was blind in regard to the basic problematic. Instead of getting down to the basic problematic, the council passed it over. Why?

a. Instead of the infallibility of the Church (which was presupposed), the infallibility of the pope was made the subject of reflection.

b. In regard to the question of papal infallibility, attention was concentrated first of all on the pastoral, ecumenical, political opportuneness of a definition, then on the conditions and limitations of papal infallibility, finally on the question of an infallibility of the pope with or without the consent of the Church.

c. Both supporters and opponents, majority *and* minority, presupposed that the promises given to the Church relate to infallible propositions. Certainly, by no means all the opponents of a definition were merely—as Catholic historiographers suggest in order to smooth over the antagonisms —"inopportunists," considering such a definition in fact as true and merely "inappropriate." What stood in the way were rather different ecclesiological conceptions in regard to the relationship between pope and Church (episcopate). But whether they regarded a definition of papal infallibility as inopportune (all opponents of a definition) or as opportune (the majority); whether they demanded the consent of the Church or of the episcopate for papal infallibility (the moderate "Gallican" opponents of a definition) or regarded this consent as unnecessary (the majority); whether they were for the infallibility of ecumenical councils, but not for that of the Roman pontiff (the radical opponents of a definition such as Döllinger and various bishops of the minority) or for the infallibility of ecumenical councils *and* that of the Roman pontiff (the majority); they all, without exception, presupposed that the promises given to the Church or in particular the "infallibility" of the Church were dependent on *infallible propositions* (whether of the ecumenical council or of the pope, whether of the pope with or of the pope without the consent of the Church).

Seen in this perspective, majority and minority were therefore in the last resort closer than it might appear: "A cross-section through the pro and contra of the discussions shows that opponents and supporters of the doctrine frequently used the same arguments. Those on the one side thought that something had to be done to strengthen the pope's authority and to make the papacy visible as a lighthouse for the salvation of shipwrecked human society. The others answered that this view was largely mistaken: a rigid, monarchic-absolutist papacy would repel both separated Christians and unbelievers. Behind these arguments therefore stood prejudgments, strongly marked by divergent ideas of Church and society; by comparison, the real theological objections to the doctrine disappeared into the background. Everything suggests that an agreement between the two parties would have been possible if the text of the infallibility decree had emphasized more strongly the union of the pope with the Church as a whole."[44]

The Church as a whole: in order to reach a real clarification and agreement, *both* parties would have had to clarify what *both* falsely or—better—naïvely presupposed as clarified, the infallibility of the Church as a whole and thus the question of ecclesiastical infallibility altogether. Fascinated and retarded by secondary questions of theological and ecclesiastical policy, therefore, they did not discuss this fundamental question. But perhaps that would have been asking too much.

Is this argument not perhaps anachronistic? By no means.
It would, admittedly, have meant the taking up by Vatican I
of the questions raised by the Reformers of the sixteenth
century, which even the Council of Trent had not solved
and indeed never discussed. This was not to be thought of at
Vatican I.

Whatever counted as Protestant was regarded by the majority of the council as a priori outside discussion. The revised
schema "On the Catholic faith," laid before the council in
the proem, had ascribed to Protestantism all the errors of
the day: rationalism, pantheism, materialism, and atheism.
Bishop Strossmayer, in a speech that became famous,[45]
pointed out that these errors had existed for a long time before
Protestantism and that among Protestants many distinguished
men had opposed them; that in the midst of Protestantism
there was a large group of men in Germany, England, and
America, who loved our Lord Jesus Christ and deserved to
be described in the words of Augustine: "They err indeed,
but they err in good faith." At this point there was increased
murmuring in the assembly in St. Peter's.

When Strossmayer nevertheless continued the quotation from
Augustine, "they are heretics, but no one takes them for
heretics," he was interrupted by the president of the council, Cardinal de Angelis and told to refrain from words
that gave scandal. When Strossmayer went on again, the other
council president, Cardinal Capalti, interrupted: they were
not talking about Protestants as persons, it was not an offense
against charity to say that the monsters of modern error were
derived from Protestantism. A heated discussion followed
between Capalti and Strossmayer, leading to a veritable
storm of indignation when Strossmayer, in face of the murmuring from all sides, said: "I attribute this to the deplorable
conditions of this Council." And when Strossmayer then threw
into the debate the question of "moral unanimity," which he
considered necessary for the council's decisions (a query on

which the bishops of the minority had not had an answer for a month), he was simply shouted down.

Many of the Fathers almost raged (*obstrepunt, vix non fremunt*) and called on him to step down. There were more exchanges and mutual protests. And when Strossmayer reluctantly got ready to step down the indignant Fathers left their seats murmuring all kinds of things. Some said: "These people don't want the infallibility of the Pope; is this man infallible himself?" Others: "He is Lucifer, anathema, anathema!" Others again: "He is another Luther, let him be cast out!" And all cried out: "Come down, come down." But he kept on saying: "I protest, I protest," and came down.

Great stress is laid on the fact that this incident was the only real "scene" in the course of the council. It is however very revealing both of the atmosphere at the council and particularly of the attitude of the majority toward Protestantism (and infallibility). Nevertheless in the definitive proem the assertion of a link between Protestantism and the errors of modern times was modified and some directly insulting expressions (such as *impio ausu, opinionum monstra, impiissima doctrina, mysterium iniquitatis, impia pestis*) were omitted. But nothing good was said of Protestants (even as persons), the Counter-Reformation version of history being substantially maintained: "For everyone knows that the heresies rejected by the Tridentine Fathers gradually broke up into many sects, because the rejection of the Church's divine teaching office meant handing over matters concerning religion to the judgment of each and every individual, and while in their disunity they were disputing among themselves, for many all faith in Christ was finally shattered" and so on up to "abyss of pantheism, materialism and atheism . . ."[46] As if naked, systematic materialism and atheism had not first broken through in Catholic France.

There is no need to say any more about the "ecumenical" aspect of the council. Vatican I even less than the Council of Trent evinced no genuine ecumenical readiness to face

seriously the grave questions of the Reformation in regard
to the claims of the teaching office. At the Second Vatican
Council, on the other hand, this readiness was present at
least in principle with the majority and came into operation
in some questions: for example, in the declaration of the
importance of the Bible for worship, theology and the whole
life of the Church; in advocating an active, simplified and
more compact, people's Mass in the vernacular; in the theoretical and practical revaluation of the laity as the people of
God and the universal priesthood; in a certain decentralization and adaptation of the Church to the various nations;
in the acknowledgment of a Catholic share in the guilt of
schism; in the recognition of other Christian communities
as ecclesial communities or Churches; in the demand for an
ecumenical attitude and practical co-operation with other
Christians; and in being ready to make concessions particularly to the Orthodox Churches in regard to mixed marriages
and intercommunion.

With many other questions of the Reformation, however,
the question of infallibility as it had been radically stated
by the Reformers was not taken up. But what was not seen
as a problem either at Vatican I or Vatican II was not
answered either by Vatican I or by Vatican II. That is no
reason why theology should have to wait for Vatican III.
For this much was clear at Vatican II: the Holy Spirit obviously does not act as a *deus ex machina* at councils. What
is not prepared theologically for a council is normally not
settled at the council.

IV. AN ANSWER

1. The problematic of propositions as such

We are not going to be so bold here as to attempt *the* answer. The question is too complex for that and the implications too many. But, in the present state of the Church, *an* answer must be attempted calmly and resolutely, in which importance will be attached not so much to setting out all the consequences as to the correct approach. There is to be no *ex cathedra* speaking here about infallibility—a single infallible pope is preferable to a lot of infallible theologian-popes—but certainly discussion in a spirit of theological and pastoral responsibility.

Articles of faith are propositions. Formulas of faith, professions of faith, and definitions of faith, are propositions—simple or complex—and are not a priori free from the laws that govern propositions. Nor are propositions of faith ever directly God's word, but at best God's word attested and mediated by man's word: perceptible and transmissible by human propositions. But, as such, propositions of faith participate in the problematic of human propositions in general. It would certainly be very exciting to deal with our special question in the light of modern linguistic philosophy (as expounded by M. Heidegger, H. G. Gadamer, H. Lipps, B. Liebrucks, K. Jaspers, M. Merleau-Ponty, L. Wittgenstein, G. Frege, C. W. Morris, H. Lefebvre, N. Chomsky). Any broad development of the theme of linguistic philosophy however would not only disturb the relatively rapid rhythm and changes of tempo in this necessarily compact work, but would also give this section—which is only meant to provide a kind of auxiliary argument within the whole—too great an importance. Infallibility is to remain our main theme and normally this subject is not a problem for philosophers, although in fact—if we may venture to say so—philosophers too sometimes like to speak *ex cathedra*.

Our aim in this section then is a very modest one. With the aid of some brief, but basic and scarcely disputable observations, it will be made clear that propositions—of which the Church's faith has to make use—are a problematic affair. The obvious conclusion will be that a Church which summarizes or defines its faith in propositions and perhaps has to do this, cannot get away from the problematic inherent in propositions as such.[1]

(1) Propositions fall short of reality: this is fundamental. I can never totally capture reality either by a word or by a proposition, simple or complex. There always remains a difference between what I *want* to state and what I do state, between my intention and my spoken word. Language is at once both rich and poor. This fundamental inadequacy and deficiency of language is something that has constantly occupied the great tradition of linguistic philosophy from Heraclitus, Plato, and Aristotle onward, by way of Augustine and Aquinas, up to the moderns.

Take an example from theology: what would be conveyed if the Church were to define the proposition (which is certainly fundamental), "God exists"? Everything—and yet so infinitely little and almost nothing at all by comparison to what might be said on this proposition.

(2) Propositions are open to misunderstanding. Whatever I say can be misunderstood, and not only as a result of lack of good will. Words have different, often ambiguous and fluid meanings. And if I qualify their meaning, these qualifications too have again various meanings and often the variable factor itself in these meanings cannot be precisely grasped. Even if I want therefore to express myself unmis-

takably and to make myself so clear to the other that he cannot fail to understand me, nevertheless what is unthought and unsaid—but perhaps thought also by the other or, likewise, not thought—still leaves sufficient scope for all possible misunderstandings and non-understandings: perhaps worst of all when someone does not or does not any longer understand himself. Linguistic analysis and linguistic criticism are constantly trying to make clear what language in the concrete really can accomplish and what it cannot accomplish.

And again as theological application: "God exists." "God": perhaps the noblest word in human speech, rising to the greatest heights, and what other word has been more understood *and* misunderstood? "Exists," "is": perhaps the most universal, most comprehensive word in human language—and how its meaning varies. There is about as much fighting among theologians over the word "God" as among philosophers over the word "being."

(3) Propositions can be translated only up to a point. Every instrument plays the high C in its own way, but it sounds different on the violin from what it does on the cello; the sounding board is different. And there is more to language than simply: "The tone makes the music." For certain words there seems to be no translation at all; they are taken over untranslated into other languages. Play upon words can rarely be preserved in translation. And there are so many words that can be translated only if the translation is not too literal. In fact, paraphrase has to replace translation. Here too lie the difficulties of the constantly recurring idea of a universal language (from Lull and Leibnitz up to modern theoretical-formal attempts or even such material attempts as Esperanto and the like). Here too lie the limits of a dead language for which people claim a universality that is bought largely at the price of intelligibility (the translation of the Latin liturgy into the vernacular shows that no translation is adequate).

And even our simple example of a theological proposition,

"God exists," which is easy to translate in our familiar languages, constantly presents unsuspected difficulties when it
has to be translated into certain Asiatic and African languages,
outside the European-American cultural sphere, where the
corresponding words have a different usage and simply cannot be taken over as a translation.

(4) Propositions are in motion. My language is not mine
alone. Language comes to be in communication. Language
comes to be as conversation. But words are not handed on like
bricks, for the simple reason that they are not bricks but
spirit. Language is not a static shape, but a dynamic event,
embedded in the stream of the whole history of man and the
world. An unchanging language fades out and becomes a
dead language. In a living language however words and
sentences receive fresh stimuli and also provide fresh stimuli.
Words and sentences can completely change their meaning
in a new situation. But on the other hand words and sentences for their part can also completely change a situation;
for there are words which make history. Language then is
always on the way to reality, a basic phenomenon of man's
historicity.

The proposition "God exists" is also a historical proposition:
understood differently by a Greek of the time of Pericles
and a Jew of the time of the Maccabees, differently by an
early hellenistic Christian and by a Christian Frank; differently
too by a medieval scholastic and a neoscholastic of the
nineteenth century, differently by Luther, by a representative
of Lutheran orthodoxy and by a Lutheran of the twentieth
century . . .

(5) Propositions are ideology-prone: words and sentences
are at our service. They can be used, abused, and exploited:
for the purposes of advertising, of propaganda, of jargon,
and also for pious purposes. Words and sentences are then
subject to a dominion that they can scarcely shake off: they
are wholly, exclusively confiscated by a particular idea,
a particular ideology, a particular system, so that at times

they are made to say the very opposite of what they
originally meant (for instance, "democracy," "freedom," "order"). They are distorted. Or even ruined: scarcely usable
any longer, empty shells without content. It may go as far
as a veritable corruption of language.

The proposition "God exists" is also ideology-prone: With
the invoking of this proposition (or—similarly—"God with
us!") wars have been waged, the poor have been put off,
innocent people tricked and killed. The proposition can be
misused by right and left. Conservative ideologists of the
status quo can distort it just as much as the fanatical
ideologists of revolution. It would often have been better
to keep quiet about God.

These five observations should be sufficient for our purpose,
to bring out in the concrete the problematic of propositions.
But—in order ourselves to exclude misunderstandings as
far as possible—we do not mean that propositions are incapable of stating the truth, that all propositions are equally
true and false, that they cannot correspond to the reality
which they claim to express, that understanding is impossible.
We mean simply that propositions are by no means as
clear as they seem to be, that they are rather fundamentally
ambiguous and consequently can be understood differently
by different people, that with the best intentions not all
misunderstandings and misuse can be a priori excluded.

And to this extent it is clear how problematic it is in the
theological field when the Church wants or occasionally
has to recapitulate or define her faith in certain propositions.
The limits of a binding, abbreviative or defensive statement
or still more of a dogmatic pronouncement meant to hold
forever cannot be overlooked and are not transgressed with
impunity.

Of course, many a scholastic theologian of the time of
Vatican I or Vatican II might object that, in spite of all
this, there are propositions—even propositions of faith—clear
enough in themselves to exclude all misunderstandings, al-

most as clear in fact as 2×2=4. Now for 2×2=4—that is, for mathematics—this objection has in fact some weight. It cannot however be overlooked that the propositions of mathematics are least exposed to the above difficulties only as long as no questions are raised about the foundations of mathematics, which indeed are as much disputed as some of their applications, for instance in statistics ("You can prove anything with figures"). But it is understandable that mathematics (and more and more the experimental, exact sciences based on it), especially from the beginning of modern times, should have had a great fascination for philosophers and theologians in their striving for clarity. And this phenomenon is in fact connected with our question about the definition of infallibility.

2. Rationalist origin of the theory of clear propositions as the ideal of knowledge

There is no doubt that the tendency appears much more intensively at Vatican I, than—say—at the Council of Trent, not only to answer definite attacks of opponents in a definite way, but furthermore—as in the previous, comprehensive Syllabus of Errors and the encyclical connected with it— to strive for a general clearing up and at the same time to clarify the official teaching of the Church as thoroughly as possible. The Constitution of Vatican I on the Catholic Faith shows such features, even though—together with the Constitution on the Pope, itself only the smallest part of the projected Constitution on the Church—it remained the sole schema that could be passed. But how many schemata had been prepared by the curial commission and described before the Council by the central commission as ripe for discussion? There were originally forty-six schemata, of which only seven came to be discussed at all at the council, without—apart from the two exceptions mentioned—being passed.

Notable also in connection with this comprehensive clarification of the faith is the project of the Curia, which led

to a long discussion at the council, for a universal catechism
binding on the whole Church. Notable too is the way in
which Thomism (to be clearly distinguished in practice from
Thomas' own system), from Vatican I onward and particularly under Leo XIII, began to be established by every
means available and practically made absolute as the normal
Catholic theology: the encyclical on Aquinas, *Aeterni Patris*
(1879) and the declaration making him an authentic doctor
of the Church; then a new critical edition of his works
ordered by Leo XIII (from 1882); in 1914 the promulgation
of the twenty-four thomistic (not necessarily Thomas') basic
theses by the Roman Congregation of Studies, which fortunately at once became grist for the mill of rivalries
among the schools of the Orders; finally, as the culmination
and as a late return present from the Roman canonists
to the theologian who deserves credit more than any other
for the introduction of the new canon law into Catholic
dogmatics, the ruling in the Code of Canon Law of 1918
that philosophy and theology in Catholic seminaries were
to be taught "according to the method, doctrine and principles
of St. Thomas Aquinas" (Can. 1366 §2).

Nor is there any doubt that the curial preparatory commissions of Vatican II largely worked in the same direction.
What had failed at Vatican I was now to succeed (we may
recall the "successful" Roman diocesan synod just before
Vatican II): in dogmatic and moral theology a far-reaching
systematic clarification from the foundations upward was
sought and prepared in schemata. And prominent members
of the theological preparatory commission, before the council,
could be heard saying that now finally the questions not
hitherto clarified—from the doctrine of creation to eschatology
—would have to be definitively decided, so that at last
there would be certainty in the Catholic Church about what
had to be believed (this undoubtedly meant the clear textbook theses of neoscholasticism).

This enterprise failed a second time completely, even more

completely, and neoscholasticism in general and neothomism in particular have been unable to recover from this blow of fate. But, in this connection, it is worth while for us briefly to follow the trend toward clear propositions and to systematic clarification. At the same time it would be interesting to examine more closely the question as to how far Greek intellectualism was taken up in medieval scholasticism and in certain respects surpassed; and again to what extent neoscholasticism continued the intellectualism of medieval scholasticism and for its own part surpassed it. But, as in the preceding section we had to deny ourselves extensive reflection on linguistic philosophy, so now we must refrain from lengthy reflection on the history of philosophy. A brief allusion to the history of philosophy is necessary however, in order to indicate a thread of development which may reveal how the mentality of Vatican I and neoscholasticism has not yet been disentangled from the trappings of restoration, romanticism and traditionalism. There was also— and this has often been overlooked in studies on the subject —quite a shot of rationalism present in it.

Between scholasticism and neoscholasticism, between Thomas and neothomism, stands Descartes. Descartes marks a break, not only because from his time onward the philosophical tradition of the middle ages has been largely forgotten in modern philosophy. It was Descartes and not St. Thomas Aquinas who set up clarity as the ideal of knowledge. Descartes' famous demand for clear and distinct knowledge—unlike Aquinas, he ignored the problematic of linguistic philosophy—in the *Principles of Philosophy* has to be quoted here:

There are even a number of people who throughout all their lives perceive nothing so correctly as to be capable of judging of it properly. For the knowledge upon which a certain and incontrovertible judgment can be formed, should not alone be clear but also distinct. I term that clear which is present and apparent to an attentive mind, in the same way as we assert that we see objects clearly when, being present to the regarding eye, they operate upon it with sufficient strength. But the distinct is that which is so precise and different from all other objects that it contains within itself nothing but what is clear.[2]

This is obvious to common sense, just as the older, representative theory of knowledge taken over by Descartes is really obvious, if knowledge is naïvely understood as representation. But this last is the very thing that is by no means clear. And consequently the objection has been raised against Descartes that such a clarity of the object is simply unattainable. This kind of demand for clarity presupposes in fact that the objects themselves are adapted to the demand for clarity and distinctness, that they are really so immovably static that the eye can simply seize on them, as static as only numbers and geometrical figures are in reality.

But this is precisely how Descartes saw the sensible-spatial world, from which—according to him—the eye should derive physical certainty and thence the ideal of clarity. For him this world is simply extension (*res extensa*, by contrast with thought) and thus identical with the object of geometry. And Descartes looked to the clarity of mathematics and geometry for his grand design of a universal scientific method: the mathematical ideal of knowledge was extended to all sciences, and evidence—that is, clear and distinct insight into the matter—was made the criterion of truth, while truth itself was identified with certainty.

Such a procedure however is costly. For only if the object of knowledge is forced into shape (spatial objects too can be turned in the last resort into geometrical figures), is the required norm of clarity fulfilled. On the other hand, however, Leibnitz and Kant draw attention to the fact that concrete knowledge is richer, that clarity and unclarity cannot by any means be so sharply divided, that there is rather a continuous transition from obscurity to clarity of the idea, with infinitely many grades and levels.

Descartes started out from a naïve conception of subject and object. He had not reflected either on the dynamism of the object or on the dynamism of the subject. And it was Hegel who drew attention to the dubiousness of such a static view of things and of the separation of subject and object, demanding a dialectical knowledge of truth which attempts to do justice to the dynamism of object and subject, which in fact cannot be separated in knowledge.[3]

The dynamism of the object: what I know is not something that passes by me as if in a vehicle, but is itself in motion and therefore quite unlike the Cartesian geometrised object. The dynamism of the subject: when I know, I myself am not immobile, not static like the camera on its tripod, but in knowing I am moving myself in harmony with the moving object.

In order to do justice to this dynamism of subject and object, perception and knowledge must be part of the whole movement and not dependent on apparently evident, fixed definitions and clear theses. Rationalism does depend on these things and that is why it never catches sight at all of the living reality in its mobility, concreteness, and fullness. For Hegel therefore it was not a mere fancy or a game with the number three for his circling thought to proceed so often, both on a small and on a large scale, in threefold divisions (or in triads of triads). Underlying it was the basic insight, never forgotten since his day, that I cannot really tell the truth by means of a single sentence in isolation. I need basically three sentences, to give definiteness and precision to what I have said, to deny it and to integrate it into a further assertion. Our train of thought could be: "That's what it's like"; "No, it's not just like that"; "Ah, but *this* is what it's like." And so the process can go on. Truth then lies in the totality, not in the particular steps, propositions, or elements of which it is made up.

But we must bring this brief excursus on the history of philosophy to a close. Theology obviously could not adopt uncritically Descartes' mathematical concept of knowledge. Consequently it came under the inspiration more of Leibnitz and Christian Wolff, who of course shared Descartes' rationalism. Wolff, likewise both philosopher and mathematician, a practitioner of philosophy *more mathematico,* had Jesuit friends, and it was his clear, rich, and comprehensive rationalistic system which on the one hand absorbed many insights of scholasticism and on the other transmitted many rationalistic influences to neoscholasticism. This holds even though it is scarcely possible to establish a direct genealogy from the Jesuits of the eighteenth century to the Jesuits of the nineteenth, whose theology dominated the First Vatican Council: the "Roman School," which included G. Perrone, who played a substantial part in preparing both the definition of the Immaculate Conception and the First Vatican Council, and his disciples and colleagues, J. Kleutgen, C. Schrader, J. B. Franzelin. In this connection it is not unimportant that the real inspirers of Italian neothomism (which started off earlier than German), L. Taparelli (+1862) and M. Liberatore (+1892), were partly under the influence of rationalism.

Some details ought to be examined here. It is sufficient in the present context to see that neoscholasticism (and with it also Vatican I), as distinct from high scholasticism, was marked by the very spirit of rationalism against which otherwise violent protests were being made. It is only in this way that we can understand why there was so much interest in clear and unequivocal propositions, in definitions of the official teaching of the Church as far-reaching as possible, and in a system as much "closed" as possible. But the leading philosophy of the time had already progressed far beyond such a naïve rationalism. And how clear, unequivocal, and unproblematic these clear and distinct definitions were to be, the subsequent times and especially Vatican II have shown. When studying the propositions of Vatican I and

not least those of the Constitution on Catholic Faith, it
often seems as if a noble beast in motion had been fixed
on a photographic plate, but not at the most absolutely
favorable moment. Which then raises the question: and is
this supposed to be our faith? A question which, according
to Hegel, could presumably be answered only with Yes *and*
No.

Here too we must be more precise, in order to avoid
unnecessary misunderstandings. The criticism above of clarity
as the ideal of knowledge is not opposed to a critical,
reflective *striving* for clarity, without which theology would
be abandoned to confusion and destruction. In theology also
teutonic profundity—for instance—can only gain from Latin
clarity and conversely, particularly since these two qualities
are not distributed simply according to nationalities. Theology
therefore will aspire to clarity, even though it cannot expect
to find the kind of clarity offered by mathematics and the
cognate sciences, as long as these latter simply claim to
depict the object and the objective sphere without asking
what lies behind them.

But there is a difference between theology striving for
clarity in its propositions and claiming to have attained
definitive clarity by its propositions. There is a difference
between attempting to grasp its subject at any precise point
and putting it on ice in clear propositions. There is a difference
between being able to state distinctly the obscurities and
incomprehensibilities and thus also clearly to express what
is unclear, and not wanting to admit the existence of
obscurities and incomprehensibilities and thus attempting to
remove them altogether with the aid of unclear distinctions.
There is a difference between theology in all its wrestling
for truth remaining open to the ever greater truth and
theology enclosing truth and itself in the golden cage of a
closed system. Briefly: there is a difference between a theology
committed to the clarity of rationality and one that is tied
to the pseudo-clarity of rationalism. Neoscholasticism cannot

be completely cleared of rationalism in this sense, and
the two last councils had to pay for this.

This may suffice as an explication of the problematic of
so-called clear propositions. And, still more than at the end
of the preceding section, the question is urged upon us:
How would it affect the existence of the Church if she
were to make her faith wholly dependent on certain clear
propositions? The theologian particularly should be the first
to remind himself and others that clarity (*doxa*) was originally
not a matter of method nor even a matter of awareness,
but a predicate of the Divinity.

3. *The problematic of ecclesiastical definitions*

In the present chapter scarcely a word has been said yet
about error. Not however because it had no place in this
context, but because it is presupposed in the context as
a self-evident possibility. For all that had to be said on
these human propositions, on these propositions always falling
short of reality, always open to misunderstanding, only
translatable up to a point, constantly changing, so easily
ideology-prone and in fact also never absolutely to be clarified,
sums up for everyone what is self-evident: propositions are
prone both to double meaning and also to nonsense, both
to confusion and to error. And there are so many sources of
error that it is scarcely worth while to classify them in
any sort of form: we speak of tacit identification and false
analogy, of incomplete disjunction and the tendency to
fabrication, permutation of the modes of being and adul-
teration of pure knowledge by emotional and voluntary
factors, and other things, as special sources of error. It
seems to be only too obvious: propositions can be true *or*
false.

Error really seems to become a special problem only with
regard to those propositions from which it is sought to exclude
error a priori and in principle. And this in particular where
it is not—for instance—a question of self-evident (which is

disputed anyway) first principles of philosophy (principles of identity, contradiction, causality), but of propositions which are regarded precisely as not evident in the philosophical sense, yet as free from error in the theological sense. Doesn't such a claim call for the most profound skepticism? All that has been said in the two previous sections makes it seem scarcely probable that even the Church's propositions of faith—which are admittedly human propositions—could be freed a priori from the human weakness, inadequacy, dubiousness, and therefore also the capacity for error, which are inherent in propositions. Indeed, it could even be further shown how propositions of faith in the form of negative definitions particularly bring out the problematic of propositions. Hence a former study of ours on the problematic of ecclesiastical definitions had to go beyond the above observation—propositions can be true *or* false—and add to it: propositions can be true *and* false.[4] This requires some clarification.

If every human statement of truth, as humanly limited, borders on error and easily turns into error, this holds in a special way for polemical ecclesiastical definitions. A definition has in fact a particular objective; it is directed at a specific error. But since there is no error without any core of truth, there is an inherent danger that a polemically oriented proposition may strike not only the error, but also the core of truth in the error: that is, the true concern behind the error, the truth within the error. For instance, as long as an Evangelical Christian unpolemically observes that "the just man lives by faith," the shadow of error, which accompanies the proposition, does not come to the fore. But if he asserts polemically that "the just man lives by faith," against a legalistic Catholic who is exaggerating the importance of good works, then there is a danger that the shadow of error may obscure the truth of his statement with the unexpressed secondary meaning: "The just man lives by faith (and does no good works)." Conversely the same holds. As long as a Catholic unpolemically observes that "the just man does works of charity," the shadow of error accompanying the proposition does not come to the fore. But if he asserts polemically, against the error of a quietist Protestant attaching too much importance to faith, that "the just man does works of charity," then there is a danger that the shadow of error may obscure the truth of his statement with the unexpressed secondary meaning: "The just man does works of charity (and does not live by faith)."

This classic example from Catholic-Evangelical controversy shows that a statement of truth polemically defined, from whatever side, is liable to be understood merely as the denial of an error. But in this way it necessarily neglects the core of genuine truth in the error. This statement of truth is then a *half*-truth: what it states is correct; but what it does not state is also correct. From the point of view of the speaker, such a statement strikes the error; from the point of view of the person addressed, it strikes the truth. For the speaker it seems—rightly—to be true; for the person concerned it seems—not wrongly—to be false. In brief: because a half-truth can also be a half-error, we don't understand one another. Each clings to *his* truth, each sees the other's error. While the truth of the one includes the truth of the other, each excludes the other because of a lack of truth.

This sort of thing has occurred only too often in Church history. The definition struck the error, but did not expressly exempt from condemnation the truth within the error. Thus the true condemnation of the error seemed to the other to be a false condemnation of the truth. The Council of Trent for instance condemned a theory of justification "through faith alone," in the sense of an empty, arrogant, obstinate belief that one is justified. It did not however define what *can* rightly be meant by "through faith alone" and what the Reformers precisely meant: true, sound faith that places its whole trust solely in the Lord. The true condemnation of the false *sola fide* was thus for the other the false condemnation of the true *sola fide*.

In this way it becomes clear why a reflection on ecclesiastical definitions had to allow for the fact that every proposition can be true *and* false, in each case in the light of its objective, its context, the meaning intended by it. At the same time it must be remembered that it is more difficult to discover how a proposition is intended than how it is said. It should be the theologian's task in every case to take seriously the truth in the other's error and the possible error in his own truth. In this way, in turning away from the supposed error there would be the encounter with the intended truth.

If a theology, if a Church, does not take seriously this dialectic of truth and error, then it is inevitably on the way from dogma to dogmatism; the functional character of a definition and the way it is tied to the matter in hand are then overlooked; the concept of dogma is overtaxed, overcharged, overstretched; the particular dogma is forced into an undialectical and uncritical isolation and acquires an absolute status: this is dogmatism, which consists in exaggerating and overvaluing the dogma, in isolating it and making it absolute. The doctrinal character of dogma is turned into doctrinalism and its binding character into legalism. The partial character of dogma becomes particularist, the authoritative character authoritarian, the intellectual character rationalist, and the trend to formulate and objectify leads finally to formalism, objectivism and positivism, crushing the truth with truths. This is the dogmatism which Josef Nolte in his impressive study has recently subjected to a complex criticism, perhaps irritatingly severe for some, but bitterly necessary. In face of this dogmatism he rightly vindicates for theology and the Church a "meta-dogmatic" way of thinking which takes seriously "dogma in history."[5]

If a theology, if a Church, takes seriously the dialectic of truth and error, then it is also protected from dogmatism in its dealing with dogmas. It becomes modest and therein wise. It allows itself to be sustained by the faith for which every definition remains a venture: necessary *in extremis,* but never without risk; a demarcation which only too easily means passing close to the frontier, which is not a bad thing as long as we do not stop there. What results is the faith of Homo Viator who knows that he has not appropriated knowledge and understanding, but must constantly wrestle afresh and pray for them. He knows that he will not be spared any darkness on his way, either of sin or of error. It is the faith therefore of the *Ecclesia peregrinans,* which knows that in all the chaos and confusion of her pilgrimage error is not the most shameful, but only the most human of her human weaknesses. And yet the question is not to be suppressed: Are we not rendering the promises to the Church meaningless?

4. The dilemma and its solution

Where do we stand now? If we look closely—and, after going into the matter so thoroughly, a short, sharp glance is sufficient—then we must say: in a more or less hopeless situation.

a. The dilemma

On the one hand: the *promises* given to the Church must be acknowledged. No sincere Christian who relies on the New Testament can dispute this. We need only recall here briefly the classical texts constantly quoted in this connection. Matthew 16:18: "The gates of the underworld can never hold out against it." Matthew 28:20: "And know that I am with you always; yes, to the end of time." John 14:16: "And he (the Father) will give you another Advocate to be with you for ever, the Spirit of truth." John 16:13: 'The Spirit will lead you to the complete truth." 1 Timothy 3:15: "The Church of the living God, which upholds the truth and keeps it safe."

On the other hand: the *errors* in the Church must be acknowledged. No critically thinking person can fail to see this. There is no need here for a wide-ranging survey; a brief summary will suffice:

(1) We must allow for errors even in the Church's propositions of faith (in the broadest sense of the word) so far as these are human propositions; it is admitted also by Catholic theology that, at least with certain officeholders and communities, with a number of propositions of faith and formulas of faith, errors (fallible teaching) cannot be excluded.

(2) We must allow for errors particularly in negative definitions (in the broadest sense of the word), so far as these polemical propositions, aiming at the error, can easily condemn the truth also; nor is it disputed in principle in Catholic theology that errors are possible, particularly in negative definitions, which may indeed be pronounced by very diverse officeholders and organs in the Church.

(3) The question is only: are there not perhaps, exceptionally, propositions of the Church which are a priori free from error and simply cannot be erroneous? To summarize the answer amounts to this:

1. Our opening problematic already showed that at least one doctrine that, according to the ordinary teaching office, must count as infallible teaching of the Church (the immorality of "artificial" birth control) is regarded by a large part of the Church and of theology as false and erroneous.

2. The decisive thing is that hitherto no one—neither Vatican I nor Vatican II, nor textbook theology—has substantiated what would have to be substantiated: that the Church, her leadership or her theology, can produce propositions which a priori cannot be false. The burden of proof lies with those who would make this claim.

3. If we are honest, we cannot dispute factual errors of the ecclesiastical "teaching office," both ordinary and extraordinary. All apologetic, as we have seen, only gets us into deeper difficulties, whether by twisting or even denying

historical facts or by having to work with anachronistic
distinctions (denying the *ex cathedra* character of past statements, etc.).

Is there a way out of this dilemma? With the disappearance
of infallible propositions, the promises given to the Church
also seem to have disappeared, and the infallibility of the
Church itself seems to have gone. But does the infallibility
of the Church really stand or fall with infallible propositions?
This is the very question which, as we saw, Vatican I
did not raise. It is a question which certainly calls for an
answer.

b. Solution of the dilemma

(1) The dilemma cannot be overcome by a decision—
skeptical or credulous—for one or the other side of the
alternative:

Either: the promise has failed. This is the opinion of an
unbelieving world, which the believer cannot accept.

Or: there are certain errors that can never be admitted.
This is the standpoint of a triumphalist Church, which the
believer likewise cannot accept.

(2) Nor is it possible to overcome the dilemma by innocuously harmonizing the one alternative at the expense
of the other. Formerly an infallibility in principle of the
teaching office was largely defended in practice; errors were
regarded as exceptional. This thesis could not be maintained
and, in spite of all the efforts of extremist ultramontanes,
came to an end with Vatican II. Later the fallibility in
principle of the teaching office was asserted, except for
certain infallible propositions. This thesis too, defended long
before Vatican I, could not—as it turned out—be maintained.

(3) The dilemma can be overcome only by *raising* the
alternatives to a higher plane: *The Church will persist in
the truth IN SPITE OF all ever possible errors!* Of this
position we may say first of all very briefly:

1. Such a view can be defended in the light of Scrip-

ture, which does indeed attest a maintenance of the Church in truth, but in no way speaks of any infallible propositions of the Church.

2. Such a view does justice also to the facts of Church history: on the one hand, the numerous errors of the ecclesiastical teaching office; on the other, the endurance and persistence of the Church and her proclamation for two thousand years.

3. It was just this statement of the problem and its solution that was not considered either at Vatican I or even at Vatican II, nor did it appear in neoscholastic textbook theology.

4. Finally, such an answer to the difficulties in connection with all the discussions before the encyclical *Humanae Vitae*, our opening problematic, had not been considered.

On this last point an observation at once strikes us: the Achilles heel of the Roman doctrine of infallibility has become nowhere more clearly evident than in connection with this encyclical. In our first chapter we admitted much—for some perhaps more than might be expected—that was right in the position of the conservative minority of the papal commission on birth control. But on one point an energetic protest must be raised. The report of the minority, on which the Pope based his decision, culminates in these sentences: "What is more, however, this change (in regard to the doctrine of contraception) would inflict a grave blow on the teaching about the assistance of the Holy Spirit promised to the Church to lead the faithful on the right way toward their salvation. . . . For the Church to have erred so gravely in its grave responsibility of leading souls would be tantamount to seriously suggesting that the assistance of the Holy Spirit was lacking to her."[6]

And here it seems we have to say that the Achilles heel of the Roman theory of infallibility—contrary to the intention of its defenders, who talk so much about faith—is ultimately a lack of faith. Is this not clear? At the very point where

faith is particularly challenged there is failure and despond-
ency: in face of error! In face of error on the part of the
Church. People have become so accustomed to identifying
the "Church" (or, better, the "hierarchy") with the Holy Spirit
that, if certain errors, aberrations, deviations and mistakes of
the Church have to be admitted, they think they have to
burden the Holy Spirit with those errors. As if the misleading
and misdirection so indisputably attributable to the hierarchy (and to theology) were due to the Holy Spirit, and the
errors, deviations, and digressions of the Church were those of
God himself.

Certainly in the Spirit God himself acts on the Church,
is attested by the Church, founds, maintains, and rules
the Church: and this God is the *Deus qui nec fallere nec
falli potest,* the God who cannot deceive or be deceived.
But the human beings who constitute the Church, can mis-
count, miscalculate, say the wrong thing and write the wrong
thing; they can fail to see, fail to hear, fail to grasp, can
blunder, fall short and go astray: *homines qui fallere et
falli possunt,* men who can deceive and be deceived. Faith
that is placed in God will have to allow for all this, coolly
and deliberately. Such a faith will not identify, but distinguish the Spirit of God and the Church. Thus liberated,
it will be able to see without illusions that the Church's
development always includes wrong developments and her
progress always includes setbacks.

Faith in God's guidance and providence in the history
of man and of the world has no room for doubts, even
though things of great or of little moment go completely
wrong. It perseveres in the face of ineptitude and adversity,
in the face of personal blows of fate and world-catastrophes.
And faith in the special presence and assistance of God's
Spirit in the community of the faithful does not fail or lose
heart, even though faults can and often do occur in all
fields, with all people and in all cases. Rather does it
persevere particularly in the face of wrong conclusions, wrong

valuations, and wrong attitudes in the Church, in the face of false moves, false steps, and mis-hits on the part of her leaders and teachers.

When the ship of the Church rides into the storm, there are always nervous and doubting disciples who think they have to wake the Lord, because they are perishing. The answer has already been given: "Why are you so frightened, you men of little faith?" (Mt. 8:26).

5. *The Church on the road to truth*

The Church composed of human beings—all the faithful, including their leaders and teachers—is always wanting to settle down in peace, to be accepted and assimilated by society, content with things as they are. Content also with the truth which she has received and "possesses" as "the deposit of faith." Yet this truth—like the Spirit which the Church has received—is merely a "pledge": the truth of the gospel of Jesus Christ, which calls her out on to the road, into that future which alone will bring the whole truth, the complete revelation, the kingdom of God.

It is the truth of the promise that summons the Church—which indeed can never be end and aim in itself—constantly to make a fresh start, a new emigration. The Church is the "Exodus community" (*Exodusgemeinde*, as J. Moltmann puts it), whose road leads through the desert with only a few oases here and there, living indeed not only under the mysterious sign of the cloud, but also under the cross expressly set up as sign: "Let us go to him, then, outside the camp, and share his degradation. For there is no eternal city for us in this life but we look for one in the life to come." This summons is the culmination of the Epistle to the Hebrews (13:13–14), the same epistle that describes the Church so vividly and impressively as the wandering people of God.[7]

Under the truth of the promise, which she herself proclaims

and announces, the Church may constantly venture on the exodus anew. Israel wandering through the desert remains the proto- and antitype of the people of the New Covenant (cf. especially Heb. 3:3–4:13). As to the old, so also to the new people of God, the "word" of revelation has gone out (4:12–13): not so that it may settle down in "possession" of the truth, but so that, summoned by the word of truth, it may set out on the road in obedience and faith. As the old, so too the new people of God is by no means secure: it must continue on its way through temptation, trial, and sin, menaced by weariness, weakness of faith, and hopelessness. As on the old, so too on the new people of God, a promise is bestowed, assuring entry into rest only after all the effort and upheaval of a long journey, only after a long probation in faith, endurance and perseverance, in firm trust and unshakable certainty, through struggle, suffering, and death.

There is only the one decisive difference: the "word" of revelation that has gone out to the new people of God is no longer provisional; it is the final and definitive word. Danger and threats therefore can never finally overwhelm the people of God: in spite of all weakening, its salvation is certain. The promise given to the new people of God is the eschatological promise, which can no longer be robbed of its force, which is absolutely and securely guaranteed by a better covenant of God with this people and thus gives them a final confidence in their journeying. But it remains a journeying with all the risks and dangers in which the individual—and Christ alone as the new Moses and leader of the people of God is excepted here (cf. 3:7–4:11; 4:15)— can be isolated, go astray and finally fall behind in the desert of this world, in which the people of God has no abiding home. Ultimately only nomads and strangers on earth, a great cloud of believing witnesses, all are on the road to the homeland that can never be lost (Chap. 11). Only

there does faith, "guaranteeing the blessings that we hope
for, proving the existence of the realities that at present
remain unseen" (11:1), pass over into vision and into the
festival of "the city of the living God" (12:22). But until
then all "created things" remain perishable, fallible, shakable
(12:27). Only in the repose of the consummation will the
faithful receive the infallible, "unshakeable kingdom" (12:28).

Thus the Epistle to the Hebrews sees the Church as the
pilgrim community of the faithful, exposed in all her members
to temptation, trial, error, upheaval, possessing truth only
as the great promise revealed in Christ. The warning is
clear and exempts no one in the Church, not even the leaders,
whose faith is set up as an example (13:7).

> So hold up your limp arms and steady your trembling
> knees and smooth out the path you tread; then the injured
> limb will not be wrenched, it will grow strong again.
> Always be wanting peace with all people, and the holiness
> without which no one can ever see the Lord. Be careful
> that no one is deprived of the grace of God and that
> no root of bitterness should begin to grow and make
> trouble; this can poison a whole community. And be
> careful that there is no immorality, or that any of you
> does not degrade religion like Esau, who sold his birth-
> right for one single meal (12:12–16).

The magnificent fresco of the wandering people of God
in the Epistle to the Hebrews is not by the Apostle Paul,
but in many respects belongs to the pauline tradition. Paul
himself had stated still more clearly than the author of
the Epistle to the Hebrews the provisional character of all
our knowledge by faith. And what the apostle says, holds
for every human word in the Church, even the most solemn:

> Our knowledge is imperfect and our prophesying is im-
> perfect; but once perfection comes, all imperfect things
> will disappear . . . Now we are seeing a dim reflection
> in a mirror; but then we shall be seeing face to face.

The knowledge that I have now is imperfect; but then I shall know as fully as I am known (1 Cor. 13:9–10, 12).

If however this is the situation in regard to the imperfection, the unfinished condition, the enigmatic character, the fragmentariness, of all our formulations of faith; if the consummation, the real sight of unsullied truth is still to come: is it good then to speak of an "infallibility" of the Church?

6. Infallibility or indefectibility?

One *can* speak of "infallibility" of the Church. And, having critically substantiated it in a much more thorough fashion, we fully maintain the statement made in an earlier book[8] about the "infallibility" or "indeceivability" (*Untrüglichkeit*) of the Church: so far as the Church is humbly obedient to God's word and will, she shares in the truth of God (*Deus revelans*) himself, who can neither deceive (*fallere*) nor be deceived (*falli*); then lying and fraud (*omnis fallacia*) and all deceit (*omne fallax*) are remote from her. Infallibility, indeceivability in this radical sense, therefore means a *fundamental remaining of the Church in truth, which is not annulled by individual errors.*

What is meant here is that, no matter how ominous the Church's deviation from truth in a particular instance may be, no matter how the Church—like Israel before her—may be constantly undecided and doubting, and sometimes even erring and falling away, ". . . he will be with you for ever, that Spirit of truth" (Jn. 14:16–17). The Church will not succumb to the power of lies. Because of God's promise, we know by faith that she is undeceivable; on her, because of God's promise, infallibility, indeceivability, is bestowed. In spite of all erring and misunderstanding, she is kept in the truth by God.

Nevertheless, the question cannot be avoided as to whether we *must* speak precisely of the Church's "infallibility," or

whether perhaps there is not a better word for what we are
talking about here. We pointed out above that the open-
ness of the word "infallibility" to misunderstanding is largely
admitted today, and indeed that it was admitted by the
spokesman for the deputation on faith at Vatican I. Ought
we not to draw some conclusions from this? In view of possible misunderstandings, would it not be better to sacrifice
the word in order to save the reality, instead of saving the
word and sacrificing the reality?

There are two reasons particularly which, today at least,
make the term "infallibility" open to misunderstanding and
frequently misleading. *First:* the word has a moral undertone, particularly in certain translations, in the sense of impeccability, from which it simply cannot be freed; when
used of a person today, it is mostly in a negative-censorious
sense ("he thinks he's infallible"). *Second:* the word has
become far too much assocated with certain infallible propositions. What we saw to be a naïve misunderstanding—that
the infallibility of the Church is tied to infallible propositions—is the very thing that has to be prevented.

We would like therefore to give preference to the concept
of *"indefectibility" or "perpetuity" in truth* over that of "infallibility." The concept of "indefectibility" (unshatterability,
constancy) and the positive concept of "perpetuity" (indestructibility, continuance) are just as much traditional
concepts in ecclesiology as "infallibility." In practice they
can often scarcely be distinguished. And if perpetuity or indefectibility in textbook theology have been linked more
closely with the existence than with the truth of the Church,
it must be remembered that the Church's being and being
true simply cannot be separated from each other. If the
Church is no longer in the truth, she is no longer the Church
at all. But the Church's being true is not absolutely dependent
on quite definite infallible propositions, but on her remaining
in the truth throughout all—even erroneous—propositions.
However, in order to bring out the fact that the Church's be-

ing means being true, for clarity's sake we shall speak, not simply of the indefectibility or perpetuity of the Church, but of her indefectibility or perpetuity *in the truth*. What is meant here then is that the Church remains in the truth and this is not annulled by the sum total of individual errors. It should thus be clear that we are holding fast to the *reality* of infallibility, even though for the reasons given we prefer the words "indefectibility" or "perpetuity" for the same reality.

In this way the word "infallibility" would remain ultimately reserved to the one to whom it was originally reserved: to God, to his word and his truth, to God who can neither deceive nor be deceived and who alone is infallible in the strict sense.

A confirmation from history may be appended here. Yves Congar, a short time ago, went thoroughly into the interpretation of the concept of "infallibility" in the middle ages: "The basic conviction, universally shared, is that the Church herself cannot err (Albert the Great, Thomas Aquinas, Bonaventure, decretists). This is understood as the Church in her totality, as *congregatio* or *universitas fidelium*. One part or another of the Church can err, even the bishops, even the pope; the Church can be storm-tossed: in the end she remains faithful. In this sense Matthew 28:20 is quoted and even 16:18; Luke 22:32; John 16:13. In the light of this basic conviction in regard to the Church other statements are formulated in regard to one hierarchical authority or another."[9]

On the basis particularly of Gratian's *Decretum*, it was assumed that the "Roman Church" had never erred in faith. But in this connection what was meant was not the Roman local Church, which certainly can err and has erred, but the universal Church, which must be regarded as *inerrabilis* or at least *indefectibilis*. With the pope, however, it is different: "It is generally assumed that the pope can err and fall into heresy, even though some today have scruples about saying so. Sometimes a distinction is made between the unerring see,

the Sedes, and the person who occupies the see, the *sedens;*
sometimes a distinction is made between the pope as a private individual and the pope as head of the Church, but
this distinction is not used. They prefer to say that a pope
fallen into heresy *ipso facto* ceases to be head of the Church
because he has ceased to be a member of the Church."[10]

Consequently—less with the canonists than with the theologians—infallibility came to be linked in a certain fashion on
the one hand with ecumenical councils and on the other hand
with the pope, but the latter's infallibility was always considered only in connection with the Church, so far as he is
and remains her head. Along with the teaching office of the
pope, there is a parallel teaching office of the *doctores*, the
theologians.

Congar concludes in regard to the high middle ages: "It
cannot be said that the dogma of 1870 is accepted in our
epoch otherwise than in germ. Substantially, importance is
attached to the infallibility or rather indefectibility of the
Church. It is not yet completely decided to which hierarchical
person this inerrancy is guaranteed, but that step is about
to be taken. Meanwhile it will still be necessary to raise
and to solve the problem of the supremacy of the pope over
the council. In the thirteenth century the two authorities are
not regarded as competitive."[11]

Is it not surprising then that throughout the whole of the
middle ages, so deeply marked by papal absolutism, the
only agreed and explicit teaching was on the infallibility or—
better—indefectibility of the Church as such? And even in
regard to modern times Congar observes: "Evidence of the
uncertainty of numerous minds at the beginning of the sixteenth century about the pope's primacy by divine right and
particularly his infallibility is abundant. The Church was infallible, but what precisely was the *subject* of this infallibility?
On this unsettled issue uncertainty and indeed disputes continued until the middle of the nineteenth century. There
existed one certain tradition, that of the infallibility of the

Church. And this continued to be firmly maintained."[12] The emphasis on papal infallibility in the thirteenth century—especially by Aquinas—was taken up again however in the fifteenth, after the conciliar epoch, by Torquemada and others and then pursued further in the Counter-Reformation period particularly by Bellarmine and Suarez, and of course notably by the popes themselves (especially Innocent XI and definitively Pius IX): "In the climate of excessive insistence on authority and obedience as opposed to the Reformation, the infallibility of the Church tended to become predominantly and almost exclusively the infallibility of the bishops and particularly of the pope."[13]

Our own conclusion is this: if once more, as against the infallibility of the bishops and particularly of the pope, we place a renewed emphasis on the infallibility or—better—indefectibility or perpetuity of the Church in the truth, then all that we are really doing is to return to a good old and—fortunately—never extinguished tradition.

7. *The Church's remaining in the truth*

The basic question of ecclesiastical infallibility may now be regarded as answered. God alone is infallible in the strict sense of the term. He alone is a priori free from error (*immunis ab errore*) in detail and indeed in every case: he is therefore the one who a priori can neither deceive nor be deceived. The Church, however, composed of human beings, which is not God and never becomes God, can constantly and in a very human way deceive herself and others on every plane and in all spheres. Therefore, in order to avoid all misunderstandings, it is better to ascribe to the Church, not "infallibility," but—on the basis of faith in the promises—"indefectibility" or "perpetuity": an unshatterability and indestructibility; in brief, a fundamental *remaining* in the truth in spite of all ever possible errors.

Within the scope of the present study it is not possible to

survey all the presuppositions and consequences of such an answer. But at least some obvious queries ought to be briefly answered.

a. If a Church errs to such an extent, isn't it the same as all other human organizations?

The answer is this. The Church of Christ—and under this we include all churches which have the will to be the Church of Christ—is certainly not distinguished from other human organizations by the fact that there is no error in her or that in her there is less or less great error, or that at least in certain fields, with certain persons or in certain cases there is no error. One merely needs to run through once again the brief list of examples of error with which we introduced our first chapter or perhaps the Index of forbidden books to agree. To err is human. To err is also ecclesiastical, to err—as we have recently added—is papal: simply because Church and pope are also human and remain human. Since this has often been forgotten in the Church, we need to be reminded of it very forcefully.

The Church is distinguished from other human organizations—and this distinction is certainly decisive—only in the fact that the promise is given to her as to the community of those who believe in Christ: that she will survive all wrong conclusions and mis-hits and also all sins and vices; that in all upheavals her truth is never simply shattered and destroyed; that in her the message of Jesus Christ will endure; that thus Jesus Christ himself will remain with her in the Spirit and thus keep her through all errors and confusions in the truth of Christ. This promise makes it superfluous for the believer to speculate on what it would be like if there were no longer any community of the faithful. The promise means that God assures the continuance of faith and Church and sees that, in all her straying and wandering, the Church in the last resort keeps her direction and carries with her the truth of Christ.

Her faith is often weak, her love lukewarm, her hope

wavering. But that on which her faith is based, in which her love is rooted, on which her hope is built, this endures. And so she too endures, not by her own power, but by God's power, the unshatterable and indestructible "pillar and bulwark of truth"* (1 Tim. 3:15). She did not give herself her indefectibility, nor can anyone take it from her. The Church may forsake her God; he will not forsake her. On her path through time she may go astray, she may stumble and very often even fall, she may come up against robbers and remain lying half-dead. Yet her God will not pass her by, but will pour oil into her wounds, raise her up, and pay also what could not be foreseen for her healing. So the Church will be able to continue on her way, living on the forgiveness, the healing, and the strengthening of her Lord![14]

This promise then and all that it involves by way of truth, life, power, distinguishes the Church even now as the community of believers in Christ from other human organizations. The only question that remains is: is all this not a truth too beautiful to be true?

b. Isn't this indefectibility in fact merely an unreal, verbal theory?

The answer is this. This indefectibility is a truth of faith. It is not based on evidence that I can observe, without myself being personally involved. It is based on the promise that challenges me to venture and commit myself confidently. Anyone who accepts the challenge of faith knows this. Only the believer can know what the community of believers really is, just as the lover alone knows what love really is. The Church, although certainly not invisible, is only relatively visible. In spite of her often only too solid visibility, that from which, in which and for which she lives, is hidden. And therefore the promise of remaining in the truth is a challenge to faith. And anyone who responds to the challenge with faith has at the same time a share in the truth.

* Revised Standard Version.

This is not to say that the Church's indefectibility is completely unverifiable. For it is impossible to overlook the fact that the Church of Christ has behind her a history of twenty centuries. This history has many, all too many shadows: the faults, sins, and vices in this long history are numerous. And if we look at certain centuries of the Church's history—the tenth perhaps, that *saeculum obscurum,* or the fifteenth, of the Renaissance papacy—we might get the impression that just about everything was done at that time to corrupt the Church and her truth. The Roman Empire also exhibits a long, imposing history and much truth was invested in it (the idea of justice, of law, of order, of peace). But men— from the highest to the lowest—corrupted the empire, and it fell, more from within than from without. The old ideas no longer inspired and sustained it, the truth of the empire had perished. Shattered inwardly and finally destroyed, it never revived.

And what guarantee have we that nothing like this will happen to Christ's Church? The answer can be given: no institution and no constitution. But up to now, at any rate, that hasn't happened. And two thousand years of Christendom provide an illustration (not an argument) that is not to be despised for our answer: in spite of all error and all sin, Christ's Church in the last resort has not in fact been corrupted but kept in the truth. All the numerous prophets of doom in the Church have proved to be false prophets. After the tenth and after the fifteenth century things went on: in spite of all reverses, after the decline there came an ascent, after all the decadence a fresh, renewed knowledge of the truth.

Out of history, admittedly, nothing can be extrapolated for the future. As in the past, so too in the future, the Church's being and being true depend on the promise and this cannot be exploited but only trustfully grasped. As in the past, so too in the future, the Church's being and being true depend on the living faith and love of Christians. Who then is it who insures that the indefectibility of the Church does not remain merely an unreal theory or even merely an empty, divine promise, but rather a genuine reality in this communion? Where was the Church's indefectibility manifested particularly in her darkest times?

Was it manifested through the "hierarchy," relying on its apostolic succession and its rights? At such times, the sight of the behavior of popes and bishops must have led people to believe more in the decline of the Church than in her indestructibility; and popes like Alexander VI—succession or no succession—are certainly not precisely witnesses for the truth of Christ. Or was it manifested through the theologians, confident in their wisdom and scholarship? At such times theology very often failed just as much as the "hierarchy"; and only too often, when the bishops were chasing power, money, and pleasure, the theologians were silent or sleeping, or even producing apologias to excuse or justify the hierarchs in whatever they did or failed to do. They too then—scholarship or no scholarship—were scarcely witnesses to Christ's truth.

Where then, in these dark ages, was the Church's indefectibility really manifested? Not in the hierarchy and not in theology, but among those innumerable and mostly unknown Christians—and there were always some bishops and theologians also among them—who, even in the Church's worst periods, heard the Christian message and tried to live according to it in faith, love, and hope. Mostly they were not the great and powerful, the prudent and wise, but—wholly in accordance with the New Testament—the "simple people," those "of no account," who are the truly great in the kingdom of heaven. They were the true witnesses of the truth of Christ and manifested by their Christian life and Christian conduct the indefectibility of the Church in the truth.

If "people" is understood in this sense, and its role as one given by grace and deliberately accepted, then with Vatican II it can be said of the people of God: "The holy people of

God shares also in Christ's prophetic office. It spreads abroad
a living witness to Him, especially by means of a life of
faith, and charity and by offering to God a sacrifice of praise,
the tribute of lips which give honour to His name (cf. Heb.
13:15). The body of the faithful as a whole, anointed as they
are by the Holy One (cf. Jn. 2:20, 27), cannot err in matters
of belief" (Constitution on the Church, art. 12). Admittedly,
if this claim again is linked with certain propositions and
the "sense of the faith . . . from the bishops down to the
last member of the laity" is regarded uncritically and in-
discriminately as the revelation of "the Spirit of truth," then
in the course of the centuries we should have had to consider
some very odd things as the revelation of the Spirit.

Here it must be remembered that the "sense of faith of the
People of God under the lead of the sacred teaching authority" can never become the source and norm for the
revelation of the Spirit. Rather is it the other way around:
the revelation of the Spirit is and remains always the source
and norm for the Church's sense of faith. This means that
whoever wants to know what is Christian revelation cannot
ascertain the people's "sense of faith" merely—so to speak—
statistically by an opinion poll—we know from experience
that the people's faith (and occasionally also that of the
"teaching office") is mingled with credulity and often even
unbelief—but must examine critically this "sense of faith" of
the people in the light of the original Christian message. The
gospel remains in every case the source, norm, and power
for the faith and for the perpetuity and indefectibility of the
Church in the truth.

c. Is certainty still possible with
this kind of indefectibility?

Certainty is essential for faith. Faith should give certainty.
Can the "hierarchy" or theology produce certainty of faith?
Both would be overestimating their capacity if they were to
claim to produce faith or the certainty of faith. Only the

Christian message itself—whoever preaches it—confers certainty of faith. It is Jesus Christ, given us in the Christian proclamation, who bestows faith. He in his person is the invitation, the challenge, the encouragement to faith, so that the individual through his person is placed before God in a way that is unparalleled in its critical and promising character, in order to assent before God to his life and death. Both "hierarchy" and theology—each in its own way, which will be explained later—may *serve* all future proclamation of the Christian message. By serving they can prepare indirectly for the faith which the Christian message—which Jesus Christ himself in the Spirit—rouses and confers.

The Christian message then—the person it proclaims—produces certainty of faith. To this extent the certainty of faith depends on the *truth* of the Christian message. But this truth is not to be confused either with evidence or infallibility. The truth of the Christian message is not a system of evident propositions which might produce certainty in Descartes' sense. The reality of God is not evident in this way. But neither is the truth of the Christian message a system of infallible definitions which might provide certainty at least in the neoscholastic sense. Nor can the reality of God be grasped in this way.

There was certainty of faith indeed for at least a thousand years before there was any talk at all of infallible propositions; the Church existed for almost two thousand years before infallibility was defined. Propositions which are a priori infallible however, as we have shown, are given neither to an individual believer nor to certain believers. Both the individual believer and the community of faith should certainly strive for *true* propositions in proclamation, although an ultimate ambivalence can never be excluded even in propositions of faith and all language even in matters of faith remains dependent on dialogue. Certainty—different from mathematical certainty, but certainty none the less—does not arise however through these true propositions. It emerges only when the person addressed commits himself to the message, whether the individual proposition is more or less true, more or less adequate to this message: when he commits himself to the Person who is proclaimed in this message.

Believing in this sense does not mean accepting true or still less infallible propositions: believing this or that; nor does it mean accepting a person's truthworthiness: believing this person or that person; but it means, throughout all perhaps ambiguous or perhaps in particular even false propositions, committing oneself in one's whole existence to the message, to the person proclaimed: believing *in* Jesus Christ. It is this faith alone that can give certainty: the peace that surpasses all reason. How am I to become certain of another person's love? By looking for declarations of love from him? These are needed, but are there infallible declarations of love and would it help if there were? Or by demanding evident signs of love from him? These too are needed, but are there infallible signs of love and do they produce of themselves unequivocal certainty? In the last resort I can be certain of love—at times in spite of clumsy declarations of love or abortive signs of love—only by committing myself to it and thus experiencing love. I become certain even of the love of God only when I myself love.

This does not mean at all that the individual believer is to be isolated. The individual is called to believe. But, without the community which believes and professes and proclaims the faith, the individual too does not come to believe. He has faith neither from himself nor directly from God, but through the community which rouses, invites, challenges him to believe and which then, too—if it is really a community of faith and love—constantly encircles and helps to sustain his faith. In this way the faith of the individual may share in the faith of the community and in the common truth. And modern man particularly—who also in his faith has become only too well aware of his historical relativity, isolation and loneliness—will be able to experience constantly not only as a burden, but also as liberation, the fact that his faith—in spite of all his own responsibility—is sheltered in the more comprehensive and manifold, old and young faith of the community of faith, which is the Church. As expressions of this faith of the believing community, as we explained, creeds, definitions of faith, professions of faith, and dogmas of faith also have their profound meaning and their important function, without claiming infallibility for their individual propositions.

8. Ecumenical perspectives

The question of infallibility divides Christendom. From the outbreak of the Reformation, this question has been waiting for a fundamental answer on the part of Catholic theology. The former appeal to tradition—which becomes questionable particularly at this point—was obviously no more convincing than the later statements of the two Vatican councils. Yet, if we are not to be fighting the wrong battles at the wrong points, we must here examine more closely—though necessarily briefly—what the Reformation position really is. There are two aspects of the problematic.

a. It was undoubtedly simpler to tie down Luther to the formal question of the *capacity of pope and council to err* than to deal with the decisive, material theological questions (particularly the doctrine of justification). In his answer to Prierias in 1518, Luther had frankly stated that both pope and council can err.[15] And in 1519 at the famous Disputation of Leipzig he was skillfully trapped by John Eck in the statement that councils have also in fact erred (in the concrete, the Council of Constance, which had condemned Huss a hundred years earlier and burned him in spite of all promises of a safe-conduct).[16] And finally, in the decisive year of 1521, at the Reichstag at Worms, Luther's insistence on the capacity of councils to err was the main reason why the Emperor Charles V dropped his support and punished him with the ban of the Empire.[17] Summoned by the imperial orator to concede the inerrancy of councils and to reject the propositions condemned at Constance, Luther answered unequivocally: "Unless I am convinced by the testimonies of Scripture or evident reason (for I do not believe either pope or councils alone, since it is certain that they have both erred frequently and contradicted themselves), I am convinced by the Scriptures I have quoted and, since my conscience is caught in the words of God, I neither can nor wish to revoke anything, since to act against conscience is neither safe nor honest."[18] It is in this connection that Luther is said to have made his famous statement: "I can do no other. Here I stand. God help me. Amen."[19]

Luther stuck to this profession of faith throughout his whole life.[20] And it was the common view of all the Reform churches that councils, and of course popes even more, can err and have erred. Calvin in his *Institutio* displays a very lively sense of history as he demonstrates how there were true councils, later recognized by the Church, and false, not recognized by the Church; how often council was opposed to council; how the truth also may be opposed to the councils and how blind obedience to councils would be irresponsible.[21] Calvin also rejects quite definitely the view "that councils cannot err; or if they err, it is not lawful for us to discern the truth, or not to assent to their errors."[22] And, in regard to the Reformation confessions of faith, Benno Gassmann observes in his thorough inquiry: "For the confessions, however, the Church is free from error only as long and as far as she relies on Christ and on 'the foundation of the prophets and apostles', that is, on Scripture. Inerrancy is not an undisputed possession of the Church; any Church can fall away from the truth, just as it can dissociate itself from Scripture. The congregation confronts Scripture as its standard and norm. Inerrancy is a relative factor, lying between these two poles."[23]

Finally in the Thirty-nine Articles of the Anglican Churches there is the sober observation: "As the Churches of Jerusalem,

Alexandria, and Antioch, have erred; so also the Church of
Rome hath erred, not only in their living and manner of
Ceremonies, but also in matters of faith."[24] In regard to the
authority of general councils, it is noted: "And when they be
gathered together (forasmuch as they be an assembly of men,
whereof all be not governed with the Spirit and Word of
God) they may err, and sometimes have erred, even in things
pertaining unto God."[25]

b. However strongly the Reformation Churches reject the
infallibility of pope and councils, they affirm just as strongly
the *infallibility or indefectibility and perpetuity of the
Church*. For Luther the councils have authority, certainly not
of themselves as formal representations of the Church, but
factually on the basis of the truth of their decisions: that is,
when they have the truth of the gospel behind them. Ecclesiastical legitimacy must be sustained by spiritual legitimacy. Luther too believes in the guidance of the Church by
the Holy Spirit. And for that reason he can expressly ascribe
infallibility to the Church: to no one after the apostles may
it be ascribed "that he cannot err in faith, but only to the
universal Church."[26]

This Church, however, is not simply to be equated with
the official Church, with pope and bishops. It is rather the
hidden, but completely real Church of those who truly believe, which cannot err, because Christ in accordance with
his promise remains with her to the end of the world; she is
"the pillar and bulwark of the truth" (1 Tim. 3:15).[27] To
this extent the Church has been preserved even under an
erring and failing papacy. Luther "sees in the real history
of the Church, in spite of everything, a continuity of truth in
as much as the promise that the Holy Spirit will lead the
Church was always fulfilled anew. The true Church in this
sense then is the object, not only of a 'faith-nevertheless',
but also of historical experience, in a manifest continuity which
Luther constantly acknowledged. But this continuity of the
Spirit's guidance, the preservation of the true Church, is simply

not identical with the official tradition and supposed apostolic
succession of ecclesiasticism and is not guaranteed by these.
God chooses for himself his witnesses to the truth at all
times, how and where he wills . . . We may not therefore
understand the guidance by the Holy Spirit in a hierarchical
or supranatural evolutionist sense. God also permits the official Church to err, in order to break down that trust in men to
which she is constantly inclined, instead of trust in his word
alone. But then he sends her again witnesses of his truth."[28]

The famous article VII of the Augsburg Confession must
be seen against this theological background: "They teach
that the one Holy Church will remain for ever (*perpetuo
mansura sit*). Now this Church is the congregation of the
saints, in which the Gospel is rightly taught and the sacraments rightly administered."[29] The perpetuity and indefectibility of the Church are here emphatically affirmed. The
article is interpreted by Melanchthon in his apologia for the
Augsburg Confession in this way: "In order that we may be
certain, not doubt, but firmly and entirely believe that a
Christian Church will really be and remain on earth until
the end of the world; that we may also not doubt that a
Christian Church lives and is on earth, which is the Bride
of Christ, although the troop of the impious is more and
greater; that also the Lord Christ here on earth in the troop
which is called Church is active daily, forgives sins, daily
answers prayer, daily animates his followers with abundant
and powerful consolation in their temptations and constantly
raises them up: for all this we have the consoling article of
our faith, 'I believe in one Catholic, universal Christian
Church'. Hence no one may think that the Church, like an
external state-organization, is tied to this or that country,
kingdom or class, as the pope wants to say of Rome; but this
certainly remains true that the troop and men are the right
Church who continually in the world, from the rise of the
sun to its setting, truly believe in Christ; who then have
one gospel, one Christ, one sort of baptism and sacrament,

are ruled by one Holy Spirit, although they have different ceremonies."[30]

Calvin too affirms an infallibility or indefectibility of the Church, which however—according to him, in contrast to his Catholic opponents—remains tied to the word:

> Their statement that the church cannot err bears on this point, and this is how they interpret it—inasmuch as the church is governed by the *Spirit of God,* it can proceed safely *without the Word;* no matter where it may go, it can think and speak only what is true; accordingly, if it should ordain anything beyond or apart from God's Word, this must be taken as a sure oracle of God.
>
> If we grant the first point that the church cannot err in matters necessary to salvation, here is what we mean by it: The statement is true in so far as the church, having forsaken all its own wisdom, allows itself to be taught by the Holy Spirit through God's Word. This, then, is the difference. Our opponents locate the authority of the Church *outside God's Word;* but we insist that it be *attached to the Word,* and do not allow it to be separated from it.[31]

The Church's remaining in the truth is not annulled by errors of councils.

> I am quite convinced that truth does not die in the church, even though it be oppressed by one council, but is wonderfully preserved by the Lord, so that it may rise up and triumph again in its own time. But I *deny* it to be *always* the case that an interpretation of Scripture adopted by *vote of a council is true and certain.*[32]

The Thirty-nine Articles of the Church of England do not enter into this question more closely, but, in regard to the Church as community of believers in which the pure word of God, preaching and sacraments, are administered in accordance with Christ's mandate,[33] they take the same line as in regard to the authority of councils, the conclusions of which have authority only when they are "taken out of holy Scripture."[34]

c. What are we to conclude from all this? An *ecumenical agreement* on this perhaps most difficult point of the Catholic-Protestant controversy is entirely possible; in fact, if the critical new approach of Catholic doctrine suggested in this book should prove acceptable, an ecumenical agreement on the question of principle could be *attained*. For there is no need of long explanations in order to make clear that the Reformers, on the basis of their own presuppositions, could assent to the view put forward here of an indefectibility or perpetuity of the Church, which depends on the presence of the Spirit, on the proclamation of the word, on the community of believers, but not on infallible propositions.

It is wholly within the realm of possibility that the view put forward here will come to prevail in the Catholic Church. In recent Catholic publications on the problematic, even though the problem of infallibility of propositions or infallibility of the Church is not tackled directly, a development towards clarification can be noted in two respects:

1. Papal infallibility is often interpreted restrictively, going beyond Vatican I, and linked with the infallibility of the Church[35];

2. The infallibility of the community of the faithful is given a more prominent place by comparison with an infallibility of office.[36]

The infallibility of the ecclesiastical teaching office has been directly contested by Francis Simons, Catholic missionary bishop of Indore (India).[37] Even though we cannot share certain opinions of this amazingly courageous Dutchman on faith, evidence, and miracles—which are too much influenced by a neoscholastic fundamental theology—or his judgment on modern exegesis, particularly on form-criticism, we must agree with his main thesis that the infallibility

of the ecclesiastical teaching office must be proved from
Scripture to be acceptable, but plainly cannot be proved.
Simons, however, assumes that the infallibility of the Church
stands or falls with infallible propositions, to which he opposes
the all-too-simply conceived counter proposal of "evidence."

The author of the present book can completely identify
himself with the statements with which W. Kasper concludes
his article on the road from Vatican I to Vatican II:

> The overcoming of ecclesiastical triumphalism by Vatican
> II affects also the Church's understanding of truth and
> demands a new and more profound interpretation of the
> concept of infallibility, which is so open to misunder-
> standing. This concept belongs more than any other to the
> still unmastered past of Vatican I. Rightly understood, it
> means the confidence of faith that, in spite of some in-
> dividual errors, the Church is maintained fundamentally
> by the Spirit of God in the truth of the gospel. Infal-
> libility would then have to be understood dynamically and
> not statically: in and through the Church there occurs
> constantly the eschatological conflict with the powers of
> untruth, error and lying; according to the conviction of
> faith, through all this, truth will always prevail and never
> finally be lost. Thus the Church, because of her faith,
> can be a sign of hope for human society, precisely in the
> struggle for the right knowledge of the truth. By her own
> example she must bear witness that it is never absurd,
> but in fact constantly necessary to seek further and to go on
> further in the certainty that the truth will prevail. The
> road on which the Church herself has gone from Vatican
> I to Vatican II is a testimony of this hope.[38]

On this road, the encyclical *Humanae Vitae*, in so many
respects, was a misfortune for the Catholic Church. If, however, it were to turn out to be a catalyst, to hasten re-

flection on ecclesiastical infallibility, then it would nevertheless not have been in vain—and particularly also for the
oikumene.

9. *The truth of councils*

There is no question of ecumenical importance addressed
to the Catholic Church which does not imply its counterquestion. The critical reflection just completed on Catholic
teaching in confrontation with that of the Reformers should
not give rise to the impression that the theme of infallibility
presents a challenge only to Catholic theology. Some questions
put now to the Orthodox theology of the Eastern Churches
will make this clear:

It is questionable whether there is a uniform *Orthodox*
doctrine of ecclesiastical infallibility, shared by all Christian
Churches of the East. Plainly the question of ecclesiastical
infallibility has not been considered in the East with the
same intensity or regarded with the same urgency as in the
West: which need not be in any way a bad sign. Nevertheless, Orthodox theology could join in the ecumenical consensus just noted, at least to the extent of considering "infallibility"—if it seems necessary at all to talk about it—
as founded in the *Church* as the whole people of God. While
Rome fixed on the infallibility of the pope, Orthodoxy remained concentrated on the infallibility of the Church as
a whole: an infallible Church, not infallible persons. This
is how the Orthodox partriarchs answered Pius IX in 1848,
without however deterring him from promulgating either the
definition of the Immaculate Conception of Mary or that of
his own infallibility: "Among us, neither Patriarchs nor Councils could ever introduce new teaching, for the guardian
of religion is the very body of the Church, that is, the people
(*laos*) itself."[39] Commenting on these explanations, the important Russian theologian Alexei Khomiakov, wrote at the
time: "The Pope is greatly mistaken in supposing that we

consider the ecclesiastical hierarchy to be the guardian of dogma. The case is quite different. The unvarying constancy and the unerring truth of Christian dogma does not depend on any hierarchical order; it is guarded by the totality, by the whole people of the Church, which is the Body of Christ."[40]

How far the infallibility of the Church requires infallible propositions may not have been subjected to close scrutiny by the Orthodox. This becomes clear from a recent study by John Karmiris, who however, as we shall see, cannot be regarded as representative of Orthodoxy as a whole:

> In regard to the Church's infallibility mentioned here, it seems necessary to declare from the very beginning that the Church is infallible as a whole, as *pleroma*, which consists of all orthodox believers, clergy and laity. As organ of her infallibility she needs only the ecumenical synod, which alone has the right to formulate dogmas infallibly and to whose supreme leadership and authority all are subject. Both the patriarchs themselves and the popes, as well as the other hierarchs, are included, just as all the apostles together with Peter were subject to the apostolic synod. The totality therefore, the *pleroma*, or the body of the Church, is regarded in Orthodoxy as bearer of infallibility, while the ecumenical synod serves as organ and—so to speak—as mouthpiece of the Church. At the ecumenical synod the ecclesiastical *pleroma* is represented by its bishops, who lay down dogmas under the inspiration of the Holy Spirit. "The Church consequently is infallible, not only when assembled at ecumenical synods, but also as totality independently of the synods, so that from the infallibility of the Church as a whole the infallibility of the ecumenical synods follows and not conversely the infallibility of the Church from the infallibility of the ecumenical synods" (K. Dyovouniotis). It must be observed that neither the ecclesiastical *pleroma* nor its two large sections—clergy and laity—each for itself alone, nor—

which would be still worse—one person, a bishop, a patri-arch or pope, could authoritatively define dogmas, since this —as we said—is the sole and exclusive right and work of the ecumenical synods and of the bishops taking part in it.[41]

If we identify in this way a priori the infallibility of the Church with the infallibility of propositions—if not in fact of the pope, yet nevertheless of the ecumenical councils— in spite of all opposition to Rome, we are exposed in prin-ciple to the same difficulties from which the Roman doctrine suffers: difficulties in regard to the artificial restriction of the apostolic succession to the bishops, difficulties in regard to the legitimacy of concluding from the infallibility of the Church to the infallibility of an ecumenical council, and— finally—difficulties in regard to the possibility of infallible propositions at all. Here too a theologian could not merely make an assertion, he would have to substantiate his claim theologically. The above arguments for the infallibility of ecumenical councils seem however to be shooting beyond the target: if a hundred officeholders can represent the Church infallibly, why not in principle even one single person? But in fact all misgivings in regard to a proposition-infallibility of the Roman pontiff are valid also in regard to any assembly of bishops, which—as we have seen—has not been promised infallibility anywhere in Scripture.

It is, however, more than questionable whether a fixation of the Church's infallibility on the propositions of an ecumenical council is really *the* Orthodox interpretation of ecclesiastical infallibility. The emphasis of certain Eastern theologians on conciliar infallibility seems at times to be decided less by their own ancient tradition than by opposition to the Roman pontiff and a desire not to be inferior to him in the matter of infallibility.[42] But, by adopting this attitude, such an Orthodox theology accepts the opponent's superficial statement of the question and at the same time takes too easily for granted its identity with the Church of the New

Testament and with the early Church. Among recent Orthodox theologians, Timothy Ware is much more discriminating and at least clearly formulates the difficulty: "But councils of bishops can err and be deceived."[43] Thus the problem is raised that Karmiris briefly dismisses, as to how we can really be certain whether a particular assembly of bishops is an ecumenical council or not.

Two groups of questions may be brought forward here, from the early Orthodox and at the same time common Christian tradition, which suggest that we cannot speak of an automatic and a priori infallibility of an ecumenical council.

(1) The *ecumenicity* of a council is *not a priori certain*. From the First Ecumenical Council of Nicea in 325 recognition by the Church as a whole was regarded as fundamental (Athanasius, its protagonist, often listed the names of all the particular Churches).[44] The recent *soborant* theory, going back to Khomiakov and maintained by many Slav theologians (in the present century especially by Sergij Bulgakov) sees recognition by the Church as a whole as a necessary and important qualification for the ecumenicity of a council. Certainly recognition of an ecumenical council by the particular Churches must not be understood as a kind of subsequent referendum, which would deny the right of making binding decisions on questions of faith to an ecumenical council.[45] But the necessity—which can be observed in history—of the recognition or reception of a council by the Church as a whole implies at least this much: the fact that a council has been convoked and carried out as ecumenical does not at all mean that it has a priori the truth on its side. The fact of having truth on its side becomes evident only when its propositions come to prevail in the Church: that is, the Church recognizes again in these propositions her own experience of faith.

Actually there were councils which were not convoked and carried out as ecumenical and which, nevertheless, have

come to be regarded as ecumenical: the Second Ecumenical
Council (Constantinople, 381) and the Fifth (Constantinople,
553). The canons also of smaller Eastern synods—like those
of Ancyra in 314, Neocaesaria (Pontus) in 320, Antioch
in 329 (?), Gangra (Asia Minor) in 342, and Laodicea
(Phrygia) in 350—by being accepted have acquired importance also for the West. But the converse is also true.
Councils which were convoked as ecumenical failed to establish themselves as such: the Council of Sardica, the Second
Council of Ephesus in 449, the Second Trullan Synod, and
also the general synods of the West, of Arles in 314 and
Rome in 341.

The historian H. Jedin rightly observes: "Until after the
first millennium the intention and will of the person convoking a council is not the criterion of its ecumenical character; nor has the recognition of the decisions by the pope
during this period a priori the character of a formal confirmation, as it clearly had for later ecumenical councils.
The recognition precisely of these twenty councils as ecumenical does not go back to a legislative act of the popes
embracing all of them together, but has become established
in the theory and practice of the Church."[46]

If the ecumenicity of a council is not a priori certain,
then still less an infallibility of the council. What is decisive here is not the will to make infallible definitions,
but the intrinsic truth of the council's decisions which as
such must impose itself on the Church's sense of faith.

(2) Councils have *corrected* one another. When ecumenical councils began, people felt by no means bound—as
they did later—by the quasi-inspired letter of the council's
decrees. Terms and concepts were constantly changing, particularly in the early christological councils: the Councils of
Nicea and Sardica presupposed, with many of the Fathers,
that there is only *one* hypostasis in God; the First Council
of Constantinople and the Council of Chalcedon presup-

posed with many others that there are three hypostases in God.

Moreover, an earlier council may be expressly rejected: the Council of Chalcedon in 451 rejected the decisions of the Second Council of Ephesus of 449, making it impossible for the latter to be accepted as ecumenical, although it had been convoked as such; the Council of Constantinople in 754 rejected the veneration of images, the Second Council of Nicea in 787 approved it.

Finally, there is the factual correction of an ecumenical council by a later ecumenical council: thus the Council of Chalcedon in 451 corrected in fact the First Council of Ephesus of 431, recognized as ecumenical, which, under the leadership of Cyril of Alexandria, had condemned and excommunicated Nestorius of Antioch. Although Chalcedon commended Cyril and upheld the condemnation of Nestorius, by its new formulation of faith it nevertheless recognized in fact the concern of antiochene theology and expressly rejected the central doctrine of alexandrian christology, which had dominated the two councils of Ephesus: the idea of the *one* nature in Christ. Hence the Patriarch Nestorius, condemned at Ephesus in 431 and 449, would certainly have been able to subscribe completely to that formula of faith of Chalcedon in 451, to which Cyril, the leader at Ephesus I, could have subscribed only with open or secret reservations, and to which Dioscorus, the leader at Ephesus II (excommunicated by Chalcedon), could not have subscribed at all (Ephesus II came to be known in history as the "Robber Synod").

There is a *locus classicus* of Augustine on the priority of Scripture which runs:

Who would not know that the holy *canonical Scriptures* both of the Old and New Testament have a priority over all subsequent writings of bishops such that there cannot be any doubt or dispute at all as to whether whatever is written there is true or right; but that *the writings of bishops* after the settlement of the canon may be refuted both by the perhaps wiser words of anyone more experienced in the matter and by the weightier authority and more scholarly prudence of other bishops, and also by councils, if something in them perhaps has deviated from the truth; and that even councils held in particular regions or provinces must give way without quibbling (*sine ullis ambagibus cedere*) to the authority of plenary councils of the whole Christian world; and that even the earlier plenary councils are often (*saepe*) corrected (*emendari*) by later ones, if as a result of practical experience (*cum aliquo experimento rerum*) something that was closed is opened, something that was hidden becomes known?[47]

If, however, ecumenical councils deviate from one another, disavow, expressly reject or factually correct one another, in this way, it is impossible—as we have shown—not only in the light of the biblical message, but also in the light of the history of the councils, to accept as a priori certain the infallibility—in the sense of infallible propositions—of an ecumenical council. The Second Vatican Council, consciously under the influence of John XXIII, although without deep theological reflection, did well therefore to refrain from any infallible definitions.

To sum it up: ecumenical councils *can* be an expression of the infallibility or indefectibility of the Church. But they are not so a priori in virtue of the will of those who convoke them or take part in them, as if the latter were granted infallibility a priori by the Spirit of God in response to their desires and prayers: this is exactly what cannot be substantiated from any source. Councils are an expression of the infallibility or indefectibility of the Church rather a posteriori, *if* and *in so far as*—that is—they authentically attest the truth of the gospel of Jesus Christ. Hence there are not indeed a priori infallible conciliar statements. But there are certainly factually *true*, conciliar statements: those, namely, which are in harmony with the original Christian message and are also recognized by the Church as being in harmony with it. Councils cannot dispose of the truth of Christ. They can and may strive for the truth of Christ. For this the Spirit of Christ is promised to the bishops and all participants, as also to every Christian.

"Is it not astonishing to see how many theologians question the infallibility of councils?" The Catholic theologian, M.-J. Le Guillou, sounds almost indignant in his reproach to Orthodox theology, quoting the names of S. Zankow, B. Zenkowsky, N. Arseniev, N. Milasch, adding: "this influence is visible even in Bratsiotis. . . . and, even more surprisingly, in V. Lossky."[48] Is such a very far-reaching consensus so astonishing? Certainly it is surprising only for the Catholic theologian who does not permit himself to be seriously questioned by Orthodox theology and thinks instead that he can dismiss this problem with an allusion to the wicked Luther and the Disputation of Leipzig and generally the devastating influences of Protestantism on Orthodox theology.

If we confront Orthodox theology *and* the Orthodox tradition frankly and without prejudice, we see delineated a thoroughly gratifying ecumenical consensus in regard to *true* infallibility or—better—indefectibility of the Church. J. Meyendorff—"perhaps the following text is still more typical of present-day Orthodox ecclesiology"[49]—therefore has our full assent when he says:

Not "ecumenicity", but the truthfulness of the councils makes their decisions binding for us. We are touching here on the basic mystery of Orthodox teaching on the Church: the Church is the miracle of God's presence with men, beyond any formal "criterion" and any formal "infallibility." It is not sufficient to convoke an ecumenical council so that it may proclaim the truth, whatever historical reality may be understood in this concept of the council; what

also of him who said: "I am the Way, the Truth and the
matters is the presence in the midst of those assembled
Life". Without this presence, the assembly, however numerous and representative it may be, is not in the truth.

Protestants and Catholics usually have difficulty in grasp-
ing this basic truth of Orthodoxy. Both Protestants and
Catholics materialize God's presence in the Church: the
former in the *letter* of Scripture, the latter in the *person*
of the pope. They do not thereby evade the miracle, but
give it a concrete form. The sole "criterion of truth"
for Orthodoxy remains God himself, who lives mysteriously
in the Church, leads her on the way of truth, and makes
known his will in the wholeness ("catholicity") of her life.
The councils—particularly the "ecumenical" councils—in the
course of history have been merely means of declaring
the truth: for it is quite plain that the Orthodox faith
is not exhaustively contained in the decisions of the seven
councils, which merely established some basic truths about
God and about Christ.

The totality of the Orthodox faith remains in the Church
continuously: it finds its expression in local councils (for
example, in the councils of Constantinople in the four-
teenth century, which defined the Orthodox doctrine of
grace) and in the works of various theologians; it is likewise always and everywhere known in the Orthodox liturgy, in the sacraments and in the *life* of the saints.
This life did not come to a standstill with the last ecumenical council (787): the truth is always and everywhere
living and active in the Church. It can also be made known
in a new "ecumenical" council, gathering together not only
the Orthodox Churches, but also the Western Christians.[50]

The question so formulated by the Orthodox theologian
must now be put as a Catholic counterquestion to Protestantism: the question of the infallibility of the Bible.

10. The truth of Scripture

The counterquestion to *Protestant* theology must be: is it
sufficient to replace the infallibility of the ecclesiastical
teaching office with the *infallibility* of the Bible? Instead
of the infallibility of the Roman pontiffs or of ecumenical
councils, are we to have the infallibility of a "paper pope"?

Against the Catholic insistence on tradition and the infallibility of certain propositions of church teaching, Protestantism set up at an early date a principle of Scripture
(*sola scriptura*) and an infallibility of biblical propositions.
As a result of this polemic, here too, a distorted statement
of the question was adopted. The Reformers themselves had
brought up against the accepted traditions in Church, theology, and piety, not the infallibility of Scripture, but the testimony of the content of Scripture; and, while Calvin practiced
philological and historical criticism, Luther had already occasionally (on the Epistle of James or on the Book of Revelation) practiced objective criticism. Nevertheless—on the
defensive against the claims of the Church newly reinforced
at Trent—Lutheran and Reformed orthodoxy developed systematically the theory of inspiration shared by the Reformers
and Trent, without undue strain, in the sense of a *verbal
inspiration:* this was extended to the smallest detail, both
from the subjective (how inspiration takes place in the
sacred writer) and the objective aspects (how inspiration
takes objective form in the book).

In this way revelation was identified with the production
of the word of Scripture as it took place through the Holy
Spirit at the time, once and for all, in the biblical author.
The authors of the books of the Bible thus appear as un-
historical-phantom beings through whom the Holy Spirit
effects everything directly. In such a conception every word
of Scripture shares with monotonous uniformity in the per-
fection and inerrancy of God himself. Human imperfection

and capacity for error must therefore be completely excluded in the human authors of Scripture: the slightest
error would in fact have to be charged to the Holy Spirit,
who can neither deceive nor be deceived. Thus "inspiration"
and the inerrancy deduced from such a conception is extended rigorously and systematically to each and every word
of the Bible (verbal inspiration and verbal inerrancy) so
that even the Hebrew vocalizations of the original text
(but not the translations) are regarded by some as inspired.
The Bible is thus declared to be in every respect—linguisti-
cally, stylistically, logically, historically—the perfect and infallible sacred book. Infallibility, complete inerrancy, belongs
a priori to the word of the Bible as such.

The theory of a verbal inspiration and verbal inerrancy
was deeply shaken by the Enlightenment. As a result, his-
torical-critical exegesis brought to light in an unexpected
way the truly human character and historicity of the
biblical authors. Thus, at the same time, the capacity for
error of the biblical authors became more than clear. Nevertheless, biblicism has remained a constant danger for Evangelical theology, and the idea of a verbal inspiration has
been upheld, not only in numerous sects, but also in some
Protestant Churches, particularly in modern American fun-
damentalism, and in some trends of European pietism. The
Christian message, Christ himself as preached, is no longer
the real ground of faith, but the infallible word of the
Bible as such.

Just as some Catholics believe less in God and his Christ
than in the Church (confusing credere in Deum with credere
Ecclesiam), so do many Protestants believe in the Bible.
As the living, proclaimed Christian message has been absorbed for the former into infallible propositions of the ecclesiastical teaching office, so for the latter it has been absorbed into the infallible propositions of the Bible. And to
the apotheosis of the Church there corresponds exactly the
apotheosis of Scripture: on the one side, blind faith in a

person, "I believe it because Father said so"; on the other,
blind faith in a book, "I believe it because it's in the
Bible." Even in scholarly Protestant theology up to the
present century some odd and unverifiable ideas were held
and put into writing about the "personal inspiration" of the
apostles or biblical writers, the "Author-Spirit" active in them,
their "power of memory" increased by the Spirit, ecstatic
"seizure" and charismatic "enthusiasm."

Now of course the fact cannot be overlooked that even
in the early Church a doctrine of inspiration had developed
which was subject to a variety of extra-Christian influences
and provided an occasion for misunderstandings. While Pal-
estinian Judaism did indeed see God himself at work in the
biblical authors, but took seriously their human and historical
peculiarities, wholly in the sense of the Old Testament;
in hellenistic Judaism (especially Philo) an attempt was made
to exclude these peculiarities, since human autonomy is dissolved in ecstasy under the divine frenzy.

Early Christian authors then saw in the biblical authors
instruments who wrote under the "inspiration" or "dictation"
of the Spirit (in the manner of secretaries or even like the
flute as the flute-player's instrument). Finally, it was Augustine particularly, influenced by hellenistic theories of inspiration, who saw man merely as the instrument of the Holy
Spirit: the Spirit alone decides the content and form of the
biblical writings, so that the whole Bible is bound to be free
from all contradictions, mistakes and errors, or has to be kept
free by harmonizing, allegorizing, or mysticizing.[51] The influence of Augustine in regard to inspiration and inerrancy
remained decisive throughout the middle ages and right up
to modern times. The Council of Trent too declared that the
books of the Bible and the unwritten traditions were received "orally from Christ or dictated by the Holy Spirit"
(DS 1501).

It is significant however that there is no mention at all

in the Tridentine decree of the inerrancy of the Bible as
a result of inspiration. Verbal inspiration is asserted and
thought out rigorously and systematically only in Protestantism. It was only toward the end of the nineteenth century,
under the pressure of a destructive critical exegesis, that
the popes took over—with a remarkable switch of phases—
the theory of verbal inspiration worked out by Protestant
orthodoxy. Even Vatican I, which made an explicit statement
on the inspiration of the biblical writings ("under the inspiration of the Holy Spirit, they have God for their author"),
in this connection makes only the indirect and reserved
observation that the Scriptures "contain revelation [!] without error" (DS 3006).

From the time of Leo XIII, however, and particularly
in the modernist confusion, the complete and absolute inerrancy of Scripture was constantly explicitly and systematically
defended (DS 3292–4, 3411, 3652–4, 3887) in papal encyclicals. It was thought possible to tackle the destructive
efforts of rationalism only—as in the case of ecclesiastical
infallibility—by applying the rationalistic concept of truth
(under Cartesian influences) and asserting a propositional
inerrancy also to Scripture even in matters of natural science
and history. A theory of this kind was to be pressed even
on the Second Vatican Council by the curial preparatory
commission in the schema on revelation.[52]

Wholly in the style of nineteenth-century apologetics, an
"absolute immunity from error of the whole of Scripture"
is deduced "directly and necessarily" from the universal extension of divine inspiration, and in fact expressly for the
whole religious and secular sphere, this being described as
the ancient and constant conviction of the Church. The whole
schema however was rejected by the Council with an overwhelming majority at the first session in 1962 and—to counter
a curial voting trick—removed from the order of the day by
John XXIII in a personal intervention. To everybody's sur-

prise Paul VI then placed the renewed discussion on revelation on the order of the day for the third session.

Precisely these discussions, however, in the third session of
the council were to signify a turning point on the question
of inerrancy. The lengthy six articles were combined in the
new schema in a single, brief article (under the chapter-
heading, not of inerrancy, but of inspiration).⁵³ The sacred
writer is no longer described as "instrument" but as "true
author," and God no longer as "principal author" but simply
as "author." Inspiration does not mean the exclusion, re-
pression, or replacement of the human activity of the hagi-
ographers. Any memory of old theories óf *verbal inspiration*
was to be omitted, and hence any form of an impersonal,
mechanistic interpretation of the origin of Scripture."⁵⁴

On the question of the inerrancy of Scripture—the negative
expression "inerrancy" had meanwhile been replaced by the
positive expression "truth"—the speech of Cardinal König
of Vienna on errors in Scripture proved to be fundamental
and received favorable comments from later speakers. Orien-
tal studies showed, he said, "that the Scriptures in matters
of history and natural science are sometimes lacking in truth
(*a veritate quandoque deficere*)." According to Mark 2:26,
for example, David had entered the house of God under
the high priest Abiathar and eaten the loaves of offering;
in fact, however, according to Samuel 21:1ff., it was not
under Abiathar, but under his father Ahimelech. In Matthew
27:9 the fulfillment of a prophecy of "Jeremiah" is reported,
which is in fact a prophecy of Zechariah (11:12ff.), and so
on. According to the Cardinal, on the question of inerrancy,
therefore, we should "speak sincerely, unambiguously, without artificiality and without fear." An unhistorical attitude in
these matters does not save the authority of the Bible, but
only renders exegesis incredible. Today a deviation from the
truth in historical and scientific questions in no way endan-
gers the authority of Scripture. In theological terms, this
would rather be evidence of divine condescension (*condescen-*

sio Dei). God takes the human author with all his weaknesses and failures and still achieves his aim of teaching man the "truth" of revelation. "Thus Cardinal König implicitly gives up that premise that comes from the aprioristic and unhistorical thinking that has dominated teaching on inerrancy since the age of the Fathers: if one admits that a sacred writer has made a mistake, then one is necessarily admitting that God has made a mistake."[55]

At the council—as in a good number of other important matters—only a compromise was reached. Apart from the constant curial pressure on the council and the theological commission, "this new view and motivation of the doctrine of inspiration and inerrancy . . . was unfortunately insufficiently prepared in theological writing, and therefore unfamiliar to the majority of the fathers."[56] The clear solution would have been to *drop* the expression "without any error" (*sine ullo errore*) and, instead, to formulate positively that the biblical books "teach the truth intact and unshakably (*integre et inconcusse*)." This was just what Cardinal König had suggested (a fact that should not be passed over in silence in the commentaries). But what happened? The commission adopted two positive words (*firmiter* and *fideliter*) and left in at the same time the "without error"! Only, instead of "without any error," they now simply said "without error"! This solution had a lot to do with policy and little with theology.

The ambiguous text (author's italics) now runs: "Therefore, since everything asserted by the inspired authors or sacred writers must be held to be asserted by the Holy Spirit, it follows that the books of Scripture must be acknowledged as teaching *firmly, faithfully, and without error* that truth which God wanted put into the sacred writings for the sake of our salvation" (art. 11). Thus, after a whole series of curial maneuvers and forcible interventions by Paul VI in the theological commission, the problem of inerrancy, together with that of inspiration and that of the determination of the relationship between Scripture and tradition, was left over to postconciliar theology. "The development of the text has shown us that 'monophysitism' in the understanding of inspiration and inerrancy is to be given up, as presented in the thesis of verbal inspiration, but also in the version of the teaching on inerrancy found in the form of 1962 (and in the scriptural encyclicals). So much can be said on the basis of Article 11. It remains for theology to examine inerrancy even more thoroughly on the basis of the new approach."[57]

We have no intention here of clarifying all questions arising in connection with the theory of inspiration. A "demythologization" and "depsychologization" (Grillmeier) of the doctrine of inspiration seem to be urgent anyway.[58] In this connection, two points of view seem to be of special importance for the problem field of infallibility; there really ought to be unanimity on these points among Catholic, Orthodox, and Protestant Christians:

a. God himself acts with us and on us through the human word of Scripture, so far as he thereby stirs us to faith and makes the word of man in proclamation the instrument of his Spirit: behind all mythological notions and often misleading concepts, this could be the real *concern* of the theory of inspiration.

b. The Scriptures are at the same time thoroughly human writings, by human authors with their gifts and limitations, possibilities of knowledge and of error, so that errors of the most varied kind cannot a priori be excluded: in all positive statements about the efficacy of the Spirit this could be the true *limit* of the theory of inspiration.

But how are the two to be combined? As in the Church composed of men, so too in the Bible composed by men, God gains his end, without doing any violence to men, *through* human weakness and historicity. Through all human fragility and the whole historical relativity and limitation of the biblical authors, who are often able to speak only stammeringly and with inadequate conceptual means, it happens that God's call as it finally sounded out in Jesus is truthfully heard, believed, and realized.

As it is false with regard to the Church to tie the operation of the Spirit of God (in the sense of an *assistentia*) to any particular definitions of a pope or council, so it is false with regard to Scripture to limit the operation of the Spirit of God (in the sense of an *inspiratio*) to any particular pieces of writing of an apostle or biblical author. No: the whole course of the origin, collecting, and transmission of the word, the whole process of accepting in faith and handing on the message in proclamation, is under the guidance and disposition of the Spirit. Not only the history of the recording, but the whole pre- and posthistory of Scripture altogether is in this sense "inspired" by the Spirit: not dictated by the Spirit, but Spirit-effected and Spirit-filled.

Hence it is not a question here of a miracle, as—for instance—with the Koran, which was directly revealed from heaven (by angels) to the prophet as a sacred book, free from error, with nothing but infallible propositions: a book that must then be accepted verbally and therefore may not even be interpreted or made the subject of a commentary. Before taking up the Bible, we do not have to wash our hands. Nowhere do the books of the New Testament claim to have fallen directly from heaven: rather do they often enough insist quite frankly on their human source (Luke 1:1–2 is particularly revealing about the origin of the gospels). And if the witnesses are already aware of being moved by the Holy Spirit, they do not present to their hearers or readers an act of inspiration as something that must be acknowledged, but simply presuppose that any reception or proclamation of the gospel occurs from the very beginning "through the Holy Spirit" (1 Pet. 1:12; cf. 1 Cor. 7:40).

The revelation of the Old and New Testaments therefore

cannot in any case be simply identified with Scripture. Scripture *is* not revelation: it attests revelation. Only indirectly and in a hidden way is God at work here. Only in faith is the gospel as proclaimed experienced as in truth God's own word to men (cf. 1 Thess. 2:13). Thus the human weakness, autonomy, and historicity of the biblical writers remain completely untouched. They are never at any time made inerrant, almost superhuman: which would mean that they were not really human at all, but tools, without will and without responsibility. The operation of the Spirit excludes neither defects nor faults, excludes neither concealment nor dilution, neither limitation nor error. The testimonies of the New Testament, however much they all proclaim the God who acts on us through Jesus Christ, are neither uniform nor of equal value; there are brighter and darker, more clear and less clear, stronger and weaker, more original and more derivative testimonies: all in all, supremely variable testimonies, which can diverge, contrast and—up to a point —contradict one another.

In Scripture, therefore, it is a question of something effected by the Spirit in unrestricted human historicity, which not only makes biblical criticism possible, but demands textual and literary criticism, historical and theological criticism. Serious biblical criticism can only help to prevent the glad tidings from remaining shut up in a book, and to secure at all times its constantly fresh and vital proclamation. This message can and should of course never simply be transmitted in the form linked with a particular time. As the first witnesses—and as such they remain fundamental—did not receive the gospel dictated in fixed formulas or as a rigid doctrine nor slavishly transmit it in this way, but rather took it up at their particular place with their special peculiarities and proclaimed it in their own interpretation and theology, so the modern heralds ought to transmit the gospel in a new form at their place, at their time, in their way.

Certainly Scripture is and remains the record, acknowl-

edged by the Church, of the original testimony. As such
it has a lasting normative authority and importance that
cannot be withdrawn by any later testimony; it remains
the standard by which all later ecclesiastical proclamation
and theology are constantly to be measured. But the freedom, variety, and diversity of the testimony at that time
justify the freedom, variety, and diversity of the testimony
today, which has its unity and simplicity in the message
of God's saving act to men in Jesus Christ.

What do we really believe in? What is the ground of
Christian faith? Is it the Church or the Bible? This is a
false alternative. It is neither the Church nor the Bible.
The ground of faith is God himself in Jesus Christ: it is
therefore this Jesus Christ himself, who is attested originally
in the Bible and constantly proclaimed anew by the Church.
As the Christian does not believe in the Church, neither
does he believe in the Bible: rather does he believe in
God in Jesus Christ. He believes, not in the gospels, but
in the gospel and in him who speaks in the gospel. Thus
Jesus Christ remains Lord also of Scripture: as source and
measure of its authority, he is himself the final authority
also for faith and theology. He himself constitutes the power
of the Spirit in Scripture, so that the latter, through all
biblical criticism, as the history of exegesis testifies, is constantly able to assert its validity afresh and to obtain recognition. I believe then, not—as it were—*first* in Scripture
or still less first in the book's inspired character and *then* in
the truth of the gospel, in Jesus Christ. But I believe in
the Jesus Christ originally attested in Scripture and, by thus
experiencing Scripture as gospel in faith, I become certain
of Scripture as Spirit-effected and Spirit-filled. It is in Scripture that my faith in Jesus Christ originates, since this is
the testimony of Jesus. But my faith is not based on Scripture: Jesus Christ, not the inspired book, is the ground of
faith.

To which therefore does infallibility belong: to the Church

or the Bible? As it does not belong to the Church, neither does it belong to the Bible, but in the strict sense to God alone and to his word: to his word that became flesh in Jesus Christ; to the gospel message as such, which is the unerringly faithful testimony of this salvation-event. Scripture—for Christians primarily the New Testament and, as its prehistory, also the Old—is the written record of this originally unerringly faithful testimony: in itself not infallible, but certainly through all human and all-too-human weaknesses, all imperfections and errors, announcing "the truth" of the gospel, which is Jesus Christ himself.

As errors of natural science and history in one of Shakespeare's historical plays in certain circumstances can even help us to perceive, not worse but better, through all its temporal relativity, the intention and statement of the drama, so too with errors of the Bible in natural science and history: God however, quite unlike Shakespeare, writes straight even on crooked lines. Taking the account of the work of the six days in Genesis 1 as verbally infallible, propositional truth frequently meant overlooking the great message of this first page of Scripture about the good God and his good world. Now that we have given over surrounding every sentence of this chapter with an apologetic that glosses over the difficulties, seeking a false concordance with the natural sciences and spiriting away scientific inaccuracies, we can see with quite new eyes what the text is really about. It is more or less the same with original sin in Genesis 3, with the conflicting traditions about Christ's resurrection, the mythical descriptions of the end of man's history.

Just as there is no a priori infallible teaching office, so there is no a priori infallible teaching book in Christendom. As the community of believers, the Church does not possess any propositional infallibility, but she certainly does have a fundamental indefectibility in the truth. Scripture as the record of the original faith in Christ does not possess any inherent propositional inerrancy. This does not mean at all

however any withdrawal of Scripture's unique precedence
in the faith of Christians. On the contrary: the influence
it exercises comes in fact from the one whom it announces.
By speaking of him it exercises a living *authority* in virtue
of its content (power of truth), by which faith is constantly
subdued afresh. Both to the person who proclaims the message and to the one who hears it, in decisive matters, it
is always freshly clear and accessible (*perspicuity*). It provokes assent and rejection and thus, in a completely un-
magical and elusive way becomes truly effective (*efficacy*).
And its unity in the context renders intelligible precisely that
salvific action of God which was shown in Jesus (*unity*).
Understood in this way, this testimony of the original Christian faith, basic for the whole of Christendom at all times,
seems to be not lesser, but greater.

In this comprehensive, but relative sense we can speak
of the *truth* of Scripture. Not in the sense of an a priori
inerrancy of its propositions, but certainly in the sense of
a testimony to Jesus Christ that, through all defects in detail, is sound and faithful as a whole. And even though
there are no propositions in the Bible which are a priori
free from error, nevertheless there are in fact *true* propositions
attesting the gospel. Truth of Scripture therefore means
more than simply truth as conformity of intellect with reality,
as it has been defined in the light of Greek philosophy
from the middle ages onward. The more recent doctrine
of inerrancy, just like Protestant orthodoxy's doctrine of inspiration, is a product of that rationalism which sought to
make a divine origin of Scripture clear and distinct, illuminating and evident, in its propositions: which, however,
sooner or later could not fail to be turned into a domination
of reason over Scripture.

Truth of Scripture means in the last resort truth beyond
all true propositions, as the term is used in the Old and
New Testament; "truth" (*emet, alétheia*) means, over and
above the truth of words and sentences, *fidelity,* constancy, re-

liability: the fidelity, that is, of the God of the Covenant to his word and to his promise. There is not a single passage of Scripture that speaks of Scripture as not containing any error. But every passage of Scripture witnesses in its narrower or wider context to this fidelity of God, who never lies, who remains faithful to himself and his word and thus also to men, who finally made his word definitively true by fulfilling all words of God in the one Word: in him who is "the Word" and "the Truth" (Jn. 1:1ff.; 14:6). In this sense Scripture, which is by no means free from error, attests unrestrictedly *the* truth as the perpetual fidelity of God, who cannot deceive or be deceived. In this sense Scripture attests the infallibility of God himself.

11. A teaching office?

The question is obvious. There is no theological substantiation for infallible propositions of Scripture, of councils, of bishops and pope: what then can be the position of a teaching office? On this broad and complex theme we shall offer here only some suggestions for discussion.

It is perhaps in order, toward the end of our study, to repeat clearly one basic point. This whole book is meant to be open to comment, open to discussion. It is to be understood as a question or, rather—the subtitle states this clearly—as an *inquiry*. An inquiry is admittedly a deliberate, urgent question, a question that calls for an answer. If anyone knows a better answer than the person raising the question, he will not keep it back. If he does not know any or—at least—any better answer, he will not dispute the question itself.

a. The expression *"teaching office"* is used a great deal in the Catholic Church today. On every possible occasion appeal is made to the "teaching office." But "the teaching office" is a concept that was introduced at a late stage in time and its content is far from clear.

(1) It is a *late* concept.[59] "The teaching office" in the

modern ecclesiastical sense—as the college of prelates who possess public teaching authority—presupposes the introduction of the distinction between the Church teaching (*Ecclesia docens*) and the Church taught (*Ecclesia discens*). This distinction too, often as it is used today, was introduced only in modern times: at the end of the seventeenth and the beginning of the eighteenth century, significantly in the context of the distinction we have already discussed between active infallibility (of the pope, or of the bishops) and passive infallibility (of the Church, or of the faithful). But it is only from the beginning of the nineteenth century that the distinction between Church teaching and Church taught began to occur more frequently. It soon became common however in theological discussion; and a particularly important witness for this distinction was one of the theological "fathers" of the definitions of the Immaculate Conception and of papal infallibility, the Roman Jesuit G. Perrone. The technical expression, "magisterium," in the modern ecclesiastical sense however turned up for the first time with unaccustomed frequency in the discussions and texts of Vatican I: "It has the meaning sometimes of teaching, sometimes of the teaching function and competence to teach, and sometimes finally—and this is new—of the body of prelates who possess public teaching authority: the magisterium."[60]

It is clear then that the term "teaching office" has no basis either in Scripture or in the older tradition but was introduced for the first time in connection with the doctrine of infallibility of Vatican I and the distinction between Church teaching and Church taught. We have already criticized this distinction because in this exclusive sense it is completely unscriptural.

(2) It is an unclear concept. The Latin, *magisterium,* has as Greek equivalents both *hegemonia* (leadership) and *didascalia* (teaching). The Latin *magisterium* also has frequently an affinity with *magistratus*. And this is echoed com-

pletely in the modern ecclesiastical sense of "magisterium": the bishops, who are the leaders of the Church, are therefore supposed to be also her teachers. At the same time, it is apparently presupposed that teaching takes place through an office or authority ("teaching office" as a kind of parallel to "home office" or "foreign office").

But this also raises the problem: is it then so obvious that there is in the Church a teaching office as an authority, that the bishops and particularly the Roman pontiff in personal union are leaders of the Church and teachers of the Church? It will not be disputed that the bishops—in this respect anyway not distinct in a dogmatic sense from the presbyters—are leaders of the Church. But it cannot be claimed with equal certainty that they are also teachers in the Church and still less—as textbook theology states—the sole authentic teachers in their dioceses and—together with the pope—in the Church as a whole. What we previously[61] pointed out in regard to the apostolic succession of the bishops and particularly of the Roman pontiff suggests some doubt about this. But let us examine the matter more closely.

b. The basic question arises here: who can and should really teach in the Church? It depends what is meant by "teach." If by "teaching" is meant the *proclaiming" of the message*, which is always fundamental for the Church in small things or in great, then it must be said that *every* member of the Church, *every* Christian, may and should proclaim.[62] To this extent there is no distinction between the Church teaching and the Church taught or hearing.

The explicit testimony of the word belongs to the universal priesthood (cf. Heb. 13:15). The proclamation of the word is not committed only to some few people, but to all: "But you are . . . a royal priesthood . . . to sing the praises of God who called you out of the darkness into his wonderful light" (1 Pet. 2:9; cf. 3:15). The saying about darkness and light recalls the logion of Jesus in Matthew 5:14, which likewise relates to all believers: "You are the light of the world." Therefore: "What I say to you in the dark, tell in the daylight; what you hear in whispers, proclaim from the housetops" (Mt. 10:27). The proclamation of the message is the primary commission of Jesus to all his disciples (Mk. 1:35-38; 16:15; Mt. 28:18-20; Acts 1:8; 1 Cor. 1:17). For that reason there is almost a superfluity of words in the New Testament—about thirty different terms, to describe preaching and proclamation: proclaim, call, preach, teach, declare, expound, speak, say, testify, persuade, confess, charge, exhort, reprove . . . The abundance of different forms of proclamation permits each and every one to make his particular contribution to it.

It is the word that creates and constantly assembles the Church anew by rousing faith and obedience; the word must constantly go out afresh from the believers (cf. Rom. 10; 14-17). Precisely as those who are "called" by the word (Rom. 1:6; 1 Cor. 1:24; Heb. 9:15), believers are to be concerned about the word. All are to hear the word of the apostles, bear witness in deed before the world and pray for the success of the proclamation of the word (cf. 2 Thess. 3:1); but not only this. They are also to proclaim the message themselves, even to take up the word at divine worship, according to the charism granted to each individual: "At all your meetings, let everyone be ready with a psalm or a sermon or a revelation, or ready to use his gift of tongues or to give an interpretation; but it must always be for the common good" (1 Cor. 14:26). And, by the very fact that all believers seize the opportunity and the right to the word in any sort of form, they bear all together a mighty witness of faith that can also conquer unbelievers (cf. 1 Cor. 14:24-25).

The Christian message could be spread so rapidly from the very beginning only because it continued to be proclaimed, not only by some few missionaries with a special mandate, but by all, each according to his gifts and opportunities: not only by apostles and evangelists, but also by merchants, soldiers, seamen . . . The Acts of the Apostles too attaches importance to the fact that "they were all filled with the Holy Spirit and began to proclaim the word of God boldly" (4:31; cf. 8:4; 11:19). And Paul frequently confirms this (cf. 1 Thess. 1:8; Phil. 1:12–18). When Paul commanded women in New Testament times to be silent in the congregation (1 Cor. 14:33–35; cf. 1 Tim. 2:12), this must be understood as a contemporary measure and not as a principle for all time. According to Hebrews 5:12, it should be possible to give all Christians not only milk but also solid food, if they are not to be initiated again in the grounds of Christian faith, but are themselves to be teachers.

If however for Paul in 1 Thessalonians 4:9 the faithful "have learnt from God," this idea is even more emphasized in the first Epistle of John. "Anointing" by the Holy Spirit gives true Christians complete knowledge in regard to everything that is decisive for salvation: "You have all received the knowledge" (1 Jn. 2:20; cf. Jn. 14:26; another reading is "you have received all knowledge"). And, since the Spirit remains in the faithful, they can be told: "you do not need anyone to teach you" (1 Jn. 2:27; cf. 2:21). This does not mean that the faithful have no need of the testimony transmitted by men (cf. Jn. 1:15; 2:17, 24; 3:11). But the Spirit is the power operating inwardly in them and independently of men, the power that gives them truly convincing instruction and final certainty.

Hence it is clear that only someone who is taught by God, by the Holy Spirit, over and above human testimony, can authoritatively transmit the message. But every Christian is such, according to the testimony of the New Testament. Every believer, having been taught by God, can and should in principle teach others; as recipient of the word of God, he can and should also be its herald in some way.

Every Christian is therefore called to the proclamation of the word in the widest sense, even though, because of the diversity of gifts, by no means everyone can or should do everything. Here, at least briefly, we must mention *lay preaching*, which—as we have just seen—was quite usual in the strongly charismatically influenced congregations of primitive Christendom, but which by the time of the second and particularly in the third century was pushed into the background in favor of preaching by officeholders.[63] But, in spite of all prohibitions, lay preaching continued to be practiced and tolerated, and—from the twelfth century—even expressly approved again for certain renewal movements. The Council of Trent, however, reserved preaching in the strict sense to the bishops and their assistants, and finally lay preaching came under a general prohibition in the Code of Canon Law of 1918.

For the present time a suitably adapted and ordered renewal of lay preaching is a pastoral necessity: not only justified and desirable in principle in the light of the New Testament, but also urgently required by the present situation of society (unchurching, a secular world come of age) and Church (lack of preachers on the one hand, maturity of the laity on the other). To this extent in fact Vatican II provided for the service of the word as revived by the council to be led by lay people. In this connection also the sociological and psychological inhibitions which would reserve preaching to males must be overcome. There are no dogmatic arguments against sermons by women (and radio and television should not be overlooked in this connection). There must be an end of the defamation of woman in the Church, in the Church's law and in the Church's worship.

This does not mean at all that any man or woman who wants to do so should go up into the pulpit on Sunday. Even though every Christian, who—as a Christian—is called to proclaim the word and to bear Christian witness, is also in principle empowered to preach, this does not mean that he is called now to preach in this particular congregation: according to Paul there is a diversity of gifts. And the very person who likes to "preach" at home and elsewhere will not always be suitable as the preacher in the pulpit. For preaching in the strict sense, the proclamation of the gospel to the assembled congregation, someone in the congregation must be called.

Bishops and parish priests may and should gratefully acknowledge the charisms of preaching granted also to lay people and let them come into effect. If public preaching by the laity takes place in this way, then it will not be without the Church's mandate or even perhaps specific training. In passing it should be observed that, even in Protestantism, lay preaching, like the universal priesthood, has remained largely a matter of theory, a program announcement (except for Methodism and the Free Churches). The Orthodox Churches too, in theory, permit laymen to preach in the church.

c. We must ask, however: even though *every* Christian is called to proclaim the word and is authorized at least in principle to preach, is he thereby called also to teaching in the proper, technical sense of being a teacher in the Church? Is the *Church leader* automatically also *Church teacher?*

It is essential for any church order inspired by the New Testament to exhibit, not a uniform, single-shaped ecclesiastical "hierarchy" ("sacred dominion," an expression first introduced by the person known as Dionysius the Areopagite in the fifth or sixth century), but a multiform, many-shaped ecclesiastical "diakonia" ("ministry" in the completely ordinary sense of "ministering to"): a "multiplicity of the Church in the multiplicity of disciples, witnesses and ministers."[64] The position of the "pastors" or *Church leaders*—today, normally, bishops and presbyters—in such a biblical-pluralistic view is in no way impaired but rather fortified.

Certainly it cannot be proved either historically or theologically (as we have previously pointed out) that the bishops in the often claimed direct and exclusive sense are the successors of the apostles (and still less of the college of the

twelve): the modern order of three offices—bishops, presbyters, and deacons—is a later historical development, although
quite appropriate in itself.[65] Apostolic succession is primarily
an affair of the *Ecclesia apostolica* as a whole, in as much as
every Christian should strive for agreement with the fundamental apostolic testimony (Scripture, succession in the
apostolic faith and confession) and for the connection with
the apostolic ministry (missionary advance into the world
and building up of the community, succession in the apostolic
ministry and life). But, within the apostolic succession of
the Church as a whole, there is a particular apostolic succession of Church leaders or pastors, in as much as they
carry on the special apostolic function of Church founding
or Church leadership, without themselves being apostles. As
such they are not indeed a ruling class with sole power to
command, in a way that would require blind obedience. But,
in the light of their special ministry, they have also special
authority and—if they fulfill their ministry in the spirit of the
gospel—they may count on co-operation and subordination.

It would certainly be an unbiblical clericalization of the
Church if we were to deduce the authority of the community,
of the universal priesthood, simply from the ministry of
leadership. On the other hand, it would be an equally unbiblical secularization of the Church if the authority of the
ministry of leadership were to be deduced simply from the
authority of the community, of the universal priesthood. All
authority in the Church, according to the New Testament,
comes from the Lord of the Church by virtue of the Spirit.
Leaders and community therefore must be seen in their
solidarity and in their distinction. The general empowering
of each and every individual Christian to proclaim the word
and participate in the sacraments is one thing; quite another
is the special authority of individuals who are called—normally by imposition of hands or ordination—to public ministry
to the community as such: in the proclamation of the word,

the administration of the sacraments, the manifold care for the members of the community.

For all the necessary and frankly expressed criticism of the present Church leadership in the Catholic Church, nothing said here is opposed to a Church leadership as such. We do not need *no* Church-leadership, we need a leadership according to the gospel; we do not need less authority but qualified authority: authority based on service and able to subordinate itself to the subordinate, if the latter has the gospel and reason on his side. The ministers, bishops, and presbyters, exist in fact for the Church, not the Church for them. Bishops and priests at their election and in their whole conduct in office should be sustained and also constantly tested by their community. For all their (relative) autonomy, the leaders should respect the right of the community to have a say in community matters and foster the active cooperation of all in every way.

A Church leadership is truly according to the gospel only when it does not "rule" with spiritual power and veiled force, by forcing laws on people and using authoritarian methods, but leads the Church and the Churches with the helping, encouraging, exhorting, and consoling word of the gospel. This holds for all grades of the Church leadership and particularly for the bishops. The first (and chronologically prior) task of the bishops cannot be going around confirming, blessing bells, attending spiritual-secular functions of all kinds: these are all things that others can do or are entirely superfluous. The primary task of the bishop ought to be the proclamation of the gospel (which cannot be accomplished by pastoral letters and confirmation addresses) and in practice this necessitates the visitation of the parishes and their priests to help and strengthen them.

A teaching office, then, of the bishops (and the pope)? If this means the proclamation of the gospel (in as many forms as possible), there is nothing to be said against it, but rather everything to be said in its favor. If only it would happen! Then the Church would have that spiritual guidance, that true leadership, which she so sorely needs. Admittedly, it would then be better to speak not of a "teaching office," but of an "office of leadership" or—better—"ministry of leadership," or simply in brief of "Church-leadership."

If however by "teaching office" of the bishops (and the pope) is meant, not the proclamation of the gospel, but the official regulation of all teaching, so that the Church leaders would be the sole authority for teaching and thus the Church leaders would also be the Church teachers, then the objection must be raised that such a limiting, canalizing, and monopolizing of the charisms in a hierocracy of pastors clearly contradicts the New Testament message and the New Testament Church. No one has the right to imagine himself alone as originally in possession of the Spirit and to deny possession to the others. "Are all of them teachers?" (1 Cor. 12:29). It means giving to ministry an absolute value in an unbiblical way when a leader considers himself simultaneously as apostle, prophet, and teacher, and so wants to be everything in one, even if he should invoke in his favor the triple office of Christ (king, prophet, and priest). The New Testament does not know of any one-man system. Each one has *his* charism. The one has this gift, the other that (cf. 1 Cor. 7:7, 17). No one, not even a bishop, not even a pope—according to Paul—can be everything: "Are all of them apostles, or all of them prophets, or all of them teachers?" (1 Cor. 12:29).

d. The "teachers" (*didascaloi, doctores*), for Paul, form the third group—after the apostles and prophets—of those who exercise public charismatic functions in the congregation, continuously and regularly. While the apostles are the original witnesses and original messengers of the living Lord, so the prophets—named together with the apostles in Ephesians 2:20 as foundation of the Church—are those in whom the Spirit directly speaks and who, in a particular situation in the Church, aware of their vocation and responsibility, light the way in the present and future. But the teachers are those who may take endless pains to find the tradition, the teaching and the correct interpretation of the original Christian message. Both—prophets and teachers— speak in the light of the original apostolic testimony for the present and future of the community; but, while the prophet makes his announcement in a more intuitive fashion, the teacher will reflect and develop the message in a more theological and systematic way.

In this context it is not so important to analyze the original function of the teachers—especially in regard to the interpretation of the Old Testament, the articles of faith and the directives of the early Church. It is more important, if we rightly speak of a succession of the apostles in the different pastoral ministries, to speak with the same right of a succession of the prophets and teachers. In postapostolic times too the teachers proved to be indispensable, even though their position and status—like those of the pastors—had been greatly transformed. According to the Didache, it was only when there were not sufficient prophets and teachers in a congregation that bishops and deacons were to be chosen, who "minister unto you the ministry [leitourgia, which meant in fact the Eucharist] of the prophets and teachers" (15:1). "In the light of Scripture then it might be asked whether there has not been an unbiblical shifting of structures in a Church which seems to attach supreme value to a succession of bishops, but does not speak of the successors of the charismatic teachers or of a proper, permanent class of such teachers."[66]

Here the author can only say what he has already formulated elsewhere[67] in a systematic exposition. What becomes of a Church in which the teachers are silent? The question is easier to understand if, in accordance with present-day usage, we speak of theologians instead of teachers. What becomes of a Church where no one any longer makes an effort at scholarly reflection on the original message and its interpretation or tries to find the genuine tradition, to translate the message of that time in terms of the present? A Church in which the theologians have to be silent will become an untruthful Church. Doctrine may perhaps be very correct, more or less unchanged, very securely transmitted; faith may seem to exist without doubts and teaching be passed on without problems; but very often precisely the decisive questions of human beings are evaded. No one notices how far a theological system wholly belonging to a particular time is dominant, how far received opinions and traditional conceptual shells are handed down as truth and how remote are doctrine and life from the original message.

The leaders, however, who do not want to hear the theologians in the Church, because they have little interest or time for solid theology, because—perhaps through fear—they do not want to be disturbed in their faith or because they naïvely imagine that they already know all the essentials: these leaders in their ignorance will seek to impose their personal teaching as the teaching of the Church so much the more securely, will so much more readily confuse the ideas they have acquired with the genuine tradition, will close their minds so much the more to instruction and—being themselves incompetent—will want to be judges over the competent. They will then claim, although the gifts are diverse, to be not only successors of the apostles, but also successors of the teachers. There *can* be pastors who are also teachers, but this—according to Paul—is not the rule.

How fruitful it can be however for them and for the Church if these leaders listen—as the best of them have always done—to the theologians, who want to help the Church by their critical examination of current teaching and by reflection on the original message; who in the last resort exercise their theological talent, not for their own sake, but for the sake of human beings, of the Church, of the world; who, by their critical examination of the Church's proclamation in the light of the gospel, really do not want to destroy but to build up, to stimulate and lead the way to better proclaiming and action. By raising the question of truth, theology does an immense service for those responsible for preaching, instruction and pastoral care. Theology helps them and the Church to distinguish, in the light of its origins, the great, genuine, abiding tradition from all that has been handed down with it, from all the false and distorted petty traditions in doctrine and life; in order to perceive again and continue to proclaim the message in all its purity. In the light of this message, continually thought out afresh with all the resources of scholarship and research, theology is able to find again the Church's mislaid keys and to reopen locks grown rusty in the course of centuries, in order in this way to lay open to her the way to renewal, to a teaching more faithful to the gospel. What would the Church be without Origen, without Augustine, Thomas Aquinas, or even without Luther and Calvin, or moreover without the many—great and small—teachers of the Church? The Church was never without teachers. Paul was certain that every community had its teachers. And if in the Church we are willing to listen to the teachers of the Church, then they will also speak. Here too we should not quench the Spirit, but let him speak.

We are talking about true prophets and good teachers. There are also false prophets and bad teachers, there is deceptive prophecy and sterile theology. Prophets and teachers, like leaders, must be tested by the whole community as to whether they really are what they are supposed to be: a ministry unpretentious and yet courageous, modest and yet resolute, bound and yet free, which can assist the Church constantly to gain a new alertness, new readiness and new vitality. Because of the ministry of prophets and teachers, leaders are not left alone in their heavy and responsible pastoral task, which neither prophets nor teachers can take from them. They then find support in the reciprocal ministry.

e. Pastors and teachers in the Church, leaders and theologians, have their own charism, each his own vocation, each his own function. The ministry of leadership and the ministry of teaching must be seen in this functionality, not as hypos-

tatized and therefore also in fact largely bureaucratic-anony-
mous "office" (even *Sanctum Officium Sanctissimae In-
quisitionis*), primarily interested in maintaining its own authority and power, but as "ministries," diverse and at the
same time dependent on one another, working in the same
field and with the same purpose, carried out by believers
endowed with diverse gifts.

Certainly some popes in recent times—not John XXIII—
have continually attempted absolutely and exclusively to reserve to themselves (and, when it suited them, also to the
bishops) the "authentic" explanation of the "deposit of
faith."[68] We may leave aside here the examples quoted,
which provide sufficient evidence of the way in which the
teaching authority, while declaring itself to be juridically
authentic, has proved in all too many cases to be unauthentic.
From all that has had to be said in this book, from beginning
to end, it is clear that the Holy Spirit is not given only to
pope and bishops in authentic fashion for the salvation of
the Church, that the Church is by no means identical with
the Church's leaders, that the truth of the Christian faith is
not "deposited" in Roman offices and episcopal chancelleries,
that the "authentic" proclamation and exposition of the Christian message is not "reserved" to anyone. The Spirit of God
breathes where he will: he is greater than the Church and the
Church is greater than her leadership.

In the light of the original Christian message, but also in
the light of the oldest and best tradition of the Catholic
Church, which in the middle ages still left the "teaching
office" to the theologians (practically, if not always fortunately, to the Sorbonne), there can be no question of the
Church leadership (under the title of "teaching office"), instead of the gospel, being the formal and material norm for
the truth of theology and theologians; or of dominion over
theology and theologians (in fact, in the sense of juridical
supervision and of an inquisition contemptuous of human
rights) belonging, not to the Lord of the Church, but to the

Church leaders. There can be no question of theologians being able to practice theology only as delegates of the Church leaders, which would necessarily lead—as experience teaches—to a legalizing of teaching at the cost of liberty and reducing theology to textbook level at the expense of scholarship. There can therefore also be no question of theology in the Church being content with a privacy congenial to the Church leadership and leaving to the latter the field of publicity and official action; or still less—as, for example, Pius IX wanted it—of regarding its "most noble task" as that of substantiating from the sources what has been defined by the "teaching office."

After so many unhappy experiences right up to the most recent times, there can be no more evasion on this point if things are to improve. We cannot but expressly support Max Seckler when he so clearly exposes the dilemma involved in the Roman conception—which he closely analyzes—of theological scholarship and "teaching office":

On the one side an ecclesiastical office with absolute autonomy, sovereignty and self-sufficiency, which in virtue of these qualities regards itself at the same time as "office for teaching" and wants to have immediacy to God, to the Spirit, to the truth. On the other side the picture of theology as an ecclesiastical science, which is a creature of the hierarchy, bound in conscience, regulated in its thinking, supervised in the lecture-hall, submitted to terminological rules, exposed to the threat of censures of every kind, and earning love and respect only as a theology submitting to the will of the sovereign, "in whom it lives, moves and is." Are these the structures willed by God?

The objection may be raised that things are not all that bad, that theologians are not so nervous and the dangers not so great. This is certainly true. The reality is largely different. But is not this precisely the dilemma, that what should be commended after everything else—

the *clementia Caesaris* on the one hand and the theologians' critical, scientific conscience in quest of truth on the other —appears, so to speak, in the pale light of the abnormal?

For the sake of the service that it has to perform in the Church and for the Church, theology will have to come to grips with this pattern of things. In the first place the *degree of the theological binding force* of this imposing construction must be clarified by historical, canonistic and systematic investigations. After the events connected with *Humanae Vitae*, but not merely for that reason, there is a special urgency about these tasks.[69]

We hope that in this book we have made a critical and constructive contribution to the clarification of this question. But a clarification in theory is only one side of the problematic as it emerges from the now famous declaration on the freedom of theology, addressed to the Roman authorities, at first by forty and then by 1360 professors of theology from the whole world. They introduced their concrete demands for the reform of the Roman supervision of doctrine and of the practice of supervision in these words:

> In complete, genuine and unambiguous loyalty to the Catholic Church, the undersigned theologians feel compelled in real and sober earnest to point out publicly: the freedom of theologians and theology in the service of the Church, regained by Vatican II, must not now be jeopardized again. This freedom is one of the fruits and exigencies of the liberating and redeeming message of Jesus himself, and remains a fundamental and essential aspect of the freedom of the sons of God in the Church, as preached and defended by Paul. All the teachers in the Church must therefore preach and proclaim the word, pressing it home on all occasions, convenient or inconvenient, welcome or unwelcome.[70]

There is certainly no need of any long explanation of the fact that, in all that was said here about theology and theologians, in the Catholic Church today it is a question not only of clerical, but also of lay theologians. The Church leadership too recognizes today, even though still with numerous reservations (particularly in regard to theological colleges), the theology of lay people—men and women. Here we need only point to the fact[71] that the first great Christian theologians were mostly laymen: Justin, Tertullian, Clement of Alexandria, Origen, and later many more. A large number of theologians at least began their theological work as laymen (and up to a point were pressed against their will into ordination): Cyprian, Basil, Gregory of Nazianzen, Jerome, Augustine, Paulinus of Nola, Diodorus of Tarsus. Lay theologians never wholly died out in the Church. But it is only in the present century, particularly in the context of the Second Vatican Council, that lay theology again became a widespread phenomenon, with the result that the medieval clerical monopoly of education in this field may now be regarded as obsolete. The essentially obvious result of this development ought to be open access in principle to all teaching positions in theological faculties for lay theologians— men and women—equipped with the appropriate academic qualifications. In regard to theology also certainly not everyone should think that he can do everything in the Church at all times. No one is a theologian at birth, but only becomes one through serious training. But here too the charisms that are bestowed—and lay theology in our time is one of the most gratifying effects of the Church's renewal—must be recognized and brought into service.

f. The negative criticism of the unhappy relationship between the ministry of leadership and the ministry of teaching has been expressed so clearly only in order to clear the way for positive co-operation. In the Catholic Church particularly today everything depends on the *trustful co-operation* discussed above. And should it really be so difficult?

Certainly, leaders and teachers in the Church have their

special task: bishops and priests leadership, theologians scholarship. But the two are not on different fronts: here too a class-war ideology would be quite out of place. Both have one and the same origin: the gospel of Jesus Christ, which they want to bring home to men. Through the word the leaders should effectively guide the Church: leadership by proclamation. To the word the theologians should devote scholarly reflection: scholarship by investigation. The leaders should not want to act as theologians, by getting mixed up in the complex problems of theological scholarship. But the theologians should not want to play at being bishops, by themselves deciding the difficult problems of Church leadership. Both sides have every reason to hear, to inform, to criticize, to inspire one another. For, in the last resort, both not only come from one and the same gospel and are under one and the same Lord, but both go out also to the very same human beings: human beings in all their need and hope, the numerous "poor devils" of all kinds in the whole world (they are the "poor" of the New Testament). For them Church leaders and Church teachers should be available: the former by spiritual guidance, the latter by spiritual learning; both in the same Spirit. It will be a help to the theorist if he knows the cares and desires of the practical man; it will be a help to the practical man if he can make fruitful the insight and foresight of the theorist. Discussion is nowhere more necessary in the Church than it is here.

It is a question of human beings, for whose sake exist the sabbath, all prohibitions and commandments, institutions and constitutions, all power of leadership and scholarship. It is a question of human beings when in case of need the one takes over the functions of the other: when Church leaders have to talk and act for the theologians or theologians for the Church leaders.

There is an emergency of *theology:* when the theologians

no longer cope with their problems, when—because of an unholy theological muddle and unholy theological scatter-brains—the proclamation of the gospel is scarcely assured any longer, when heresy shakes the Church to her foundations and perhaps is even identified with a political system, when therefore it is a question of the existence or non-existence of the Church of the gospel. Then there exists the *status confessionis* and the Church leaders cannot be content to look on. Then—certainly in co-operation with all theologians of good will—they will come together and, trusting in God's Spirit, say clearly what is the Christian faith and what is not. So it happened repeatedly in the past, so it can also be in the future: in *extremis* and only then, not endless discussions, but resolute, albeit unpretentious definition in the service of faith and the faithful; definition—as we have explained at length—binding on the Church *and* provisional in relation to the situation, and with clear awareness that no one is infallible except God himself.

But there is also an emergency of Church leadership: when Church leaders no longer cope with their problems, when—through nervousness or indolence, ignorance or arro-gance—they keep their eyes closed to the crushing problems of human beings, when they do not want to see or cannot see, when they endanger the unity of the Church through passivity or aggressiveness, when they obstruct renewal and want to restore what is past, when the gospel and human beings are simultaneously betrayed or forgotten, when there-fore it is a question of the existence or non-existence of the Church of the gospel. Then there exists the *status confessionis* for the theologian, then he may not be silent or retire to his academic ivory tower. Then he must speak distinctly and clearly, welcome or unwelcome, without re-spect of persons no matter how highly placed. Then he must bear witness for the sake of the gospel and for the sake of human beings; he must present the truth and not be frightened even to give concrete, practical directives. All this he must do in modesty and objectivity, being clearly aware that no one is infallible except God himself.

Thus we have reached the close of our reflections and what was said in the preface may be taken up again in the light of a deeper understanding.

OUTLOOK

THE POPE AS HE MIGHT BE

To the "look back in anxiety" as descriptive of the preface there may be added at the end a "look forward in hope."

Among Church leaders, the Primate of Belgium, Cardinal Léon-Joseph Suenens, more than any other, deserves the credit for having opened up such a prospect in the increasing darkness of postconciliar times: he it is who gave shape and form to this new hope particularly by his now famous, courageous, and forthright interview.[1] This interview found a gratifyingly positive echo, and this—strikingly enough—inside and outside the Church, in the Catholic Church not only of Europe and America, but also of the East. The opposition—which was to be expected—was essentially confined to certain curial reactions and small, notably traditionalistic circles. Otherwise it was everywhere understood that a man had here committed himself for the Church, demanding reforms long overdue and vitally necessary for the Catholic Church today. There is no need to stress the fact that the Belgian Primate sought publicity only when he had to recognize that nothing was to be attained in any other way.

There is no need to defend Cardinal Suenens' complete Catholic orthodoxy, both in theory and practice. By committing himself in this way, he spoke for so many bishops who today—to the detriment of their authority and that of the Church—present a picture of a "silent Church," without leadership, and he made an effective stand against that crisis of confidence which is making itself felt with increasingly disturbing effects on all sides—not only between pope and Church, but also between bishops and Church—and which provides an atmosphere favorable both to the defeatism of those who want reform and to the rise of extremist, fanatical movements to right and left. It is particularly gratifying to note that, even after various negative Roman reactions, Cardinal Suenens did not adopt the attitude otherwise familiar in ecclesiastical circles and water down his criticism by talking about "misunderstandings," but upheld and confirmed his criticism in every detail. Staying power such as this—requiring good nerves, strong faith and a certain sense of humor—is too rare in the upper ranks of the Church today not to be given public recognition.

Cardinal Suenens has done a great service to the Pope, whose sincerity and good will he has constantly and rightly acknowledged. He is a better apologist of the Petrine ministry in the Church than all those traditionalists who defend a past form of this Petrine ministry or—it might be said—their own positions of power within the Roman system. Who did the pope a greater service at the time of the Reformation: those who demanded a serious reform of the papacy and the discarding of its medieval trappings or those who appealed to Matthew 16:18 and to canon law in order to defend the medieval status quo? Who gave better advice to the pope in the nineteenth century: those who demanded a voluntary renunciation of the papal states and on that account were threatened with excommunication or those who again appealed to Matthew 16:18 and canon law to defend an historical state of affairs that was already out of date, although the fact had not then been noticed in Rome? And who supports the pope better today in what is certainly not an easy task: those who demand a radical reform of the papacy according to the gospel of Jesus Christ or those who want to lead Church and pope back again from

Vatican II to Vatican I, or at least think that the reform
of the papacy can be settled by some "progressive" nominations of cardinals (nominations which have hitherto at
most served merely as liberal shop-window dressing for
an unchanged system and, for the rest, were amply com-
pensated by less "progressive" nominations) and with the
setting up of a commission of theologians (which can be
largely manipulated by the still traditionalistic "Congregation
for the Doctrine of the Faith" and has still to prove its
efficiency)?

The Pope and the few even in the Curia who are real
friends of reform think that they must be given time. But
the present situation is one that does not permit any thinking
in centuries or even thinking in decades. So many inside
and outside our Church think that we have already been
waiting for all too many centuries. This does not mean
that there will be a formal schism; but as a result of
lack of confidence in higher Church leadership, it could
be—though this must be avoided at all costs—that clergy
and people will take less and less notice of the exhortations
and warnings, in the last resort even of the encyclicals
and decrees of the higher Church leaders. The encyclical
Humanae Vitae, analyzed at the beginning of this book, is
only one example of how the Pope in this situation—which
could be decisively changed only from Rome—no longer
has a following in the widest circles of the Church: not
only among the laity, also among the clergy; and not only
among the "lower" and younger clergy, but also among the
bishops.

To return to the Suenens interview, the hopeful and
important thing about it is this: *the picture of a pope as
he might be* has been presented to us, with strict objectivity,
not by a theologian, but by a leading bishop of our Church.
We need only assemble the features from the interview and
the picture becomes completely clear. And why should it not
be appropriate, at the end of this book, to describe such a

picture—so to speak—as a future prospect? It is not pure prognosis of the future, since John XXIII after Pius XII—more spontaneously than as the result of a deliberate plan, more symbolically than systematically—provided at least a sketch to prove that it is not illusory to think that the pope *could* be different. What then might the pope be like?

Such a pope would have a genuinely evangelical and not a juridical-formalistic and static-bureaucratic view of the Church. He would see the mystery of the Church in the light of the gospel, of the New Testament: not as a centralized administrative unit, in which the bishops are merely the pope's delegates and executive organs, but as one Church realized authentically in the local Churches (of the individual parishes, towns, dioceses, countries), everywhere forming one community as the one Church of God and thus linked with the Church of Rome as with the center of their unity.

This pope would not regard the decentralization of power as a dangerous prelude to a possible schism. He would not prevent, but would foster legitimate diversity: diversity in the fields of spirituality, liturgy, theology, canon law and pastoral ministry. His aim would be, not to concentrate power permanently at the center, but unpretentiously to serve the local churches in their rich diversity in the one Church; not to suppress differences of opinion among theologians with inquisitorial sanctions from past centuries, but to encourage them in their freedom and their service to the Church; not jealously to hold on to powers and prerogatives or to exercise authority in the spirit of the old order, but to make authority felt as service in the spirit of the New Testament and in response to the needs of the present time: fraternal partnership and co-operation, dialogue, consultation, and collaboration, especially with bishops and theologians of the whole Church, opportunity for those concerned to take part in the process of making decisions, and full scope for the exercise of co-responsibility.

This pope would therefore regard his function as a function of the Church: a pope not *above* or *outside* the Church, but *in* the Church, *with* the Church, *for* the Church. No extrinsicism, isolationism or triumphalism, and therefore not a solitary pope, but one who is constantly seeking and realizing anew his unity with the Church. For all important documents and enterprises he would make sure of the co-operation of the episcopates, of the most capable theologians and laymen, and never subsequently disavow them. If he could and certainly should sometimes act "alone," this could never mean "apart" and "separated" from the Church and her episcopal college, but in spiritual communion and unbroken solidarity with the Church as a whole. He would never regard the promise assured to Peter as personal inspiration, but as special assistance in discussion and co-operation with the Church, to which as a whole the Spirit is promised.

Such a pope would thus cut down the administrative machinery of the Curia and restrain its aspirations to hegemony. He would liberate the center from unnecessary bureaucratic and administrative unwieldiness and would take steps toward a genuine internationalization and a far-reaching reform with the help of theologians and experts in sociology, in management, with the assistance of international organizations, and so on. He would want both a thorough overhauling of the system of Roman nuncios and a system of nomination to the Curia freed from any suspicion of royal prerogative, based on objective and public criteria. He would organize the teamwork in accordance with the principle of subsidiarity and arrange differently or better the system of *ad limina* visits, of bishops' quinquennial reports and so many other things.

This pope then would not be against justice, but against juridicism; not against law, but against legalism; not against order, but against immobility; not against authority, but against authoritarianism; not against unity, but against uniformity. He would be a man elected, not by a college of cardinals under the domination of a particular national group, but by a representative body of the whole Church, and elected not because of his nationality but quite simply because of his suitability. He would be a man renouncing power arising from secondary and inessential titles (Metropolitan of the Roman ecclesiastical province, Primate of Italy, Patriarch of the West, Head of the Vatican State) and concentrating on his pastoral function in the whole Church and on pastoral work in his own diocese of Rome, the radiance of which ought to draw the attention of the whole world.

The pope might thus take a new view of his function in the Church and society of today. Together with the bishops, he would provide a new form of service to the ecclesiastical community and its unity; he would be able to stimulate the missionary work of the Church in the world and to continue his efforts for peace, disarmament, and the social betterment of peoples and races, with quite a new credibility. In the Christian oikumene and far beyond it, he could thus constantly make the voice of the Good Shepherd heard in his life and work. He would be inspiriter in the spirit of the gospel and a leader in the postconciliar renewal and Rome would become a place of encounter, of dialogue and of honest and friendly co-operation.

This is a kind of "model pope," after the pattern suggested by Cardinal Suenens: the portrait of a pope as he might be. It is certainly not in opposition to Vatican II. If it should be opposed to Vatican I, then Vatican I—and this was not least the intention of Vatican II—would have to be supplemented and corrected in the light of the gospel. The juridical categories of Vatican I, in any case, are not adequate to describe how a Petrine ministry might be understood in the light of Scripture itself: whatever may be the force of the exegetical and historical arguments for the succession of the Roman pontiffs from Peter—which for some is an utterly secondary question—we have to try to appreciate the meaning of a *ministry to the whole Church*, a *primacy of service* in the full biblical sense.

A primacy of service would be more than a "primacy of honor": such a primacy is not within the gift of the Church of service nor—as a complete passive reality—can it be of help to anybody. A primacy of service would also be more than a "primacy of jurisdiction": as pure authority and power this would be a basic misunderstanding; understood literally, it passes over in silence the very thing that is decisive, namely, service. A Petrine ministry in the biblical sense can only be a *pastoral primacy:* a pastoral ministry to the whole Church. As such, apart from all questions of succession, it is objectively covered by the New Testament. As such it could be of great value today for Christendom as a whole. And once again: John XXIII showed practically, at least in outline and with clear indications of where the emphasis should lie, that such a pope would be possible.

A program of this kind is one for the long term. Its realization requires patience and undaunted dedication. There can be no doubt that it will be realized in one form or another. The only question is whether this will not once again be too late and therefore with too heavy losses.

INSTEAD OF AN EPILOGUE

*So shall we walk together in charity to him of whom
it is said: "Seek his face at all times." I would like to
join with all my readers in a pledge before God to do
this, in all my books . . .*

*If any reader then says to himself, "This is badly expressed,
I can't understand it," it is my expression he is criticizing,
not my faith; and it may well be that the meaning could
have been made clearer. But what writer succeeds in making
himself understood all the time? If however readers who
feel like this can find others more expert in such matters,
by all means let them put my book down and even throw it
away and study the works which they find more intelligible.
Still they should not expect me to keep quiet because my
writings are not as intelligible as they find the others to be.*

*Books usually have only a limited circulation and so are
not always available to everybody. It may happen then that
the simpler books never find their way into some people's
hands and they may have to be content with mine. The
multiplication of books by different writers and in different
styles, about the same faith and the same problems, is not
a bad thing. It means that most people can find books to suit
their varying tastes.*

*As for those who complain that my books are obscure,
without ever having made a serious attempt to master such
topics, instead of viciously attacking me and telling me to
stop writing, let them give themselves to prayer and study.*

*And if anyone says, "I understand your meaning well
enough, but it's not true," I ask him to state his own position*

and refute mine. If he does this sincerely and without malice and will inform me of his views (if I am still alive, that is), then I shall count my efforts well rewarded. If he cannot let me know personally, then I would be delighted if others profit from his views.

If I may speak for myself, I meditate on the law of the Lord, if not all day and night, at least whenever I have a moment to spare; and I write my thoughts down, in case I should forget them. I hope God in his mercy will help me never to turn my back on teachings which I believe to be true. But, if any of my convictions are wrong, he himself will make it plain to me, either by secret warning and inspiration or by his own clear words or by the conversation of my brethren. This is my prayer and this is the undertaking which I commit into the hands of him who will not fail to protect what he entrusted to me and to make good his promises.

Augustine, *De Trinitate* I, iii, 5.

NOTES FOR PREFACE

1. "Konzil—Ende oder Anfang?" in *Frankfurter Allgemeine Zeitung,* 18.11.1964; *Tübinger Forschungen* 1964, No. 19; *Civitas* 4 (1965), pp. 188–99; KNA (Special edition on the Second Vatican Council), September 8, 1965. "The Council—End or Beginning?" in *The Commonweal* 81 (1965), pp. 631–37. "Het Concilie: Einde of Begin?" in *Elseviers Weekblad,* February 6, 1965. "Poczatek czy koniec Soboru" in *Zycie i Mysl,* Warsaw, 1 (1965), pp. 104–13.

2. Cf. "Was hat das Konzil erreicht?" in *Vaterland,* December 17/18, 1965; *Tübinger Forschungen* 1966, No. 27; *Universitas* 21 (1966), pp. 171–86; *Deutsche Tagespost,* April 8/9, 1966. "The Reform of the Roman Church" in *The Sunday Times,* London, December 12, 1965. "What has the Council done?" in *The Commonweal* 83 (1966), pp. 461–68. "Sobór Jest Poczatkiem" in *Tygodnik Powszechny,* Cracow, February 13, 1966. "Co Sabor osiagnal?" in *Kultura,* Paris (1966), pp. 69–82. In a different form, "Die 16 neuen Pfeiler von St. Peter" in *Epoca* (1966), pp. 12–19; *Neue Bildpost* 1966, Nos. 3–8. Finally, as separate print, "Konzilsergebnis," *Dokumente der Erneuerung,* Kevelaer, 1966.

3. Cf. Hans Küng, *Truthfulness: the future of the Church,* London, New York and Sydney, 1968, B6: "The beginning of a change."

4. Cf. J. Neumann, "Zur Problematik lehramtlicher Beanstandungsverfahren" in *Tübinger Theologische Quartalschrift* 149 (1969), pp. 259–81.

5. Full text in *Herderkorrespondenz* 24 (1970), pp. 230–34.

NOTES FOR CHAPTER I

1. Karl Rahner, "Zur Enzyklika 'Humanae Vitae,'" in *Stimmen der Zeit* 93 (1968), p. 204. A summary of this article appeared in *The Tablet,* London, September 14, 1968.

2. J. Neumann in a radio interview published in *Die Enzyklika in der Diskussion. Eine orientierende Dokumentation zu "Humanae Vitae"* (edited by F. Böckle and C. Holenstein, Zürich-Einsiedeln-Cologne, 1968), p. 47. This enlightening miscellany will be quoted henceforward as *Documentation.*

3. *Ibid.,* pp. 46f.

4. W. Schaab in *Die Zeit* No. 32, 1968 (*Documentation,* pp. 44f.).

5. *Osservatore Romano* June 24, 1964.

6. *Osservatore Romano* October 30, 1966.

7. September 8, 1968 in *Documentation,* p. 38.

8. Cf. also Charles Davis, *A Question of Conscience,* London, 1967, pp. 93f.; New York, 1967.

9. *Osservatore Romano* August 1, 1968. English in *Herder Correspondence,* November 1968 (Vol. 5 No. 11), p. 336.

10. *Corriere della Sera,* October 3, 1965.

11. J.-M. Paupert in *Le Monde* August 11/12, 1968.
12. A. Müller in *Neue Zürcher Nachrichten* August 6, 1968 (*Documentation*, p. 79).
13. H. Heibling in *Neue Zürcher Zeitung* July 30, 1968 (*Documentation*, p. 81).
14. On what follows cf. Hans Küng, *Structures of the Church*, New York, 1964, London, 1965, pp. 341f.
15. *Corporis Juris Canonici*, ed. A. Friedberg, Leipzig, 1881, II, 287; cf. II, 908.
16. S. Merkle, "Der Streit um Savonarola" in *Hochland* 25 (1928), pp. 472f.; St. Thomas Aquinas, In IV Sent. dist. 38, expos. textus in fine.
17. R. Bellarmine, *De summo pontifice*, Ingolstadt, 1586–1593, Paris, 1870, Book II, ch. 29, I, 607.
18. General Audience July 31, 1968, *Osservatore Romano* August 1, 1968. *Herder Correspondence* November 1968 (Vol. 5 No. 11) p. 336.
19. *Ibid.*
20. *Documentation*, p. 45f.
21. Reproduced in *Herder Correspondence* October 1968 (Vol. 5 No. 10), p. 300.
22. *Humanae Vitae* n.6. English translation by NC News Service, reproduced in *The Catholic Case for Contraception*, edited by Daniel Callahan, New York, 1969; London, 1969.
23. *The Tablet* May 6, 1967, p. 511.
24. *National Catholic Reporter* April 19, 1967, reproduced in Callahan, *op. cit.*, p. 210.
25. *Ibid.*, pp. 202–3.
26. *Ibid.*, p. 188.
27. These items are drawn from an excellently informed report in *Herderkorrespondenz*, Freiburg, 22 (1968), pp. 525–36 on "post-conciliar background of an encylical" (Quotation pp. 532ff.).
28. *Ibid.*, p. 530.
29. L. Kaufmann, "Der Vorhang hebt sich. Zur Vorgeschichte von 'Humanae Vitae'" in *Publik* November 29, 1968.
30. *Humanae Vitae* n.18.
31. *Ibid.*, nn.28–29.
32. *Ibid.* n.29. This passage is not in NC News Service translation
33. *Ibid.*, n.31.
34. Cardinal Charles Journet in *Osservatore Romano* October 3, 1968.
35. Cardinal Pericle Felici, "L' 'Humanae Vitae,' la coscienza ed il Concilio" in *Osservatore Romano* October 19, 1968. Cf. the same author's "Continuità, coerenza, fermezza di una dottrina. Dalla Costituzione pastorale 'Gaudium et spes' alla Enciclica paolina 'Humanae vitae'" in *Osservatore Romano* October 10, 1968.

NOTES FOR CHAPTER II

1. On the manipulation of the proposition, "Outside the Church no salvation," cf. Hans Küng, *Truthfulness*, New York, London and Sydney, 1968, VIII B.

2. L. Ott, *Fundamentals of Catholic Dogma*, translated by Patrick Lynch, Cork, Ireland, 1960[4], p. 299. On what follows compare, among recent Latin textbooks, J. Salaverri, *Sacrae Theologiae Summa* I, Madrid, 1955[3], pp. 552–747. T. Zapelena, De Ecclesia Christi II, Rome 1954, pp. 7–260 (esp. 171–91).

3. L. Ott, *op. cit.*, p. 300.

4. *Ibid.*

5. Daniel Callahan (ed.), *The Catholic Case for Contraception*, New York, 1969; London, 1969, pp. 179–80.

6. Cf. Ott, *op. cit.*, pp. 297–99.

7. *Ibid.*, p. 298.

8. *Ibid.*

9. On the history of the whole Constitution on the Church and the different projects compare—in addition to the council documents used here—the study of the second secretary of the theological commission, G. Philips, in H. Vorgrimler (ed.), *Commentary on the Documents of Vatican II*, Vol. I, 1967, pp. 105–37.

10. On the interpretation of articles 18–27 see the illuminating commentary by Karl Rahner in the above-mentioned volume, pp. 186–218.

11. K. Rahner, *loc. cit.*, p. 210.

12. *Schema constitutionis dogmaticae de Ecclesia* of 10.11.1962, p. 49.

13. Rahner, *loc. cit.*, p. 212.

14. *Ibid.*

14a. *Ibid.*, p. 214.

15. Quoted at length in the new version of the Constitution on the Church of 1963, p. 41.

16. On the exegetical-historical verification of the not very clear article 19 of the Constitution on the Church about the calling of the twelve or of the apostles, see *The Church*, D IV, 1.

17. On the apostolic succession of the whole Church see *The Church*, D IV, 2; the Constitution on the Church in article 10 goes directly from the mission of the apostles to the hierarchical offices.

18. On the historical development of the episcopal office see *The Church*, E II, 2a–b; this should be compared with the remarks on the universal priesthood, which becomes effective in baptism, the celebration of the Eucharist and forgiveness of sin, in D I, 2 and E II, 2.

19. On this astonishing backward development of dogma see the notes of the commission on faith to the Schema of the Constitution on the Church (Rome, 1964), 87 and 99; likewise *The Church*, E II, 2c and f.

20. On the question of teachers in the Church see *The Church*, E II, 2a and g.

21. Schema of the Constitution on the Church (Rome, 1964), p. 101.

22. Cf. Hans Küng, *The Living Church*, translated by Cecily Hastings and N. D. Smith, London and New York, 1963, Part 4, Chapter 3: "What is and what is not the theological task of this council?"

23. Cf. *The Church*, E II, 2e–i.

24. In addition to the earlier tendentious works both of J. Friedrich, *Geschichte des Vatikanischen Konzils*, Vols. 1–3, Bonn, 1867–87, from the Old-Catholic standpoint, and T. Granderath *Geschichte des Vatikanischen Konzils*, Vols. 1–3 (ed. K. Kirch), Freiburg, 1903–6, from the curial standpoint, see especially C. Butler, *The Vatican Council 1869–*

1870, London, 1962²; Westminster, Maryland, 1962, which gives a particularly lively impression of the dramatic course of the council and of individual interventions, and the most recent critical history of the council, R. Aubert, *Vatican I*, Paris, 1964, which we are following in this section, particularly for the description of the situation on the eve of the council. Cf. also the same author's *Le Pontificat de Pie IX*, Paris, 1952.

25. On the question of infallibility at Vatican I, in addition to older works, see the following which appeared on the eve of Vatican II: R. Aubert, "L'ecclésiologie au concile du Vatican" in *Le concile et les conciles*, Paris, 1960, pp. 245–84; A. Chavasse, "L'ecclesiologie au concile du Vatican. L'infaillibilité de l'Église" in *L'ecclésiologie au XIX siècle*, Paris, 1960, pp. 233–45; W. Caudron, "Magistère ordinaire et l'infaillibilité pontificale d'après le constitution 'Dei Filius'" in *Ephemerides Theologiae Lovanienses* 36 (1960), pp. 393–431; O. Karrer, "Das ökumenische Konzil in der römisch-katholischen Kirche der Gegenwart" in *Die ökumenischen Konzile der Christenheit*, ed. H. J. Margull, Stuttgart, 1961, pp. 237–84, esp. 241–64; G. Dejaifve, *Pape et évêques au premier concile du Vatican*, Paris, 1961, pp. 93–137; K. Rahner, *The Episcopate and the Primacy*, Freiburg, London, 1962, pp. 92–101; G. Thils, "Parlera-t-on des évêques au concile?" in *Nouvelle Revue Théologique*, 93 (1961), pp. 785–804; J. P. Torrell, "L'infaillibilité pontificale est-elle un privilege 'personnel'?" in *Revue des sciences philosophiques et théologiques*, 45 (1961), pp. 229–45; W. Kasper, "Primat und Episkopat nach dem Vatikanum I" in *Tübinger Theologische Quartalschrift*, 142 (1962), pp. 68–77.

On the question of infallibility as such see the important symposium, *L'Infaillibilité de l'Église. Journées œcuméniques de Chevetogne 25-29 Septembre 1961*, Chevetogne, 1963, with informative and far-seeing articles by J.-J. von Allmen ("Über den Geist, der in alle Wahrheit einführt"), B. Reyners ("Irenaeus"), B.-D. Dupuy ("Das Lehramt als Dienst am Wort"), P. de Vooght ("Das Wort 'Infallibilität' in der Scholastik"), G. Thils ("Infallibilität auf dem Vatikanum I"), N. Afanasieff (Orthodox standpoint), H. Balmforth (Anglican standpoint), J. Bosc (Reformed standpoint), J. de Satgé (Conference report). More recent literature in the next chapter.

26. See the evidence from the documents of the council in *Structures of the Church*, New York, 1964/London, 1965, VII, 2.

27. Cf. the comments, which are always relevant, on the by no means rare case of a conflict between pope and Church, the dubious proposition *Prima Sedes a nemine iudicatur*, the deposition of popes in the middle ages, the answer of modern canon law on the loss of office by the pope, the ecclesiological importance of the Council of Constance, which deposed three rival popes and represents with its decrees an opposite pole to Vatican I, in *Structures of the Church*, VII, 3–5.

28. Cf. the sifting of the certain and the uncertain in *The Church*, E II, 3b.

29. Cf. the numerous theoretical and practical implications and consequences of such a transition from a primacy of power to a primacy of service in *The Church*, E H, 3c.

30. C. Butler, *The Vatican Council* 1869–1870, London, 1962, p. 57.
31. *Ibid.*, pp. 59–60.
32. *Ibid.*, p. 61.
33. Reprinted in R. Aubert, *Vatican I*, pp. 261–69.
34. Aubert, p. 33.
35. Latin text in R. Aubert "L'ecclésiologie au concile du Vatican" in *Le concile et les conciles*, Paris, 1960, p. 280.
36. Mansi 52, 1204–30: Part 1: General report: a. Arguments from Scripture and tradition (1204–12), b. Explanations of the definition itself (1212–18); Part 2: Amendments Nos. 1–79 (1218–30).
37. Mansi 52, 1216.
38. Mansi 52, 1214.
39. *Ibid.*
40. Mansi 52, 1213.
41. *Ibid.*
42. Mansi 52, 1214.
43. We are following closely—as above noted—the authentic commentary of Bishop Gasser and the commission.
44. Mansi 52, 1213.
45. Mansi 52, 1214.
46. Mansi 52, 1213.
47. *Ibid.*
48. Mansi 52, 1215.
49. Mansi 52, 1214.
50. F. Suarez, *De Charitate. Disputatio XII de schismate, sectio 1, Opera Omnia*, Paris, 1958, 12, 733f. What we have hitherto brought forward in this section as critical counterquestions are not due to a tardy postconciliar hindsight. *Pro domo*, so to speak, it may be pointed out that our analysis of the Vatican problematic of primacy and infallibility and of the possible case of a conflict between pope and Church was already published before Vatican II in *Structures of the Church* (German edition, 1962) and rewarded with a Roman Inquisition process; nevertheless no one from the progressive majority at the Council ventured to give expression to these questions, so painful for the Curia, and to discuss them thoroughly.
51. Cf. supra II, 5.
52. According to the Emnid poll in 1967, 55 per cent of all the Catholics questioned held the opinion: "The Pope can't be infallible, since he's a human being." At the same time it is illuminating that even 44 per cent of *practicing* Catholics are of this opinion. See W. Harenberg (ed.),*Was glauben die Deutschen. Die Emnid-Umfrage. Ergebnisse, Kommentare*, Munich, 1968, p. 42.
53. J. Schmid, *Das Evangelium nach Lukas*, Regensburg, 1960, p. 332.
54. Y. Congar, *L'Ecclésiologie du Haut Moyan Age. De Saint Grégoire le Grand à la désunion entre Byzance et Rome*, Paris, 1968, pp. 159–60.
55. J. Langen, *Das Vatikanische Dogma von dem Universal-Episcopat und der Unfehlbarkeit des Papstes in seinem Verhältnis zum Neuen Testament und der exegetischen Überlieferung*, 4 vols., Bonn, 1871–76, II, pp. 123f.
56. Cf. *Structures of the Church*, VII, 6; Y. Congar, *op. cit.*, pp. 226–32. H. Fuhrmann, "Päpstlicher Primat und pseudo-isidorische Dekre-

talen" in *Quellen und Forschungen aus italienischen Archiven und Bibliotheken*, 49 (1969), pp. 313–39.

57. Congar, *ibid.*, p. 230.

58. St. Thomas Aquinas, *Contra errores Graecorum*, Pars II, capp. 32–35; the forgeries are also dealt with frankly and noted in recent Catholic commentaries, as for instance in R. A. Verardo's edition with an excellent introduction, *Opuscula Theologica* I, Turin and Rome, 1954. On this subject the studies of F. H. Reusch are of fundamental importance: *Die Fälschungen in dem Tractat des heiligen Thomas von Aquin gegen die Griechen*, Munich, 1889.

59. St. Thomas Aquinas, *ibid.*, cap. 36.

60. F. M. Reusch, *op. cit.*, p. 733.

61. St. Thomas Aquinas, *Summa Theologiae* II-II, q. 1 a. 10.

62. Cf. *Structures of the Church*, VII, 6.

63. On the question of Honorius see R. Bäumer, art. "Honorius" in *Lexikon für Theologie und Kirche*, V, Freiburg-Basle-Vienna, 1960, coll. 474f. (bibliography).

64. On the evaluation of this development we may refer once again to *Structures of the Church*, VII, 3–5, and *The Church*, E II, 3.

65. Cf., in agreement with this, K. Baus, art. "Konstantinopel" in *Lexikon für Theologie und Kirche*, VI, Freiburg-Basle-Vienna, 1961, coll. 495–97. J. Alberino (among others), *Conciliorum oecumenicorum decreta*, Freiburg, 1962, pp. 133–35. H. Aletvisatos (Orthodox), "Les conciles oecuméniques Ve, VIe, VIIe et VIIIe in *Le concile et les conciles*, Paris, 1960, pp. 119–23.

66. R. Aubert, *Vatican I*, pp. 110–11.

67. R. Aubert, *ibid.*, pp 116–17

NOTES FOR CHAPTER III

1. V. Conzemius, "Das Konzil des Papstes. Vor 100 Jahren begann das Erste Vatikanum" in *Publik* December 5, 1969.

2. *Ibid.*

3. *Ibid.*

4. H. Jedin, "Das erste Vatikanische Konzil im Lichte des Zweiten" in *Vaterland* January 17, 1970.

5. W. Kasper, "Die Kirche in der modernen Gesellschaft. Der Weg vom Vatikanum I zum Vatikanum II" in *Publik* December 12, 1969.

6. *Ibid.*

7. H. Jedin, *ibid.*

8. V. Conzemius, *ibid.*

9. W. Dirks, "Das Dogma von den fehlbaren Päpsten. Die Wandlung der katholischen Kirche seit 1870" in *Deutsches Allgemeines Sonntagsblatt* January 11, 1970.

10. Quoted in *Publik* January 23, 1970.

11. Text published in *Publik* January 23, 1970.

12. W. Küppers, "Sieben Thesen der alt-katholischen Kirche" in *Publik* January 23, 1970.

13. H. Bacht, "Dialog mit den Alt-Katholiken aufnehmen" in *Publik* January 23, 1970.

14. Especially *The Church*, translated by Ray and Rosaleen Ockenden, London, 1967; New York, 1968. E II, 3.

15. H. Bacht, *ibid.*

16. *Ibid.*

17. W. Küppers, *ibid.*

18. W. Kasper, *ibid.*

19. W. Dirks *ibid.*

20. J. Finsterhölzl, "Belastung oder Verheissung?" in *Publik* 9.1.1970.

21. *Ibid.*

22. W. Dirks, *ibid.*

23. J. Finsterhölzl, *ibid.*

24. *Ibid.*

25. *Structures of the Church*, New York, 1964; London, 1965, VIII, 3, pp. 336–37.

26. Mansi 52, 1219.

27. H. Fries, "Das Lehramt als Dienst am Glauben" in *Catholica* 23 (1969), pp. 154–72 (Quotation pp. 165–66).

28. Cf. Mansi, 52, 7, 14, 24 etc.; cf. in the Constitution itself *ab errore illibata* (DS 3070).

29. *Structures of the Church* VIII 2c., p. 335.

30. Cf. *The Church* VIII 2c.

31. K. G. Steck, "Die Autorität der Offenbarung. Das Erste Vatikanum im Urteil evangelischer Theologie" in *Publik* January 16, 1970.

32. *Ibid.*

33. *Ibid.*

34. *Ibid.*

35. *Ibid.*

36. *Ibid.*

37. Cf. E. Käsemann, "Liturgische Formeln im NT" in *RGG* II (Tübingen, 1958), 993–96; G. Bornkamm, "Formen und Gattungen im NT," *ibid.*, 999–1005. On professions of faith: O. Cullmann, *Die ersten christlichen Glaubensbekenntnisse*, Zollikon-Zürich 1943, 1949[4] (English translation by J. K. S. Reid, *The Earliest Christian Confessions*, London, 1949; Naperville, III, 1953; K. H. Scheikle, *Die Passion Jesu in der Verkündigung des Neuen Testaments*, Heidelberg, 1949, pp. 247–75; J. N. D. Kelly, *Early Christian Creeds*, London, 1950.

38. Cf., on the whole problem of Church, heresy and excommunication, *The Church* C III, 4.

39. On the concept of dogma and the distinction between dogma and dogmatism see J. Nolte, "Dogma in Geschichte. Versuch einer Kritik des Dogmatismus in der Glaubensdarstellung" (expected to appear in 1971 in the series *Ökumenische Forschungen*, Section 1).

40. St. Thomas Aquinas, *Summa Theologiae* II-II q. 1 a 10 ad 1–2; a.9 ad 2; a.10 *in corp*. Cf. also H. Küng, *The Living Church*, translated by Cecily Hastings and N D. Smith, London and New York, 1963, Part 4, Ch. 3: "What is and what is not the theological task of this council?"

41. Cf. Chapter II, 3.

42. Cf. Chapter II, 7.

Cf. Chapter II, 1.

44. V. Conzemius, "Das Konzil des Papstes" in *Publik* December 5, 1969.

45. Mansi 51, 72–77; cf. on the following C. Butler, *The Vatican Council*, pp. 236–39.

46. Mansi 51, 429–30.

NOTES FOR CHAPTER IV

1. In what follows I have made use of the five points in which a a student of mine, J. Nolte (*Dogma in Geschichte. Versuch einer Kritik des Dogmatismus in der Glaubens-darstellung;* this will appear probably in 1971 in the series, *Ökumenische Forschungen,* Section I), summarizes his reflections on linguistic philosophy, in order to place them then within a very much broader philosophical-theological problematic.

2. René Descartes, *Principia philosophiae* I, 45. English translation by Elizabeth S. Haldane and G. R. T. Ross, *The Philosophical Works of Descartes,* Cambrige, 1911, Vol. I, p. 237.

3. Hegel's basic teaching on this is found in his *Phenomenology of Mind.* Cf. Hans Küng, *Menschwerdung Gottes. Eine Einführung in Hegels theologisches Denken als Prolegomena zu einer künftigen Christologie,* Herder, Freiburg-Basle-Vienna, 1970, especially Chap, V,1.

4. Cf. *Structures of the Church,* VIII, 3c.

5. Cf. J. Nolte, *op. cit.*

6. From *National Catholic Reporter* April 19, 1967, reproduced in Callahan, *The Catholic Case for Contraception,* pp. 210–11.

7. Cf. *The Church* C I 2d. On the idea of the People of God in Hebrews: E. Käsemann, *Das wandernde Gottesvolk,* Göttingen, 1961[4]; F. J. Schierse, *Verheissung und Heilsvollendung. Zur theologischen Grundlage des Hebräerbriefes,* Munich, 1955.

8. Cf. *The Church* D III 2c.

9. Y. Congar, *L'Église de Saint Augustin a l'époque moderne,* Paris, 1970, pp. 244–48; quotation pp. 244–45.

10. *Ibid.,* pp 245–46.

11. *Ibid.,* p. 248.

12. *Ibid.,* p. 385.

13. *Ibid.,* p. 386.

14. Cf. *The Church* D III 2c.

15. Luther's works in the Weimar Edition (1883ff.), quoted here as WA. Answer to Prierias: WA I, p. 656.

16. WA 2, 303; cf. WA 5, 451.

17. Cf. J. Kolde, *Luthers Stellung zu Concil und Kirche bis zum Wormser Reichstag 1521,* Gütersloh, 1876. On Luther's conciliar theology cf. *Structures of the Church* VI, 1.

18. WA 7, p. 838.

19. *Ibid.*

20. Cf. especially his disputation theses, *De potestate concilii* 1536 (WA 39/I, pp. 181–97) and also his polemical tract, *Von den Konziliis und Kirchen,* 1539 (WA 50, pp. 509–653).

21. John Calvin, *Institutio christianae religionis,* 1559, particularly Book IV, Chaps. 8 and 9 (especially n.9). Calvin is quoted here in the

translation in the Library of the Christian Classics, S.C.M., London, Vol.
21, 1961: *Institutes of the Christian Religion*, edited by John T. McNeill
and translated by Ford Lewis Battle.

22. *Ibid.* IV, 9, 11. Trans. p. 1174.

23. B. Gassmann, *Ecclesia Reformata. Die Kirche in den reformierten
Bekenntnisschriften*, Freiburg-Basle-Vienna, 1968, p. 355.

24. Article 19 (quoted as in *The Book of Common Prayer*).

25. Article 21.

26. WA 39/I, 48.

27. Cf. WA 18, pp. 649ff.; 51, p. 511.

28. P. Althaus, *Die Theologie Martin Luthers*, Gütersloh, 1963², p.
256.

29. Translation in Henry Bettenson, *Documents of the Christian
Church*, Oxford, 1943, p. 295.

30. *Die Bekenntnisschriften der evangelisch-lutherischen Kirche*,
Göttingen, 1959⁴, pp. 235–36.

31. Book IV, Chap. 8, n.13. Trans. p. 1162.

32. IV, 9, 13. Trans. p. 1177. Calvin outlines an extensive teaching
on the Council; cf. on this *Structures of the Church* VIII, 1; on Calvin's
theory of the Church and ministry in general, see A. Ganoczy, *Ecclesia
ministrans. Dienende Kirche und kirchlicher Dienst*, Freiburg-Basle-
Vienna, 1968.

33. Article 19.

34. Article 21.

35. Cf. the recent, very stimulating publication by G. Thils, *L'Infaillibilité pontificale. Source-Conditions-Limites*, Gembloux, 1969.

36. Cf. the progressive contribution by R. Murray, "Who or what is
infallible?" in *Infallibility in the Church. An Anglo-Catholic Dialogue*,
London, 1968, pp. 24–46. Here too see the important criticism of
A. Farrer, and the contributions of J. C. Dickinson ("Papal Authority")
and C. S. Dessain ("Newman in Manning's Church"). Significant and
important for the earlier Catholic-Anglican dialogue is B. C. Butler,
The Church and Infallibility, 1954; new edition, London, 1969.

37. F. Simons, *Infallibility and the Evidence*, Springfield, 1968.

38. *Publik*, December 12, 1969. While this book was being printed, the
important volume, edited by Enrico Castelli, *L'infaillibilité. Son aspect
philosophique et théologique*, Paris, 1970, reached me. This contains
the documents of the conference held in Rome in January 1970 on this
theme. No doubt there are some contributions which could confirm
our analyses. We may draw attention to the work of the following
contributors: from the philosophical-theological standpoint, K. Rahner,
C. Bruaire, E. Jüngel, J.-L. Leuba, E. Agazzi, R. Marlé, G. Pattaro,
E. Grassi, A. de Waelhens, G. Vahanian, R. Panikkar, J. Lotz, G. Girardi,
L. Alonso-Schökel; from the historical aspect, R. Aubert, R. Manselli,
P. de Vooght, K. Kerényi, G. C. Anawati; from the ecumenical standpoint, R. Bertalot, B. Ulianich, A. Scrima.

39. Timothy Ware, *The Orthodox Church*, Harmondsworth, 1963, p.
255; New York, 1963.

40. *Ibid.*

41. J. N. Karmiris, "Abriss der dogmatischen Lehre der orthodoxen
katholischen Kirche" in *Die Orthodoxe Kirche in griechischer Sicht*,
edited by P. Bratsiotis, Stuttgart, 1959, I, pp. 18ff.

42. In this connection, see the protest of Karmiris—unsupported by any arguments—against the not unfounded assertion of the Reformed Churchman, W. Niesel, that "Orthodox Christendom does not know of any infallible teaching office" (*ibid.*, p. 19).

43. Ware, *op. cit.*, p. 256.

44. Cf. the documentation on this section in *Structures of the Church* IV, 2.

45. Cf. P. Johannes Chrysostomus, "Das ökumenische Konzil und die Orthodoxie" in *Una Sancta* 14 (1959), pp. 177–86; P. Leskovec, "Il Concilio Ecumenico nel pensiero teologico degli Ortodossi" in *La Civiltà Cattolica* 111 (1960), pp. 140–52; B. Schultze, *Die Glaubenswelt der orthodoxen Kirche*, Salzburg, 1961, pp. 149–53.

46. H. Jedin, *Kleine Konziliengeschichte*, Freiburg-Basle-Vienna, 1961, p. 10; it has been shown in *Structures of the Church*, that papal convocation, direction and confirmation of a council is merely a question of human law.

47. Augustine, *De baptismo contra Donatistas* Book III, Ch. 2 (PL 43, coll. 128–29; CSEL 51, 178). Cf. F. Hofmann, "Die Bedeutung der Konzilien für die kirchliche Lehrentwicklung nach dem heiligen Augustinus" in *Kirche und Überlieferung*, Festschrift for J. R. Geiselmann, Freiburg-Basle-Vienna, 1960, pp. 82–89.

48. M.-J. Le Guillou, *Mission et Unité*; German edition, *Sendung und Einheit der Kirche*, Mainz, 1964, p. 574. Le Guillou also lists as "being suspicious of councils" (p. 579) the important names of P. Afanasieff, A. Schmemann and J. Meyendorff.

49. Le Guillou, *ibid.*, p. 581.

50. J. Meyendorff, "What is an ecumenical council?" in *Vestnik* I, 1959 (Russian).

51. Cf. H. Sasse, "Sacra Scriptura-Bemerkungen zur Inspirationslehre Augustins" in the Festschrift for Franz Dornseiff, Leipzig, 1953, pp. 262–73.

52. *Schema Constitutionis dogmaticae de fontibus revelationis*, Rome, 1962, art. 12.

53. Cf. A. Grillmeier's excellent commentary on Chapter 3 of the Constitution on Revelation in *Commentary on the Documents of Vatican II*, London, New York, Volume III, 1968, pp. 199–246.

54. Grillmeier, *ibid.*, p. 204.

55. *Ibid.*, p. 206.

56. *Ibid.*, p. 210.

57. *Ibid.*, p. 235.

58. The different views of inspiration may be compared in the articles in encyclopedias by A. Bea, in *LThK*, Freiburg-Basle-Vienna, 1960[2], coll. 703–11; by G. Lanckowski, O. Weber, W. Philipp, in RGG III, Tübingen, 1959[3], 773–82; likewise in the various manuals of dogmatics, on the Catholic side, for instance, S. Tromp, M. Nicolau, L. Ott, M. Schmaus; on the Protestant side, K. Barth, E. Brunner, O. Weber, H. Diem, P. Althaus.

59. On the following see the documentation in Y. Congar, *L'Église de Saint Augustin à l'époque moderne*, pp. 389, 446.

60. *Ibid.*, p. 446.

61. Cf. supra Chapter II, 3.

62. Cf. *The Church* E I, 2b.

63. Cf. the excursus on lay preaching in *The Church, ibid.*

64. On the charismatic structure of the Church, along with *The Church* C II, 3 and E II, 2, see the very recent, comprehensive and penetrating studies: P. V. Dias, *Vielfalt der Kirche in der Vielfalt der Jünger, Zeugen und Diener,* Freiburg-Basle-Vienna, 1968; and G. Hasenhüttl, *Charisma. Ordungsprinzip der Kirche,* Freiburg-Basle-Vienna, 1969. Hasenhüttl in the light of Jesus' preaching examines both the authority on freedom that belongs to the basic charismatic structure of the community and the decline of the charisms to the point at which we have a community structure without charisms; thus he provides material for reflecting again on the charismatic structure of the community today. On the "charismatic states" (Hasenhüttl) of apostles, prophets, teachers, evangelists, pastors, cf. likewise P. V. Dias, B IV–IX, and G. Hasenhüttl, B III,

65. Cf. the comments in Chapter II, 3.

66. G. Hasenhüttl, *op. cit.,* p. 207.

67. *The Church* E II, 2g.

68. See the acute analysis—which in its documentation will certainly open the eyes of a good many people—by M. Seckler, "Die Theologie als kirchliche Wissenschaft nach Psiu XII and Paul VI" in *Tübinger Theologische Quartalschrift* 149 (1969), pp. 209–34. Particularly revealing is the address of Pius XII, *Si diligis,* on the canonization of Pius X, on May 31, 1954.

69. M. Seckler, *Ibid.,* p. 233. Cf., in the same issue of the quarterly, the contributions—important for the whole complex of problems on theology and "teaching office"—by P. Touilleux, "Kritische Theologie" (pp. 235–58); J. Neumann, "Zur Problematik lehramtlicher Beanstandungsverfahren" (pp. 259–81); H. Kümmeringer, "Es ist Sache der Kirche, 'iudicare de vero sensu et interpretatione scripturarum sanctarum'" (pp. 282–96). In coping with the crisis of traditional moral theology, supported by the "teaching office"—which has become clear particularly as a result of the appearance of the encyclical, *Humanae Vitae*—A. Auer's inaugural lecture at Tübingen must be regarded as fundamental: "Die Erfahrung der Geschichtlichkeit und die Krise der Moral" in *Tübinger Theologische Quartalschrift* 149 (1969), pp. 1–22.

70. Theologians' statement as in *Herder Correspondence,* February 1969, p. 46.

71. Cf. the excursus on lay theology in *The Church* E I, 2b.

NOTE FOR OUTLOOK

1. These reflections were first published in connection with Cardinal Suenens' interview (*Informations Catholiques Internationales* of May 15, 1969), under the title of "Portrait d'un pape," in *Le Monde* of August 12, 1969 and in *Publik of August* 15, 1969 (an abridged version of the article in *Le Monde* appeared in *The Tablet* of August 23, 1969). Here they appear in a slightly different form. Cf. also the collection

of documents, which has appeared in a number of different languages, *Le Dossier Suenens. Diagnostic d'une crise* (Paris, 1970), edited by J. de Broucker (published in English by Gill and Macmillan, Dublin, 1970), and also the interview with Suenens on the bishops and the question of celibacy in *Le Monde* of May 12, 1970 (see also *The Tablet* May 16, 1970).